WITHDRAWN

THE HISTORY OF THE ENGLISH NOVEL

THE HISTORY OF THE ENGLISH NOVEL

By Ernest A. Baker, D. Lit., M.A.

Vol. I	The Age of Romance: from the Beginnings to the Renaissance
Vol. II	The Elizabethan Age and After
Vol. III	The Later Romances and the Establishment of Realism
Vol. IV	Intellectual Realism: from Richardson to Sterne
Vol. V	The Novel of Sentiment and the Gothic Romance
Vol. VI	Edgeworth, Austen, Scott
Vol. VII	The Age of Dickens and Thackeray
Vol. VIII	From the Brontës to Meredith: Romanticism in the English Novel
Vol. IX	The Day before Yesterday
Vol. X	Yesterday

THE HISTORY
OF THE
ENGLISH NOVEL

By Ernest A. Baker, D. Lit., M.A.

Volume II

The Elizabethan Age and After

New York
BARNES & NOBLE, INC.

First published 1936
Reprinted 1966 by special arrangement with
H. F. & G. WITHERBY, LTD.
326 High Holborn, London, W. C. 1

Printed in the United States of America

PREFACE

It was originally intended to deal in a single volume with the history of English fiction from Lyly and Sidney to Defoe and Swift—that is, from the developments coming into view at the end of the volume published in 1924, dealing with "The Age of Romance; from the Beginnings to the Renaissance," to the time immediately preceding the advent of Richardson and Fielding. This would have resulted, however, in such an unwieldy tome that subdivision was necessitated. The present volume closes, not with any definite landmark, but with a halting-place in a period of transition. The next must needs hark back, and consider various belated survivals of romance that were more or less contemporaneous with the gradual approach to realism; it will end with Defoe and Swift. The succeeding volume, the fourth, will be concerned with Richardson and Fielding and their immediate followers. I am indebted to my colleague, Mr Oswald Doughty, for kindly reading the proofs, and to my old student, Mr Egbert E. Smart, for the compilation of an excellent analytical index.

E. A. B.

August, 1928

CONTENTS

THE ELIZABETHAN AGE AND AFTER

CHAPTER I

THE AGE OF TRANSLATION

The modern novel still in the distant future

THERE were still two centuries to run from the date reached at the end of the previous volume to the time when a writer would be able to say to himself, " I will write a novel," having a clear idea of what he was going to do and of the kind of work that would be expected of him. It was farther yet to the period when, in the absence of a living drama and in the decline of poetry, novels would be the readiest means of imaginative diversion, not only for intellectual people but for all who could read. Prior to Defoe, the only modern work of prose fiction that is undeniably a classic is Bunyan's *Pilgrim's Progress*, which is, undeniably, not a novel.

Romance had come to an end and had been buried with a stately funeral by Malory. Debased renderings of the old legends were still hawked about for the entertainment of the simple-hearted, but were despised by those writers and readers whose interest had been roused and their outlook on the world entirely changed by the new culture that was spreading from the south all over Europe. The main sap of English literature, revivified by this change of spirit, was to flow into poetry and drama. Vast numbers of prose tales issued from the press all through the Elizabethan age, some written by university wits for readers of refined taste, a far larger number for those of little education and less fastidiousness ; but of all that appeared not one has stood its ground as a classic. Certainly *Euphues* and the *Arcadia* cannot be graced with that dignity ; their interest to us is in the phases of change which they represent—as patterns of what fiction should be they were soon discarded. The period upon which we are now entering was one of haphazard or ill-directed experiment, of copious translation and adaptation and imitation ; a period of doubtful successes and manifest failures, of that process of trial and error which is normal to the transition from old to new.

The four main stems of Elizabethan fiction

A fund of unexhausted assets remained over from the earlier time, of which a rough inventory was given in the previous volume. It consisted, not of the tarnished relics of mediæval romance, but of the anecdotes and domestic stories, the jests and skits, which were the English equivalent of the *fabliaux*. These showed that even dull, or at any rate unlettered, people could be interested in the common incidents and humours of the life they themselves lived—an interest which was to persist in humble kinds of fiction, though its rights to the foremost place were not to be recognized for a long time yet. Meanwhile the wits were spinning fables of the adventures of kings and princes and shepherds in a fanciful Arcady, or making some threadbare tale a vehicle for their learning or their ingenious lucubrations on the world and man.

The fund of native assets may be distinguished as the popular contribution to the future novel. The learned contribution was threefold. First there were the translations or free adaptations of ancient and of contemporary fiction, in which the foreign, and more especially the Italian, impetus is most clearly operative. Then appeared the curious blend of moral disquisition and story typified by *Euphues*, which drew two-thirds of its inspiration from Italy and Spain. And almost simultaneously came the development of pastoral romance, now in the simple fashion of the Italian idyllists and now in combination with chivalric adventure after the manner of the Peninsula. In the learned category may also be included that form of direct criticism of life, the analytical portrait of character, which traces its main line of descent from Theophrastus ; it was a favourite in the early decades of the seventeenth century. This, even more than the didactic story, is a philosophic dissertation, or even a scientific dissection, rather than fiction in the artistic sense, though it was often handled with genuine artistry. Yet it was to have more telling effects on the rise of a true critical realism than either euphuism or arcadianism, wide as was their vogue for a time.

English varieties of picaresque story may perhaps be entered more appropriately side by side with the popular contribution, for they were not merely tales about the common people, but were also intended for the most part to amuse or edify persons of the same class ; and their generic relation to the beggar-books, the cony-catching pamphlets, and such middle-class fiction as Deloney's, was so close that it is difficult, without a list of what a given author had read, to say positively whether such a notable work as *Jack Wilton* was the offspring of Spanish rogue-fiction or of pure English stock.

The period was in the main a time of experiment and random effort

To view this rude, uncultivated tract of country with any precision, it is well to have in the mind's eye a sort of rough chart. To the north we may place the native contribution, and to the south the general mass of translated work ; to west and east respectively, or, since both were mainly of foreign origin, to south-west and south-east, we may put *Euphues* and its miscellaneous progeny, and the *Arcadia*, with the poetical or idealistic tales that were its next-of-kin. From these four quarters the waste land was gradually settled, with all kinds of intermarriages and tentative unions, sterile births, and more vigorous strains which, by dint of cross-fertilization and the lapse of time, resulted in such a posterity as would have stultified the keenest forecast. Unlimited scope for trial and experiment was what was chiefly needed for the novel to come into being. But, for the present, there could be little chance of steady progress, since the direction in which progress had to be made was not yet divined. There were, moreover, serious obstacles to progress. One vital need—one, however, of which no writer saw the real bearings—was the want of a suitable prose. Most of the current prose—all of it indeed that was employed in works to be read for enjoyment—was a much more artificial mode of expression than the diction of contemporary verse. Denied the charms of rhyme and metre, the prose writer did not reflect that poetic licence was also disallowed ; on the contrary, he tried to make up for the deficiency by an exhausting strain after point and epigram, trope and metaphor, and such artificial effects of assonance, alliteration, and iterating cadence as in verse would have been intolerable. Thus Lyly hardly ever steps down from the tight-rope ; and Sidney, in the *Arcadia*, is like the coryphee in some elaborate ballet, swimming indefatigably through the mazes of an intricate dance. Until someone realized that in fiction it is more important to be lifelike than to be literary, an appropriate style was not to be forthcoming or even sought for. Till then, with or without Spanish and Italian masters to emulate, the style of imaginative prose was

The lack of a suitable prose

bound to remain a hybrid; and, in fact, a style suitable for portraying actual life and reporting fiction as if it were fact did not appear till the seventeenth century was middle-aged, at a time when entirely new standards of literary expression were coming into usage.

General uncertainty as to the proper aim of prose fiction

The other great obstacle to the advance of the art of fiction—the one indeed which was the root of all the trouble—was the lack of any definite notion of what a story or a novel should be, what or where was the essential point by virtue of which a story was a story and not a meaningless account of chance occurrences; what the kind of interest that marked it out for prose rather than verse, and what manner of satisfaction it should provide for the reader. Writers had the vaguest and most confused apprehension of the problem to be solved; whether the main object was the story or the moral, the incidents or the picture of life; truth, insight, lifelikeness, or strangeness, ingenuity, surprise. As to form, they had everything to learn; where to begin, when to conclude; what to stress, what to leave to the imagination. Hence the value of a long spell of adventure and experiment; hence the still greater value of the tutelage and discipline afforded by translation from experienced foreigners. That the native assets were for a while neglected was all to the good; although, ultimately, in the development of mere story-telling into something of ampler scope and deeper significance, the native, the popular contribution was to pay by far the heavier dividends.

The translations were chiefly of service to drama

For the time being the unwearying labour of a large body of men on the translation of Italian and other stories was to be of chief service to the drama. We study Elizabethan collections of tales from Bandello and his fellows now, not because they provided models for English writers of fiction, but because they furnished plots for famous tragedies. Neither in short story nor in novel did the Elizabethans produce anything of intrinsic and not merely of historical importance. Prose fiction was not the form of art that came natural to them. Not a single first-rate author tried his hand at it, with the sole exception of Sidney, who did not live long enough to take it seriously. But imagine what might have been the indirect result had the Puritan opposition succeeded in closing the theatres half-a-century earlier than it actually did. What would have been the effect upon imaginative writers of the damming up of this outlet for their creative energies? Many would have remained dumb. Opportunity is the most powerful of all incentives, and without their true vocation beckoning them on they might never have found congenial employment for their talents. Some would have disported themselves in pastoral, allegorical, chivalric, and other conventional forms of poetry; narrative verse would undoubtedly have gained, and some great dramatic epic might have seen the light before Milton was born. But prose fiction could hardly have gone without profit from the theatre's loss, and Elizabethan fiction would in all likelihood have been a totally different thing from what it was. Yet if the Elizabethans had evolved the novel, it would have been a novel very unlike that of Richardson and Fielding. The genius that produced *Hamlet*, *King Lear*, *The Duchess of Malfi*, *The Changeling*, *'Tis Pity She's a Whore*, *A New Way to pay Old Debts*, would never have produced a *Clarissa Harlowe* or a *Tom Jones*. Some dim idea of what might have been produced may perhaps be imagined if we think of certain examples of modern Russian fiction, although we must remember that the Russians were not uninfluenced by the work of Fielding and his successors. Or we might think of the interfusion of prose and poetry, of intellectual realism and free imaginative creation, in the work of novelists who have also been poets—Emily Brontë, Victor Hugo, Meredith, Hardy, Gabriele d'Annunzio—making the same allowance for all that was learned from the eighteenth century.

The history of Elizabethan fiction mainly a record of failure

But speculation on such contingencies only leads us back to the general truth that fiction does not normally arise and flourish in times of intense creative energy—that is, in times when great poets abound—but rather in the quiet intervals when writers are less imaginative and more critical. The Elizabethan age was not the appointed age for inaugurating a new art of fiction, well differentiated from the rival literary forms. The mental habitudes and the circumstances that made for success in poetry and drama were unfavourable to the novel. Hence Elizabethan fiction was an obscure, slight, and unsatisfactory affair. Its history is, on the whole, a record of failure, of the exploration of misleading routes and the discovery of dead-ends. There was nothing of any importance going on in *Arcadia*. *Euphues* was a barren exercise out of a pedant's brain. Jack Wilton and Jack of Newbury were almost the only heroes whose persons and histories had any human pith and any chance of a strong lineage. It was in the affectionate regard for such low-born swains and in the warm interest men and women took in seeing the mirror held up to the life around them that the English genius for the novel was latent.

Translations

The distinguished band of educators, led by Erasmus, More, and Colet, whose mission it was to establish the new learning on solid foundations in this country, had no great regard for the native language, and taught their pupils to read the classical authors in the originals. They were more given to compiling grammars, commentaries, and other aids to scholarship, and compiling them in Latin, than to wasting time on providing the unstudious with translations into English. But when their work had been accomplished, and the study of the Greek and Latin authors was at length a regular part of the curriculum in schools and colleges, the translator began to be active. The apostles of the Renaissance had laid open vast stores of learning, wisdom and beauty, which could not fail to be exploited by the purveyor of literature for the general mass of readers. Bishop Gavin Douglas had completed his vivid translation of the *Æneid* in 1513[1]; but, although that remarkable piece of work preceded the busy season of Englishing the classics by only a quarter of a century, it really belongs more to the age of Chaucer than to that of the classical revival. In truth, Greek rather than Latin scholarship gives the surest index to the progress of the new learning, since Latin had long been almost a mother tongue to the professional writer, and a large proportion of the vernacular literature of the preceding ages had at one stage or another been done out of Latin. Before 1500, on the other hand, Æsop was the only Greek book that had come into English, and that had arrived in a roundabout way. But between 1500 and 1540 a dozen Greek books were Englished, and between the latter year and the end of the century the number was fifty-six.[2]

Marcus Aurelius, some of Cicero's works, Sallust, Livy, and no doubt others, were taken in hand before the middle of the century. There was a gathering from Diogenes Laertius and other wise men in 1550, entitled *A Treatise of Morall Phylosophye*, and from that

[1] Not printed till 1553.
[2] F. M. K. Foster, *English Translations from the Greek*, introduction, xxiv.

date onwards the translators were busily occupied. Seneca's plays and also his moral works had a crowd of interpreters. The Scottish bishop's version of the *Æneid* was superseded by that of Phaer, who had a fantastic rival in Stanyhurst. Horace, Ovid, Ausonius, Cæsar, Justin were among the Latin authors, and Thucydides, Isocrates, Epictetus, Diodorus Siculus, Demosthenes, among the Greeks, turned into English before 1579, the year when North's version of Plutarch saw the light. Like others of those just enumerated, this was a rendering, not directly from the Greek, but out of the charming French of Amyot. It was thus at a second or third, or even at a fourth, remove that many of the ancient masterpieces were transcribed into choice and racy English. Few of the translators before Philemon Holland were scholars in any strict sense of the term. They rarely went to the original text; but, having a French, Italian, or other modern version to hand, in which the antique writer had been already assimilated to the spirit of the age, they availed themselves of this to assimilate him further to the English spirit. Hence it will be seen that, although the translators began with renderings of the Greek and Latin classics and subsequently went on to the romantic literature of their own time, it was not so much the classics that led them to the moderns as the new literary spirit of Europe that led them by its own ways to the classics. In this manner was it that the Elizabethans were made acquainted with the Greek and Latin post-classical romances. Adlington published his *Golden Asse, Conteininge the Metamorphosie of Lucius Apuleius*, in 1566, translating into his stately and mellifluous English from the French of Guillaume Michel's *Lasne Dore*. Thomas Underdowne, in *An Æthiopian Historie* (1569), used a Latin rendering by Stanislaus Warschewiczki. Angel Day, again, had the advantage of Amyot's version of Longus, when he gave us *Daphnis and Chloe* in 1587; and there was a French translation, perhaps by Belleforest, in front of William Burton, when he did the English version of the *Clitophon and Leucippe* of Achilles Tatius, in 1597. How the story of *Apollonius of Tyre* came into the language centuries earlier, and was retold in successive editions, has been described in the previous volume. Petronius was kept waiting for an English translator till late in the seventeenth century, when he was discovered to be a forerunner of the picaresque novelist.

Most of the translations came through French, Italian, etc.

CHAPTER II

TRANSLATIONS FROM ITALIAN

Fiction of Italian origin

An extremely early translation of a story of Italian authorship appeared in 1550 or 1560, and was republished over and over again, in spite of having to stand the competition of several rival versions. This was *The goodly History of the moste noble and beautyful Ladye Lucres of Scene in Tuskan, and of her louer Eurialus,*[1] directly or ultimately from the Latin of Æneas Sylvius, or Enea Silvio Piccolomini, afterwards Pope Pius II.[2] The original story, *De Duobus Amantibus* (1444), was based on what the author himself knew about a love affair of his friend Count Schlick, a favourite of the Emperor Sigismund, with the wife of a gentleman in Siena.[3] The Emperor and his courtiers stayed some time in that city, before his coronation at Rome (1432-34), and it was then that the intrigue must have taken place. In the tale, Eurialus is a knight of Francony, and Lucrece the beautiful wife of a churlish citizen, Menelaus,[4] whose house he passes daily. At first, they can only correspond with their eyes; but soon there is an interchange of letters. In fact, the ten love letters that pass between them are the chief device by which the plot of the story is worked out, from the first avowal to the last farewell. Frequent examples of the letter used as a main link in the machinery occur in the Italian stories translated later by Painter, Fenton, and Pettie; but this seems to be its first appearance in English. In their stratagems to meet each other, the lovers are aided,

[1] Hazlitt dates the oldest extant English edition *c.* 1549; according to Lowndes there was one by Copland in 1547, which, according to H. H. Gibbs, is a mistake for 1567.

[2] Reprinted with *The Hystorie of the most noble knyght Plasidas and other rare pieces*, ed. H. H. Gibbs (Roxburghe Club, 1873). The *Plasydas* (alias St Eustace) is a life of the saint by John Partridge (1566).

[3] A version entitled *The Amours of Count Schlick* appeared with the Comtesse d'Aulnoy's *Hypolitus Earl of Douglas* (1708).

[4] His brother is Agamemnon, and the lovers are cheated by one Pandalus, a gentleman allied to Menelaus. In a popular story such names would be adopted as familiar labels.

after some reluctance, by the family servant Sosias. Eurialus is smuggled into the house disguised as a porter, and on the sudden return of the husband has to take refuge in a blind closet. But the husband wants certain papers which are in the closet. On the spur of the moment Lucrece upsets a box of jewels out of the window, and whilst they are being picked up the lover escapes. On another occasion, as he is hiding in a stable, he is within an ace of being pitchforked by the ostler Dromo.

The lovers express their passion in the vehement language of nature. The tale, indeed, is by no means wooden or conventional, and in the English version is given a deeper touch of pathos. Eurialus is obliged to leave Siena in the Emperor's train, and after his departure Lucrece dies of a broken heart. According to Æneas Sylvius, the bereaved lover mourns his lost lady for a decent period, and then is made happy by Sigismund, who bestows on him the beauteous daughter of a ducal house. But the Englishman prefers to dwell on the knight's constancy and unquenchable sorrow: "When he knew his true lover to be dead, moved by extreme dolour, clothed him in mourning apparel, and utterly excluded all comfort, and yet though the Emperor gave him in marriage a right noble and excellent lady, yet he never enjoyed after, but in conclusion pitifully wasted his painful life." On the other hand, the ostler Dromo is made into a racy and humorous character quite different from the featureless original.[1]

Painter's "Palace of Pleasure"

The first, and also the largest and richest, of a remarkable group of collections which now begin to appear, consisting for the most part of translated stories, but some comprising original tales written in imitation, was *The Palace of Pleasure*, of which William Painter brought out the first volume in 1566, and the second in 1567. There were sixty tales in the first, and thirty-four in the second volume; but by 1575, when the book went into a third edition, the total numbered a hundred and one. Painter was a Middlesex man, who went to St John's College, Cambridge, at a rather precocious age, and became head master of Sevenoaks School on leaving the

[1] H. J. Savage, in "The Beginning of Italian Influence in English Fiction" (*Mod. Lang. Association of America*, xxxii., 1917, pp. 1-21), collates the original and two Continental editions with the English. There were Italian, German, Spanish, and French translations before 1550, and an enormous number of Latin editions—R. A. Peddie (*Conspectus Incunabulorum*) enters sixty-two before 1500.

university. At the age of forty or a little more he held the post of clerk of the ordnance, at the Tower, where he made money by questionable practices and is stated to have died owing the queen nearly eight thousand pounds.

If, as is most probable, *The Cytie of Cyvelete*, entered at Stationers' Hall in 1562, is to be identified with the *Palace of Pleasure* in its first projected form, our author changed his title before going into print—a change that perhaps indicates a change of design. At any rate, as he explains in his dedication of the original volume to the Earl of Warwick, general of the ordnance, his plan grew upon him. He was first attracted by Livy, " viewing in him great plenty of strange histories," recounting noble facts and exploits achieved by valiant personages of the Roman state. But fearing that it was not in him to do worthily of that majestic author, he stopped when he had dealt with " such as were the best and principal," resolving to wait and see how these would be liked, and filling out the book with stories gathered from the Italian and French novelists. Besides Livy, Painter, in his list of authorities, refers to Herodotus, Xenophon, Cicero, Quintus Curtius, Aulus Gellius, and other ancients, and in the second tome to Strabo, Plutarch, Homer, Virgil, Ovid, Horace, Propertius, and the late historiographers. Though they number about a third of the sum total in the two volumes, however, the stories of antiquity bulk very much less than those of more recent days. Nor is it to be assumed for a moment that Painter went straight to the authorities he mentions. A good proportion of the antique stories were obtained from Bandello, Giraldi Cinthio, Ser Giovanni, Boccaccio, and other intermediate sources, and obtained even so through French translations and not Italian texts. To put it briefly, Painter set out to make a great English collection of stories, to rival the famous collections in Italian and French; he sought to make it as miscellaneous as was in his power, and with that intention selected what he wanted from all the available repositories in turn. The score and a half of tales reduced to a " compendious form " from Livy and other ancient writers, in volume one, are followed by ten from the *Decameron*, half-a-dozen from Bandello and his interpreter Belleforest, a few from Ser Giovanni and Straparola, and half-a-score from the *Heptameron*. In the second volume, also, the tales are in distinct groups, from Bandello, Cinthio, Boccaccio, and again Bandello, with a few from other sources interspersed.

Painter inclined to didacticism

In his choice of stories, the compiler, without harbouring any narrow idea of the interests that are conducive to a free and worthy life, shows clearly a preference for those stories which yield a specific lesson. He says in his address to the reader in the second part:

The contents of these novels from degree of highest emperor, from state of greatest queen and lady, to the homely country peasant and rudest village girl, may conduce profit for instruction, and pleasure for delight. They offer rules for avoiding of vice and imitation of virtue to all estates. This book is a very court and palace for all sorts to fix their eyes therein, to view the devoirs of the noblest, the virtues of the gentlest, and the duties of the meanest. It is a stage and theatre for show of true nobility, for proof of passing loyalty and for trial of their contraries.

He had argued, more closely, in the dedication of his first volume, that histories in which were depainted in lively colours "the ugly shapes of insolency and pride, the deform figures of incontinence and rape," nevertheless, being thoroughly read and well considered, taught old and young "how to avoid the ruin, overthrow, inconvenience and displeasure, that lascivious desire and wanton will doth bring to their suitors and pursuers." Like the other Elizabethan makers or vendors of fiction, as we shall find, Painter had a very practical end in view. Quoting from a Greek orator, he writes:

For Scientia (affirmeth he) is the only immortal storehouse of all possessions. Amongst which troop of sciences, the knowledge and search of histories deserveth a place in the chiefest rank, and is for example of human affairs, a crystal light to show the paths of our ancestors. The same displayeth the counsels, advices, policies, acts, success, and ends of kings, princes and great men, with the order and description of time and place.

Painter and his like wrote particularly for those who were about the court; hence the emphasis constantly put on lessons in statecraft and the conduct of the great. But on the conduct of life in general there is no reason to doubt that he desired to be, and thought he was, a salutary influence. Wherefore the diatribe of the worthy

Ascham, which must have been written soon after the date when Fenton's *Tragicall Discourses of Bandello* and the second tome of the *Palace of Pleasure* had come out, must be read as an ebullition of savage puritanism. Ascham was apt to see the devil's horns at every mention of Rome or priests or the age of chivalry. It is after the famous denunciation of Italianate Englishmen that the passage occurs. Ascham goes on to describe Italian books translated into English as " the enchantments of Circe, brought out of Italy to mar men's manners in England " ; and he flatly declares that they were introduced into this country by the enemies of Protestantism. Failing to persuade in matters of doctrine, " then the subtle and secret Papists at home procured bawdy books to be translated out of the Italian tongue, whereby over many young wills and wits allured to wantonness do now boldly contemn all severe books that sound to honesty and godliness." [1] Then follows the unmeasured invective against Malory as a chronicler of open immorality. " And yet ten *Morte Arthures* do not the tenth part so much harm, as one of these books made in Italy and translated in England." [1]

Painter refrains, however, from intruding moralization into the stories themselves, having done his duty by drawing attention in the preface to the lesson always implied. Thus he differs from his sermonizing colleagues, without being an exception among Elizabethan writers of fiction. Compilers of story-books, writers of moral treatises, painters of idealistic Arcadias, journalists pouring forth cautionary pamphlets and rogue-tales, or anticipators of Samuel Smiles like the historian of Jack of Newbury and Thomas of Reading : all were alike intent on teaching by example, precept, and warning, some more earnestly or more ostentatiously than others, but all with a certain sincerity, even if they nursed a private relish for the kind of story that was anathema to Roger Ascham.

His main sources—classical history, Boccaccio, etc.

The tales that Painter culled from the classical historians consisted in the main of such well-known pieces as the combat of the Horatii and the Curiatii, the Rape of Lucrece, Coriolanus, Appius and Virginia, Candaules and Gyges, Phalaris and the Bull, Cyrus and Panthea, Androdus (or Androcles) and the Lion, Timon of Athens. Already in certain of these brief anecdotes, some less than a page in length, we see the germ of Shakespearian plots ; and in

[1] *The Scholemaster* (1570), Book I., sec. 7-8.

those that come after, drawn from the *novellieri*, we recognize more, these later ones being told in full detail and at much greater length. Giletta of Narbonne, from Boccaccio, was the story used in *All's Well that Ends Well*. Painter's version of *Romeo and Juliet*, from Bandello, had been preceded by the metrical translation of Arthur Brooke, and both seem to have been read by Shakespeare. Webster, Greene, Heywood, Peele, Beaumont and Fletcher, Marston, Shirley, Massinger, Middleton, and later dramatists founded plays on Painter's narratives; and, directly or indirectly, he supplied the matter for poems and hardly less celebrated paintings from that day to this. A third volume was contemplated but was never realized. As Painter explains, at the end of the second volume, he would have liked to give "the remnant of Bandello, specially such (sufferable) as the learned Frenchman François de Belleforest hath selected," with others "out of Erizzo, Ser Giovanni Fiorentino, Parabosco, Cinthio, Straparola, Sansovino, and the best liked out of the Queen of Navarre, and other authors."

Translations from Bandello

It must be remembered that whilst Painter was compiling Belleforest was still at work on his renderings of Bandello in the *Histoires Tragiques*. The first volume, containing six stories, translated by Pierre Boaistuau, Seigneur de Launay, had come out in 1559; these were all appropriated by the Englishman. The volume ended with a sonnet to Boaistuau by Belleforest, who the same year published a *Continuation* giving twelve tales, four of them to be used by Painter. These two instalments were combined in the 1564 volume, and the following year were supplemented by another eighteen, by Belleforest. Eventually these two volumes, containing eighteen tales apiece, were extended to a total of seven volumes; and an eighth was published by another translator giving twenty-eight stories, said to have been found after the death of Bandello.[1]

[1] See G. Reynier, *Le Roman Sentimental avant l'Astrée* (pp. 160 and 366-367), for a bibliography that does not pretend to be complete. A somewhat misleading lacuna occurs between Boaistuau's volume of 1559 and the second volume, by Belleforest, mentioned here under date 1568. M. Reynier speaks of the long interruption of the work and makes Belleforest explain and apologize. But there was no long interruption, certainly not one of nine years. There had been a second volume by 1565 at the latest. In fact, both Painter and Fenton had done their extant translations and published them before 1568. But the bibliography of the *Histoires Tragiques* is very confusing, and interesting only in relation to the translators who used this writer as a key to Bandello.

Bandello was the nearest in time of the great *novellieri* to those who translated or dramatized their stories, with the sole exception of Cinthio, who was still alive when Painter's two volumes had appeared. Devoid of Boccaccio's large and tolerant humanism, the Milanese friar who became a French bishop was a story-teller more to the English taste, in that age at any rate. Bandello loved actuality, and whether his tales were relations of things he had seen done in the turbulent world he lived in, or were merely lifelike, he made them out to be facts, and his readers' appetites were whetted for more. He had a literary liking for violence, bloodshed, ghastliness; this, in brief, was his idea of tragedy. The Elizabethans were of the same mind. Nor had he more objection than could be expected of an Italian churchman in the time of the Renaissance to scenes of licentiousness, even of a corrupt and horrifying kind; though he touched the subject in a gloomy, admonitory way. Both traits appealed to English and likewise to his French admirers. Belleforest revelled in Bandello's most sombre tales. Deliberately avoiding those which were gay and comic, as too frivolous for a sensible person's attention, he succeeded in giving even a deeper grimness to some that were almost unendurably harrowing in the original. "If any one cares for the pleasant tales to be found in Bandello," says he, "let him enjoy them freely; as for me, I give way to him." No literal translator, he prided himself on not being a superstitious copyist. He cherished the privilege of his time to alter and omit at will, suppressing what did not suit his saturnine taste, interfering with the order of events, sometimes even changing the conclusion, and he fully made good the assertion that he took only the subjects from Bandello, supplementing the art of the original with his own invention.

In nothing was he more arbitrary than in the long ethical homilies which he substituted for Bandello's pithy reflections. He had chosen, said Belleforest, on the title-pages of the collective edition, "things worthy of memory, and various successful achievements and events which serve for our instruction in life."[1] To enforce such instruction, he inserted wordy disquisitions on every ethical point that arose, not

[1] Contenant plusieurs choses dignes de memoire, et divers succes d'affaires, et evenements, qui servent à l'instruction de nostre vie: le tout recueilly de ce qui s'est passé, et jadis, et de nostre temps, entre des personnes de marque et reputation.

to mention letters and pieces of verse that had no place in Bandello. By this means, and with stories extracted from other authors, he expanded the *Histoires Tragiques* to seven volumes in lieu of Bandello's three. Yet there is hardly any more mental analysis in Belleforest than in Bandello. Only one story, that of Dom Diego, who buries himself in the Pyrenees to brood on the fickleness of Ginevra, a tale retold by both Painter and Fenton, belongs to sentimental fiction. The moral is not brought out by any anatomy of motive, but simply in the crushing consequences of unruly passion, emphasized by the commentator's censorious rhetoric. The more terrible the nemesis the more was it relished by both the translators and their master, betraying a crude appetite for horrors which they mistook for righteous indignation.

Fenton's "Tragicall Discourses of Bandello."

Belleforest found a devoted translator in Geoffrey Fenton, a man of different kidney from Painter. He belonged to a knightly house, and affected, like so many of his time, to join the character of a thinker and man of letters to that of the courtier and politician. But he was lacking in the sterling qualities that enabled his magnificent contemporary, Sir Philip Sidney, to realize such an ideal, and the record of Fenton's doings as a servant of the queen in Ireland is one of callous self-seeking, meanness, and treachery. He was under thirty when his *Tragicall Discourses of Bandello* appeared in 1567, a few months before Painter's second volume. It was dedicated to Lady Mary Sidney, Sir Philip's mother, and had presumably been the employment of Fenton's leisure hours in Paris, where he may perhaps have gone with the ambassador, Sir Thomas Hoby. Having sowed his wild oats, the young man was in a moralizing mood, and found congenial themes in the *Histoires Tragiques*, just as he was a little later to find satisfaction in Englishing certain religious and philosophical disputations and an anthology of meditative passages from Guevara, which he styled *Golden Epistles*. Fenton was a sentimentalist, in that his moral obsessions were only skin-deep; but his temper was in sympathetic accord with that of Belleforest, from whom he took thirteen stories and expanded them with still further comments and elaborate embellishments.

It is worth the English reader's while to compare the four tales borrowed from Belleforest by both Painter and Fenton, and observe the different ways in which they handled the material. The stories in question are "The Countess of Celant," "The Lord of Virle," "Dom Diego and Gineura," and "Salimbene and Angelica." The first Fenton manages to expand from the thirty-six pages of his rival's unadorned version to the length of fifty-six pages ; "Salimbene and Angelica" from forty-one to sixty-eight pages ; and even "Dom Diego" to ten more pages, in spite of the fact that Painter had inserted several long sets of verses in full, whilst Fenton merely mentions songs and sonnets or gives them in a much curtailed form. There is not much difference, however, in point of length, between the two versions of "The Lord of Virle." No story was more to Fenton's taste than "The Disordered Life of the Countess of Celant; who, living long in adultery, and after she had procured divers murders, received the hire of her wickedness by a shameful death." It was long enough as retold by Painter, with the set speeches, screeds of verse, wordy letters, and prolix reflections which he took from Belleforest. At the end of his task he passes on with a sigh of relief to the next story, "Romeo and Juliet," "the history of two, the rarest lovers that ever were." Fenton amplifies the argument forming the preface,.and interlards the stroy with fulsome comments and unseasonable comparisons with other famous examples of moral obliquity. The story is tending to be a mere text, on which the retailer hangs out elaborate dissertations and exhortations, curious instances, and precious conceits. He displays many anticipations of euphuism, probably the result of cultivating the graces dear to Belleforest and the Pleiad, rather than of his study of Guevara. Painter, on the contrary, was always more inclined to condense than to amplify or embroider. His stories are told without too many interruptions, and thus attracted the dramatists by their intrinsic merits. With this preference of the essential to the supererogatory, he wrote in a businesslike and straightforward style, and his was a striking exception to the redundant artistry of the current prose in works of fiction.[1]

Two collections of stories, from Spanish and from Italian respectively, published in the next few years, need not detain us, as the English editors were not responsible for their compilation but merely

[1] Painter may have resorted to the Italian text of Bandello, merely using Belleforest as a crib. Anyhow, he often gives the Italian forms of names—*e.g.* Bianca Maria, Giachomo Scappardone, etc. ; *cp.* Fenton's Blanche Maria, James Scarpadon, etc.

Translations from Mexia and Guicciardini

translated them. Pedro Mexía's *Silva de varia leccion*, which had appeared in 1542 at Seville, was Englished from Claude Gruget's French version by Thomas Fortescue, and appeared as *The Foreste or Collection of Histories* (1571). It included the story of Timur, and was the original source of the Latin life of Tamerlane (1553) by Perondinus, which was Marlowe's source in writing his play. The book from Italian was *The Garden of Pleasure: Contayninge most pleasant Tales, worthy deeds and witty sayings of noble Princes and learned Philosophers, Moralized. No lesse delectable, than profitable* (1573), done into English by James Sanford, from Ludovico Guicciardini.[1] Put the other way about, the title would have read more correctly as short stories gathered together to illustrate moral apophthegms, for there is much more edification than entertainment in the book, such entertainment as it affords being turned to extra profit by an appendix of "Certayne Italian Proverbes and Sentences," in Italian and English. The tales are largely from Greek, Roman, and mediæval historians and biographers.

Gascoigne's "Adventures of Master F.I.": an English novella

Much more interesting than these solemn trifles is an original tale, written in the Italian manner, which makes only the most perfunctory claim to be profitable as well as pleasant. This is George Gascoigne's *Pleasant Fable of Ferdinando Jeronimi and Leonora de Valasco*, which appeared in a collection of pieces, otherwise in verse, entitled: *A Hundreth sundrie Flowers bounde up in one small Poesie* (1572). It is said to be "translated out of the Italian riding tales of Bartello," but Bartello is a mythical person, and the story may have been made up out of Gascoigne's own experiences. Ferdinando is invited home by the Lord of Valasco, ostensibly for the hunting and shooting, but really in the hope that he will become a suitor to the daughter of the house, the Lady Frances. Ferdinando, however, falls in love with this lady's sister-in-law, wife of the son and heir, and after a prolonged courtship is admitted to her favours. On the whole, the story is told in a straightforward and effective style, many pieces of verse exchanged by the lovers diversifying the narrative more agreeably than the grave sermons which any one of Gascoigne's

[1] This long descriptive title was altered in the second edition to *Howres of recreation or Afterdinners, Which may aptly be called the Garden of Pleasure: Containing most pleasant Tales, worthy deeds and witty sayings of noble Princes and learned Philosophers, with their Morals . . . now . . . newly perused, corrected, and enlarged* (1576).

contemporaries would have inserted. There are many lively and lifelike conversations, not lacking in repartee, and there is some passable character-drawing. Leonora is an objectionable heroine. She has carried on an illicit affair already with her secretary, a grotesque and repulsive rascal who is sketched in lines that anticipate Smollett's mode of caricature, as " in height the proportion of two pigmies, in breadth the thickness of two bacon hogs, of presumption a giant, of power a gnat, apishly witted, knavishly mannered, and crabbedly favoured." When " this manling, this minion, this slave, this secretary " returns from an errand to Florence, Leonora throws over Ferdinando, who endures acute pangs of suspense and jealousy. But the personage who has all the reader's sympathies is the Lady Frances. She is secretly in love with the wayward Ferdinando; and her love is so unselfish that she aids him, at least with good counsel, in his pursuit of her rival, hoping all the time that he will be sensible of his folly and discover her own worth. But the reader who expects that she will get her reward is disappointed ; Gascoigne does not execute poetic justice. The faithful lady dies of grief when Ferdinando, his eyes opened to the frailty of his mistress, departs, to throw himself into a life of dissipation. The light-minded Leonora continues her wicked life without disaster. Thus the tragedy towards which the story seems heading after the Italian manner, and the wholesome moral that English readers expected, were both eschewed, and the tale ends lamely. Its merits are not in the conclusion.

There are the makings of a fine story here, but Gascoigne missed his opportunities. In some ways he is even more thrifty and sparing of circumstance than the average *novella*. The father, the Lord of Valasco, who starts the ball rolling, makes only a few formal appearances. The husband does not come on the scene at all. No glimpse is vouchsafed into the lady's mind ; the reader is told what she says and does, but can explain her skittish behaviour only by the general rule that some women are made like that. Ferdinando's mental sufferings are recounted ; but he is not penetrated very deeply, and we are left in wonderment at his obtuseness in not perceiving the golden prize held out to him in the person of his friend and confidant, the Lady Frances. One would almost think that this pathetic figure had been created independently of the author's volition. Her place in the drama is entirely subordinate ; if it had been one appropriate to the beauty of her character, the inconsequent tale would have been a masterpiece. With all its shortcomings, however, *The Adventures of Master F. I.*, as it is oftenest called, is extremely interesting as the first original piece of English prose fiction on the new lines.

This is how the dialogue runs. Ferdinando has gone to bed in the dumps, because the secretary has returned and his mistress will not see him. The other ladies are walking in the park.

The dames (but specially the Lady Frances) gan straightways conjecture some great cause of sudden change, and so leaving Dame Elinor, walked all together into the park to take the air in the morning. And as they thus walked, it chanced that Dame Pergo heard a cuckoo chant, who, because the pride of the spring was now past, cried Cuck-cuck-Cuckoo! in her stammering voice. "Aha!" quoth Pergo, "this foul bird begins to fly the country, and yet before her departure, see how spitefully she can devise to salute us." "Not so," quoth Dame Frances, "but some other whom she espied"; wherewith Dame Pergo looking round about her, and espying none other company, said: "Why, here is nobody but we few women," quoth she. "Thanks be to God, the house is not far from us," quoth Dame Frances. Hereat the wily Pergo, partly perceiving Dame Frances' meaning, replied on this sort: "I understand you not," quoth she, "but to leap out of this matter, shall we go visit Master Jeronimy, and see how he doth this morning?" "Why," quoth Dame Frances, "do you suppose that the cuckoo called unto him?" "Nay, marry," quoth Pergo, "for (as far as I know) he is not married." "As who should say," quoth Dame Frances, "that the cuckoo envieth none but married folks." "I take it so," said Pergo. The Lady Frances answered: "Yes, sure, I have noted as evil luck in love (after the cuckoo's call) to have happened unto divers unmarried folks as ever I did unto the married."

The arch-plagiarist Robert Greene must have been familiar with Gascoigne's story. One incident, how the Lady Leonora makes a show of handing back his letters disdainfully to Jeronimi, who does not notice that she has really given him an encouraging reply till he has torn the missive to pieces, is reproduced in the tale of Valdracko, in *Planetomachia*.[1] Greene also retells, in the *Disputation betweene*

[1] Dr J. C. Jordan suggests that this may have come from Boccaccio's story of the confessor who unwittingly is employed by a married woman to give the signal to her gallant. The resemblance is certainly hard to see (*Robert Greene*, 31, n.).

a Hee Conny-catcher and a Shee Conny-catcher, the story told by Lady Frances about the gentleman who detected his wife's frailty with his bosom friend, and ever after treated her as a courtesan, leaving a piece of money every time he exercised his marital rights.[1]

Pettie's "Palace of Pleasure"

Ten years after Painter's first volume, in 1576, a quarto in black-letter, the very title of which confessed a modest rivalry with that very popular collection, came from a young Oxfordshire man, George Pettie, about whom some facts are known through his grandnephew Anthony à Wood. *A Petite Pallace of Pettie his Pleasure: Contayning many pretie Hystories, by him set foorth in comely colours and most delightfully discoursed*, is remarkable in two points. First, it shows better perhaps than any other of these books of tales what an English writer, using a free hand and owing no obligations to the authors from whom he borrowed, would make of his material. And then, its style is an almost complete anticipation of the various tricks and graces of euphuism, two years before Lyly's novel appeared. He deliberately tried to show that English, suitably enriched, was as good as French or Italian for prose fiction. There was no novelty in the actual stories which he told; they were classic examples of their kind, and already favourites with English readers. He may have taken "Icilius and Virginia" from Painter, and "Synorix and Camma" from *The Diall of Princes*, or he may have borrowed them elsewhere. He makes frank allusions to Painter, as well as to Ovid, whom he knew perhaps in Golding's translation of the *Metamorphoses*. But Pettie's manner is very unlike Painter's, and hardly more like the brooding censoriousness of Fenton.

"Amphiaraus and Eriphile"

The original affinity of the novel and the essay, the portrayal of and the discourse on life, is nowhere better exemplified. The story itself seems to be of little account, except as occasion for the moral. It is embedded in an elaborate moralistic framework. Prefixed is the "Argument," like the one explaining the story of "Amphiaraus and Eriphile," which is none too clear in the actual telling:

> Amphiaraus, a Gentleman Argive, sueth for marriage to Eriphile a widow, either liking other's possessions better than persons. Infortunio, burning in fond affection towards the same trull, seeing Amphiaraus's land preferred before his loyalty, is at point to destroy

[1] *Complete Poems of G. Gascoigne*, ed. W. C. Hazlitt (1869), i. 473-478.

himself. Amphiaraus, hiding himself to escape from the wars, is betrayed by Eriphile for covetice of reward : and setting foot within the Theban soil, the earth openeth and swalloweth him up. Eriphile, eftsoon a widow, proferreth her love to her old suitor Infortunio, by whom being repulsed, in choler she consumeth away, and dieth.

Having given out his text, the author proceeds with what is more like a sermon than a tale, a sermon on the well-worn theme, *auri sacra fames*. After a course of reflections on the evils of avarice with illustrations from ancient writ, Amphiaraus and Eriphile at length come on the scene, as the best illustration of all. But at every stage there are further reflections by the author, as well as long speeches and soliloquies in which the characters reason with each other or with themselves.

It is in these discourses that the author displays his choicest arts of expression. A typical instance is the meditation of the hero when he finds that his wife has betrayed him for a reward, and that he cannot avoid going to the front though he knows from the stars that he is fated to die in the first action.

Ah ! fond fool that I was, to repose any trust or confidence in women, whose sex is subtle, whose kind is cruel, who are constant only in unconstancy, who are witty only in wiles, who, as Aristotle saith, are monsters in nature, altogether imperfect, weak vessels, ignorant in all things, yea, which we may most lament, they are naturally endued with baits to allure men, with poison to infect men, and with charms to change men from men to beasts, as Circe did the servants of Ulysses ; yea, what man hath ever been so wise but by woman hath been seduced to folly ! as Pharo his daughter caused Solomon to fall to idolatry ! What man hath ever been so godly, but by woman hath been depraved ; as Bersabe drove King David to devilishness ! What man hath ever been so strong, who by woman hath not been made to stoop ; as Dalila took away the force of Sampson by cutting away his hair ! Who hath ever been so perfect, but by woman hath been drawn to imperfection ; as Adam by the means of Eve lost the perfection of Paradise ! Who hath ever been so faithful, but that women have enforced them to infidelity ; as a handmaid made Peter deny his master Christ ! Who so valiant, but by woman hath been vanquished ; as Omphale made Hercules serve her, and spin amongst her maids ; and after by Deianira was done to death ! Who so learned, but by woman hath been taught new

translations into verse, chiefly from Boccaccio, but in essentials differed very little from the current prose tales.

Smyth's "Tragical Histories"

Robert Smyth's *Straunge, Lamentable, and Tragicall Hystories* (1577) are described on the title-page as translated from the French, which means from Bandello, through the medium of Belleforest. One is the favourite Elizabethan story[1] of the close-fisted priest who refuses to bury a poor man because his widow cannot pay the fee. Smyth quaintly entitles it : " A just fact, but to cruell, of John Maria, Duke of Myllayne, towarde a Prieste, extreme couetous." The Duke being told of this piece of inhumanity, peremptorily orders the priest to carry out the burial, and at the last moment has the avaricious wretch bound face to face with the corpse and buried with it. Of an equally lurid complexion are the other tales : " A Gentleman Myllinois beeing amorous at the very end of his age for the extreame Jelosy of his Concubyne, was cause of the death of his Sonne and of himselfe, and lastly of the unhappy ende of the Harlot, whiche was cause of all" ; " A Mahometan slaue, reuengeth the death of his Lord upon his son that was the Homesyde "[2] ; or "The Marques of Ferraria, without hauing regarde to fatherly loue, caused his owne Sonne to be beheaded, for that he was found in Adultery with his faire Mother in law."[3]

Whetstone's story-books

George Whetstone was an adventurer with more talent for soldiering than for authorship, who is better known in the chronicles of literature for his clumsy and unsuccessful play in rhymed verse, *Promos and Cassandra*, than for his other books. He was a friend of the poets Gascoigne and Churchyard, and contributed prefatory verses to Gascoigne's *Flowers* (1575), also writing panegyrics on this and other distinguished friends in his own book of poems, *Remembraunce* (1577). He afterwards went with Sir Humphrey Gilbert on the Newfoundland voyage, served in Holland, was present at Zutphen, and gave an account of the Babington and other conspiracies against Elizabeth in the last of his diversified writings. His first volume of tales, *The Rocke of Regard* (1576), was mainly in verse, like the anonymous *Forrest of Fancy* (1579), by a certain "H. C." This was a common fashion of book-making in Tudor and Stuart times. The sub-title of the *Forrest of Fancy* runs : "Wherein is conteined very prety Apothegmes and pleasaunt

[1] From Bandello, iii. 25. [2] *Ibid.*, i. 52. [3] *Ibid.*, i. 44.

histories, both in meeter and prose, Songes, Sonets, Epigrams and Epistles, of diuerse matter and in diuerse manner. With sundry other deuises, no lesse pithye then pleasaunt and profytable." Boccaccio, Straparola, Bandello, and Giraldi Cinthio are among the sources. *The Rocke of Regard* is divided into four parts—"The Castle of Delight, the Garden of Unthriftinesse, the Arbour of Vertue, and the Orchard of Repentance: wherein are discoursed the miseries that followe dicing, the mischeifes of quarrelling, the fall of prodigalitie." One poem, in the first part, is a complaint by the Countess of Celant at the hour of her beheading, and her story is related in prose in the next book.

"An Heptameron of Civill Discourses"

Whetstone's collection of prose stories also presents itself in an ethical guise. *An Heptameron of Civill Discourses* (1582),[1] which, like the *Heptameron* of Marguerite d'Angoulême, has a dramatic framework, sets forth "The Christmasse Exercise of sundrie well Courted Gentlemen and Gentlewomen" who are supposed to be discussing marital questions. In the brief summary of the arguments handled in these seven days and one night's pleasures, the following are the heads enumerated: "Of the difference between the married state and the single life"; "Of the inconvenience of forced marriages"; "Of the inconveniences of rash marriages"—which topics are debated with illustrative stories on the first three days; "Other inconveniences" taking three more days, and "The excellency of marriage," occupying the last. Whetstone quotes learned opinions, especially from Plato, and draws many examples from life and history. *Promos and Cassandra* appears here as a prose tale, from Phyloxenus—that is, Cinthio; Shakespeare no doubt read both this and the play. Whetstone cannot be acquitted of some originality. Some of the tales in the *Rocke of Regard*, and several in the later set, though attributed to Dr Mossenigo and other mysterious people, are probably of his own invention. Mention is not irrelevant here of his prose treatise, *A Mirrour for Magestrates of Cyties* (1584), which is a survey of shady London life, full of unsavoury detail, especially in the "Addition or a Touchstone for the Time," which was inserted in the reprint that quickly followed.

[1] The book reappeared in 1593 under the title *Aurelia, The Paragon of Pleasure and Princely delights: Contayning The seuen dayes Solace (in Christmas Holy-dayes) of Madona Aurelia, Queene of the Christmas Pastimes.*

Barnaby Rich

Another soldier-novelist who apparently mixed his own inventions with what he obtained from previous writers was Barnaby Rich (*c.*1540-*c.*1617), author of several romances and of a story-book containing eight novelettes, *Riche his Farewell to Militarie profession.* He fought in the French war under Mary, and won the rank of captain in the Low Countries, afterwards enjoying a command in Ireland, which provided him with materials for *A Looking Glass for Ireland*, *A Short Survey*, *A New Description of Ireland*, and various pamphlets on Irish affairs. He wrote also on military subjects: the decay of discipline; the danger of neglecting the army; and the hardships of the soldier's profession. He quotes the authority of an eminent captain, Sir William Drury, "That the Souldiers of England had alwayes one of these three ends to looke for—to be slaine, to begge, or to be hanged." Rich himself, whose training, he said, had been more with his pike than with his pen, "not in the schools among clerks, but in the fields among unlettered soldiers," turned at last to literature for a livelihood. He also found vent in writing for a spleenful and fault-finding temper as good at general invective as that of his contemporary Fenton or any of the anatomizers of abuses who were so common. The title of one of his later works is evidently intended as a sarcasm: *The Honestie of this Age, proouing by good circumstance that the world was neuer honest till now* (1614).[1] No Jeremiah ever preached a more despairing sermon or painted his time in blacker colours. The epilogue in which he avouches his sincerity and freedom from malice summarizes the indictment thus:

> I know I shall offend a number, for I have inveighed against sins and that of several sorts: perhaps some will say I am too bitter, but can we be soo serious in exclaiming against Pride, against Adultery, against Drunkenness, against Blasphemy, and against other and so great Impiety, as I think since it rained fire and brimstone upon Sodom and Gomorrah, there was never the like, if it be not now time then both to speak and to write against those abominations, it is high time the world were at an end.

The close if hypercritical observation of the man is well displayed in this long sermon. Rich might have drawn his fellow-beings

[1] See preface by Peter Cunningham in reprint by the Percy Society (1844).

realistically in fiction, had he not been led astray by the preference for romantic stories. The bits of narrative that do occur are pointed anecdotes in the jest-book style, such as the one about the woman who was found weeping bitterly after her husband was hanged, and explained that her grief was not for the loss of her good man, " but for that he was not hanged in a clean shirt ; if his linen had been cleanly about him, his hanging would never have grieved me." The much-appreciated wit of the collections of quick answers, also, will be noticed in the remark of the Lord Mayor who was annoyed by the intrusion of a crowd of strangers at dinner. One of the officers reports: " If it please your lordship, here be too few stools." " Thou liest, knave," replies the Mayor, " there are too many guests."

" Beautified with sundry worthy histories, rare inventions, and politic devices," is the descriptive sub-title of his first book, *A right exelent and pleasant Dialogue, betwene Mercury and an English Souldier: Contayning his Supplication to Mars* (1574), a work chiefly of animadversion on the grievances under which the army laboured, collectively and individually, thrown into more painful relief by comparison with the soldierly exploits of great and mighty princes and valiant captains.

"Don Simonides"

A euphuistic story, *Don Simonides*, and the set of eight shorter pieces in the *Farewell* both appeared in 1581. Rich was probably one of those whose first incentive to authorship came from the resounding success of John Lyly—he was not, however, captured by the charms of Lyly's style. *The straunge and wonderfull aduentures of Dō Simonides, a gentilman Spaniarde : Gathered for the recreation as well of our noble yong gentilmen, as our honourable courtly Ladies* was followed by *The Second Tome of the Trauailes and aduentures of Don Simonides* (1584). It is the history of a foreign votary of Spanish and Italian culture who, like Euphues, comes to London, experiences and reflects on the ways of English society, and even runs up against the bosom friend of Euphues, Philautus. About this date was written the last novel of Barnaby Rich, *The Aduentures of Brusanus, Prince of Hungaria, Pleasant for all to read, and profitable for some to follow*. It was published in 1592, " by the great intreaty of diuers of his freendes."

"The Adventures of Brusanus"

"Farewell to Militarie Profession"

As had become the custom since *Euphues*, Rich, in his *Farewell to Militarie profession*, assumes that his chief readers will be ladies. There are no less than three addresses at the front of his book, besides several sets of verses. The first is, "To the right courteous Gentlewomen"; the second, "To the noble Souldiers, bothe of Englande and Irelande"; and the third, "To the Readers in generall." The first is a discourse explaining why he had determined to desert Mars, and in his riper years desired to live in peace among women and to consecrate himself wholly to Venus. For dancing or playing or singing he is not apt; hence he has but one gift to offer, these few rough-hewn histories. More in his own vein than this heavy politeness is the address to his old comrades, wherein he inveighs in unmeasured terms against an evil age. After an interesting allusion to his patron, Sir Christopher Hatton, to whom he had dedicated his *Allarme to England* (1578), Rich goes on:

Rich addresses himself to ladies

> And now where I left off I was telling what pride, what covetousness, what whoredom, what gluttony, what blasphemy, what riot, what excess, what drunkenness, what swearing, what bribery, what extortion, what usury, what oppression, what deceit, what forgery, what vice in general, is daily entertained and practised in England; and although it hath pleased God, by wonderful signs and miracles, to forewarn us of his wrath, and call us to repentance, yet you see the world runneth forwards, and keepeth his wonted course, without any remorse of conscience, neither making sign, nor proffer to amend.

His originals

In the address to the readers in general, Rich is guilty of some mystification regarding his sources. Three of the eight stories, "Nicander and Lucilla" "Fineo and Fiamma," and "Of Gonzales and his virtuous wife Agatha," he describes as Italian histories written by "Maister L. B."—whoever that may be. The initials do not agree with Bandello's. Of the other five, "forged only for delight," as he puts it, one at least, "Apolonius and Silla," the original of Shakespeare's *Twelfth Night*, can be traced to Bandello, but the names are altered; it is also found in Belleforest. Rich may, however, have derived it from some play that has disappeared; there were, at all events, two Italian comedies having similar features. The first and longest story, "Sappho, Duke of Mantona," largely coincides, except in names and places, with a play, *The Weakest goes to the Wall*, first printed in 1600, after it had been several times presented. The exact relationship between the story and the play, or perhaps an earlier play with a similar plot, is uncertain. Sir David Lyndsay's comedy, *Philotus* (1603), has similar correspondences to the last story, " Philotus and Emelia," another of the five " forged only for delight." But whether Rich borrowed from the theatre or the theatre dramatized stories from Rich is yet undetermined.

" Sappho, Duke of Mantona"

" Sappho, Duke of Mantona," abounds in the entanglements, wandering adventures, dangers and escapes, and ultimate disentanglement and reconciliation, characteristic of the late Greek romances. Sappho is a noble at the court of the Emperor Claudius. Of a frank and straightforward disposition, he falls a victim to a plot to discredit him with the emperor, and is banished. With his wife he retires into exile, and lives at Tariffa, in Macedonia, where they subsist in the deepest poverty. The man in whose house they live makes love to the disguised duchess ; and prosecuting the duke for his debts, compels him to leave his wife in pawn and go to seek his fortune. The duke makes his way towards the famous city of Cayre, and in a wilderness loses his little son Aurelianus. The boy is found starving by the Duke of Vasconia, who takes him to his court and brings him up as an esquire. Subsequently, the Duke of Vasconia's daughter falls in love with Aurelianus, and persuades him to run away with her. They escape to Cherona, where Duke Sappho is now the parish sexton. He takes a liking to the runaways and gives them lodging in his house. But Aurelianus, under the name of Sylvanus, goes forth in his turn to woo the goddess Fortune. He is received into the army of the Emperor Claudius, engaged in fighting the Turks. Meanwhile, Claudius has recalled Sappho, and placed him in command of the Imperial forces. The Turks are routed ; Sylvanus, *alias* Aurelianus, gains high distinction in the battle. But the Duke of Vasconia recognizes the abductor of his daughter. Sylvanus and his wife are both condemned to death. As it happens, however, Sappho overhears accidentally that Sylvanus was picked up in the desert, and that his real name is Aurelianus. Mutual recognition and general rejoicing ensue. By a like fortunate conjunction of events, his wife and daughter are also restored to him, and the son of still another duke who loves the daughter of the disguised duchess—she has been reduced to earning her livelihood as a sempstress—is thus enabled to marry her. The net result is that the banished and separated parents are reunited and regain their former wealth and honours, and both their children are brilliantly wedded.

"Apolonius and Silla"

"Apolonius and Silla" likewise has Greek affinities; in truth, it cannot be entirely unrelated to the famous old *Apollonius of Tyre*. Rich begins with one of his habitual dissertations on the theme of man's innate liability to error, especially through the estrangements from rectitude due to the passion of love. Apolonius, driven by storms to land in Cyprus, is beloved by Silla, daughter of the governor, who pursues him to Constantinople, and waits upon him in male attire. After many pretty incidents, her identity is revealed to Apolonius, who in requital for her devotion makes her his wife. There is a picturesque account of Silla's shipwreck in a terrible storm, reminding the reader inevitably of *Apollonius of Tyre*. An incident copied in *Twelfth Night* is that in which she has to carry a love-letter from her master Apolonius to the Lady Juliana whom he is courting. Some of the other stories plunge without delay into the current of events; yet they do not fail at the end or at some other convenient point to expound, with superfluous emphasis, what edification may be gathered from the events.

Colonna's "Hypnerotomachia"

The first part of that strange æsthetic romance, *Hypnerotomachia Poliphili*[1] by the mysterious Venetian friar, Francesco Colonna, was translated anonymously in 1592 as *Hypnerotomachia: The Strife of Loue in a Dreame*. Its rococo style was bound to be popular at a time when euphuistic and arcadian prose were all the rage, and the translator provided a close English or half-English equivalent. Let two specimens suffice :

The archer Cupid, in my wounded heart having his residence, like a lord and king, holding me tied in the bands of love, I found myself pricked and grievously tormented, in his tyrannous and yet pleasant regiment. And abounding in doubtful delight, unmeasurably sighing, I watered my plaints ; And then the surmounting Nymph, with a pleasing grace, incontinently gave me comfort, and with her ruddy and fair spoken lips, framing violent and attractive words, gave me assurance, abandoning and removing from my heart, all

[1] Aldine Edition (1499).

fearful thoughts, with her Olympiacal aspects, and cooling with her eloquent speeches, my burning heart; and with an amorous and friendly regard, and cast of her eyes, and smiling grace, she said thus unto me.[1]

The descriptive passages are wonderful, and worthy of the strange illustrations that adorn the book:

The seeling of the walls as aforesaid, mounted up to the bending of the Arch from the Chapters which stood upon their strict and upright Antes even to the uppermost end of the entry, which was by my perspective judgment twelve paces. From which perpolite ligature and fastened joints, the roof of the entry all the length thereof, did march with a hemicircubate flexure, answerable to the Antes and straight sides of the afore described porch full of varieties and exquisite representments, rarely engraven and of little water monsters, as in the water itself in their right and well-disposed plemitules, half men and women, with their fishy tails: some embracing one another with a mutual consent, some playing upon Flutes, and others upon fantastical instruments. Some sitting in strange fashioned Chariots, and drawn in them by swift Dolphins, crowned and adorned with water Lilies suitable to the furniture of the garnished seats: some with divers dishes and vessels replenished with many sorts of fruits, Others with plentiful copies, some coupled together with bands, and others wrestling as they did, riding upon Hipposatamies, and other sundry and uncouth beasts, with a Chiloneal defence.[2]

Boccaccio

The *Decameron* was not Englished till 1620, which at first seems unaccountable.[3] Boccaccio had, of course, been one of Chaucer's masters, and had long exercised an important influence on English writers; but he was either read in his own language or known indirectly through those who copied him. The earliest English prose version of any story from the *Decameron* was probably "The Wonderful history of Titus and Gisippus, whereby is declared the figure of perfect amity," which occurs in Sir Thomas Elyot's great treatise, *The Governour* (1531). It seems to have been translated

[1] The passage is given in the original spelling in Andrew Lang's reprint (1890, p. 193).
[2] *Ibid.*, p. 62.
[3] The *Filocopo* was translated by H. G. as *A Pleasant Disport of divers Noble Personages* (1567).

through the Latin of Philip Beroaldo.[1] Titus, a noble young Roman, is sent to Athens to study philosophy, and there makes friends with his housemate and fellow-student Gisippus, son of his father's friend, an Athenian gentleman. They love each other like the classical Pylades and Orestes or the mediæval Amis and Amile. Presently, Gisippus becomes engaged to a young lady, and takes his friend to see her. Titus falls incontinently in love. After a mental debate, and a hard struggle with himself, he sternly resolves to be true to Gisippus. But love cannot be controlled, and he takes to his bed. There Gisippus finds him, and succeeds in wringing the secret from his friend. Then comes the act of magnanimity. Gisippus realizes that Titus is the more grievously enamoured, and surrenders his betrothed. There are, of course, embarrassing explanations to be offered to the lady's kinsfolk, who, when they hear of the transaction, make themselves unpleasant. Titus returns to Rome, and Gisippus, falling into disfavour with his friends and neighbours, at last, in utter destitution, makes his way there too. But Titus fails to recognize his old friend in the beggar stationed before his door, and Gisippus believes himself to have been deliberately repulsed. Desperate, and yearning for death, he makes no defence when, through a mistake, he is arrested for a murder. He is sentenced to crucifixion. But at the critical moment Titus enters the prætorium and, recognizing Gisippus, seeks to repay his ancient debt by pretending that he himself is the guilty person. His statement is accepted, and he is about to be sentenced, when the real criminal, overcome with compassion for the two innocent men, gives himself up. All three are discharged by Octavianus, the two friends as exonerated, and the third man for his act of generosity. Titus receives Gisippus into his house, and they live in perfect friendship for the rest of their days.[2]

In 1587, in the heyday of euphuism, Boccaccio's *Amorous Fiammetta* appeared in an English dress, and the very title-page is

[1] *The Governour*, ed. H. H. S. Croft (1883), ii., c. 12. The tale is the eighth in Book X. of the *Decameron*.

[2] The initial situation, two friends in love with the same woman, to whose house the engaged man had brought his friend, with the mental debate before the latter resolves not to outrage friendship, obviously resembles that of Euphues, Philautus, and Lucilla, in Lyly's novel. Dr S. L. Wolff shows good reason for thinking that Boccaccio's "Tito e Gisippo" was Lyly's source, although the *dénouement* is different. He also traces "Tito e Gisippo" through the Old French poem, "Athis et Prophilas," to a late Greek Romance now lost (*The Greek Romances in Elizabethan Fiction*, pp. 248-261).

crammed with examples, caveats, and dehortations of the usual edifying stamp. Painter and other collectors were satisfied with choosing a few stories from the *Decameron*. Greene, who borrowed unscrupulously everywhere, took motives, incidents, and even whole stories from it without the slightest acknowledgment. But it was not through the novelists but through the playwrights, ransacking the collections of translated stories for plots, that Boccaccio made his chief contribution to English literature—at least, for the time being.

One explanation of this apparent neglect of him by the translators is that educated people read Boccaccio in the original, as of course they did many of the later *novellieri* who were Englished for the benefit of the less learned. A classic of old standing never makes the same appeal to the latter as does the current fiction of the day. Bandello, Straparola and Cinthio were famous contemporaries; Sacchetti, Giovanni Fiorentino and Massuccio were not much older. They depicted an existing Italy and Italian society as luckier and more adventurous Englishmen had actually seen it. Exciting reports of that fascinating land were in everyone's ears—none the less exciting or alluring because the strait-laced denounced it as a hell of iniquity. The strait-laced may, indeed, have been a potent reason for the lack of an English presentation of Boccaccio's masterpiece, which never affected the solemn tone of explicit edification, for even a licence to John Wolfe (1587) for an edition of the *Decameron* in the original language seems not to have been acted upon, and that to Jaggard (1620) was revoked by Whitgift, Archbishop of Canterbury,[1] although a few copies are known.

Limited influence of the novella on our fiction

The same considerations probably explain why there were not a great many more translations from the *novellieri* than actually appeared. They were read with avidity. Their influence was widespread and lasting. They set a fashion that took long to die. Italianate names were long the mode in fiction as in drama, on which the *novella* left an indelible mark. Italy was far more often the scene of a story than France or Germany, and, at certain dates, even than England. Greene, Lodge, and other makers of idyllic pastorals were deeply addicted to the Italianate tradition, and what they learned

[1] See Esdaile, preface, xvi.; and M. A. Scott: *Elizabethan Translations from the Italian*, 91-92. Jaggard printed a number of prohibited Italian books.

from the Greek romancers was largely through Italians who had studied under them beforehand. But it is easy to overestimate the influence of the *novellieri* on the actual development of English fiction. The Italian *novella* is a pleasing and sometimes an exquisite thing, but after all it is only a *novella*. It is not a novel; it is hardly a short story according to modern standards. It has incidents and situations which are diverting or affecting or terror-striking; but these are rarely given full value by means of a well-adjusted scheme. Character-drawing is at a minimum. The general view of life is, as it were, somewhat out of focus; in other words, it is not really general, partly because of the convention that only certain stock types of personage, a kind of standardized assortment, could figure in the *novella*—a more serious restriction than one that merely tied the observer down to a narrow segment of the social sphere. As a reading of life it was not to be compared with the English drama to which it gave so much that was valuable. The dramatist took the story and made it into something new and something greater; the novelist or collector merely paraphrased or copied. The task of the one was to convey the body and spirit of a story into a different artistic form, to transplant a piece of life into another element; and he performed that feat with the power over essentials that is able to use trifles for the creation of masterpieces. The other set himself a much easier task, and remained, even when he tried to be original, little more than a translator. Original stories rivalling the *novella* in accomplishment as well as in intention were exceedingly rare.

CHAPTER III

CONTRIBUTIONS FROM SPANISH AND OTHER SOURCES

The Spanish contribution

If the indebtedness of English drama to Italy was far heavier than that of fiction, Spanish literature yielded comparatively little to English drama, but, in the long run, a great deal to the novel.[1] In this case it was not merely that stories and subjects were transferred, but also that a peculiar attitude to life happened to coincide with a streak of humour in the English temperament, and a very effective way of expressing it found a ready response in English writers. Enough for the present has been said about the Amadisian romances[2]—that curious aftermath of mediæval romance. It was through these that the age of romance handed on what life remained inextinct to Sidney and other votaries of fancy and ideality; from these rather than from the authentic stock—to which they might have had easy access in Malory—the English heroic and sentimental romancers of the seventeenth century—like the French—borrowed almost all the furniture of their protracted and extravagant stories. There will be something more to be said on this subject in the next chapter. The Spanish share in the genesis of euphuism can also stand over for the present. Much more important, for it was a leaven that has never quite ceased working, was the intensely Spanish alloy of moralistic sentiment and bitter humour that reached England first through the picaresque novels.

Satirical realism in Spanish literature

A propensity for moralization and a keen eye for the absurdities of things were two immemorial traits in the Spanish character; in most writers one or the other preponderates, now and then they are seen in conjunction. The oldest Spanish story-book, the *Libro de Patronio* or *Conde Lucanor* of the Infante Juan Manuel (1282-1348),

[1] For Spanish features in English drama see J. G. Underhill's *Spanish Literature in the England of the Tudors*, 354-358.

[2] See Volume I., pp. 249-258.

was compiled expressly as a series of instructive examples; but the humorous observation and worldly experience are the salt that has kept the didactic work fresh till to-day. The didacticism of Juan Ruiz, Archpriest of Hita (*fl.* 1350), on the other hand, was a pose, assumed to give edge to his satire. He lays bare the cant and folly and baseness of mankind with a jovial cynicism, and with that sharp-eyed realism which is the deadliest weapon of satire. Although in the *Rimado de Palacio* of the chronicler Pero López de Ayala (1332-1407) moral indignation leaves the satirist little taste for merriment, yet there is the same close watch on the varied types that peopled actual society, high and low. Prototypes of the rogue, or *pícaro*, who was to figure so prominently in the most characteristic fiction of two hundred years later, may be recognized among the common folk sketched by either the Archpriest or Ayala; a specimen has even been pointed out in the earliest of the native romances of chivalry, *El Cavallero Cifar* (*c.* 1300).[1] In a more famous work—which ran the *Amadís* close in popularity and was quickly translated into Italian, French, Dutch, and German—the *Celestina*, or *La Comedia de Calisto y Melibea*, the candid and complete portrayal of the vicious classes and of those persons whose primitive natures in the stress of passion drag them down into the same depths, shows a like spirit and a more mature art. The rascally serving-men are chips from the same block as Lazaro and Guzman were shortly to be carved from.

The "Celestina"

The *Celestina*, which appeared just before the end of the fifteenth century, is in form an enormously long play, but for all intents and purposes it is a dramatic novel divided into acts and scenes instead of chapters, with lengthy passages of dialogue that serve to present and even to anatomize the characters as thoroughly as might be done by an expert novelist. Calisto and Melibea, sundered like Romeo and Juliet by inexorable circumstance, fling themselves headlong into the torrent of passion, which sweeps them to perdition. Celestina, who acts as go-between, is a creation of such towering interest and importance that her name usually takes first place in the title. Her genial rascality and hypocrisy and her ripe worldly wisdom are in the finest style of Spanish tradition. The realism that

[1] See H. Warner Allen's introduction to Mabbe's translation of the *Celestina* (Library of Early Novelists), p. xxv.

nothing escapes and that strips off all disguises, and the cynical humour that no sentiment can abash, are conjoined in this work with an intensity in the delineation of feeling against which Amadis and his kindred look pale and thin.

There is awkwardness in the way the story is presented ; there are many crudities; but as a whole the *Celestina* sums up and surpasses all that was finest in Spanish literature to that day. Probably the main reason for its superiority is that by then much had been learned from France and Italy. The old procuress was developed from an original in the *Libro de buen amor* of the Archpriest of Hita, who had drawn his humorous Trotaconventos after a character in an old Latin play and refashioned her in the spirit of the *fabliaux*. And, as the *Decameron* had by then been translated into Catalan and Castilian, it is impossible to suppose that the inspiration of Boccaccio had been without effect upon the author or authors of the *Celestina*.

The first four acts were adapted to the English stage as an interlude, by John Rastell, as early as 1530. Twice before the end of the century a comedy was licensed under the title of *Lacelestina*. But English readers seem to have preferred the ponderous, shallow, and affected Guevara, whose *Relox de principes* was translated over and over again, to fiction so vital as this. At any rate, they were content to wait for a complete translation of the book till 1631, when Mabbe performed the task with raciness and spirit. It was, no doubt, however, read pretty widely in the original Spanish, since Vives included it in his list of books [1] the perusal of which ought to be forbidden. Mabbe toned down the unflinching candour of the book to conciliate Puritans, and his title is a paragraph pregnant with literary and social history, running thus : "The Spanish Bawd, Represented in Celestina ; Or, The Tragicke-Comedy of Calisto and Melibea. Wherein is contained, besides the pleasantnesse and sweetnesse of the stile, many Philosophicall Sentences, and profitable Instructions necessary for the younger sort : Shewing the deceits and subtilties housed in the bosomes of false seruants, and Cunny-catching Bawds." But, in spite of this edifying advertisement, the *Celestina* is not in the least one of the many didactic works imported from Spain. It contains pithy maxims and moral reflections innumerable ; but they fall from the lips of that amiable old reprobate, the Spanish bawd

[1] Underhill, 100.

herself, whom no one would be abandoned enough to recommend as a moral adviser ; and it is the mingled irony and humanism concentrated in this inimitable personage that gives the philosophical sentences and the profitable instructions their right value.

"Lazarillo de Tormes"

Nor is there anything of the didactic commentator in the first *novella picaresca*, or novel of roguery, *Lazarillo de Tormes*, the oldest extant edition of which is dated 1554. This is a book which is Spanish to the core. It is an inversion of the chivalric romance, with its resplendent hero and high-sounding achievements. Spain at that time had been ruined and demoralized by a gigantic war. The whole country was in a state of destitution. Large numbers of the gentry were reduced to miserable shifts, maintaining appearances on next to nothing, forced to keep body and soul together by mean pretences; a large proportion of the lower classes were rogues and vagabonds without disguise. Such was the state of things that formed the background of the picaresque novels. We find in them the comedy and satire that emanate from despair.

Lazaro is the offspring of a miller's foreman and a trull. He gets his living as best he can, and his first job is to lead about a blind beggar. He cheats and is beaten by this first master, then drifts from one patron to another, each worse than the last—skinflint priest, starving hidalgo, seller of indulgences, friar, painter, chaplain, alguazil—attaining the summit of his career as town-crier of Toledo and husband to an archpriest's concubine. Some of the tricks and adventures of the young scamp are borrowed from the popular jest-books. But the mordant realism with which his successive masters are sketched, and the cynical humour, are what had been traditional from the Archpriest of Hita to the *Celestina*. In one sense the story —and a brief one at that—is formless, the incidents merely following one another at random as the hero passes from one protector to the next. But this, which was to be the regular scheme of the picaresque story, was not a bad device for satirical portraiture of the different phases of Spanish life. The tale is told not without economy and restraint ; there is a steady consistency in the comic view of life, the satire being directed at the same ironical angle throughout. The picaresque method—of which this is the first complete example—is by no means lacking in artistic possibilities.

Lazaro's philosophy of life—if so respectable a term can be applied to the sapience of such an imp—is that nothing can be worse than the worst, and the one alleviation of the world's ills is to enjoy their absurdity.[1] To Lazaro there is nothing sacred, nothing profane. He makes what profit he can by casual benefactors, and flouts them into the bargain. The same cynical attitude is the second famous *picaro's* main equipment against the world. Mateo Alemán, however, in *Guzman de Alfarache*, tried to combine the Spanish love of sermonizing with Spanish cynicism, and the two do not piece well together. It is like putting moral homilies in the mouth of Lazarillo. They may fall aptly and with infinite comic effect from that ripe old sinner Celestina, who has evolved a paradoxical order of right and wrong in her charitable experience of an outcast world; but in Guzman, the rascally young adventurer, with no eye for anything but his belly or his conceit, they are out of character. Le Sage was right in pruning away these concessions to philistinism when he adapted the book into French.

"Guzman de Alfarache"

In *Guzman de Alfarache* the rogue becomes a cosmopolitan adventurer. As ne'er-do-well, loafer, street-arab, man of fashion, sharper, pimp, professional mendicant, servant to a cardinal and then to an ambassador, he works his way through Spain and Italy, sketching people and manners in the liveliest style. Without the discourses the book would have been as good as *Lazarillo*, erring however on the side of length as that in too much brevity. The first part appeared in 1599. A fraudulent sequel was published by a literary rival, upon whom Alemán retaliated by putting his brother into the second part as an objectionable character. The genre was now firmly established. In 1603 appeared the *Viaje Entretenido* of Augustín de Rojas, and the *Pícara Justina* of Francesco Lópéz de Úbeda the same year. Quevedo was writing his *Vida del Buscón llamado Don Pablos* about this time, not publishing it, however, till 1626. Some of the best pieces in the *Novelas Exemplares* of Cervantes are picaresque stories, and there is manifestly a certain picaresque element in *Don Quixote*. Espinel's *Marcos de Obregón* (1618), which gave Le Sage the basis for his *Gil Blas*, and *La Garduña de Sevilla* (1634) of Alonso de Castillo Salórzano perhaps complete the list of the most famous

[1] What is the answer of Figaro, that most delectable *picaro*, to the Count's demands: "Qui t'a donné une philosophie aussi gaie?" FIGARO. "L'habitude du malheur. Je me presse de rire de tout, de peur d'être obligé d'en pleurer" (*Le Barbier de Seville*, i. 2).

Spanish rogue-stories. All these were sooner or later adapted into English, together with several of minor note.[1]

Picaresque tendencies in English works

The picaresque stories found a soil prepared for them in England. In the jest-books and merry tales which everyone delighted in, and more particularly in such attempts to string episodes of cheating and horseplay into a continuous story, as Scoggin's *Geystes* (1566), Skelton's *Merie Tales* (1567), or the *Jests of George Peele* (1607), there was something parallel, if less coherent, of native origin. The economic and social condition of England late in the sixteenth century was not altogether unlike that of Spain—or, indeed, of the Continent in general. True, she was not a defeated nation; but she was overstrained by warlike effort, the social system had been unhinged by the suppression of the monasteries, agriculture was depressed, unemployment general, and the land, especially in the neighbourhood of towns, was swarming with discharged soldiers and sailors, and others hard put to it to make a living, who were easily induced to join the regular army of vagrants and criminals. Awdeley and Harman's warnings, of which there will be more to say presently, were meant in all seriousness, and there was no doubt much truth in the picture of the seamy side painted by Greene, Nashe, and Dekker, however much they were second-hand reporters.

Translations of Spanish picaresque stories

Lazarillo de Tormes was translated, in a racy style, by David Rowland of Anglesey (1576),[2] and in this or other versions went through many editions down to the middle of the eighteenth century. Alemán's novel was fortunately undertaken by that conscientious person James Mabbe, who entitled it, certainly not with the approval of its magisterial author, *The Rogue, or the Life of Guzman de Alfarache* (1622). This also became extremely popular. The third edition was corrected and enlarged by the addition of the *Celestina*, in 1634. Later versions as a rule omitted the moral discourses;

[1] E.g. *La Hija de Celestina* (1612), by Alonso Gerónimo de Salas Barbadillo, adapted through the French of Scarron into English, by John Davies of Kidwelly, as *The Hypocrites* (1657); *El Necio bien Afortunado* (1621) of the same author, translated by Philip Ayres, as *The Fortunate Fool* (1670); the partly authentic *Estebanillo Gonzáles* (1646) and Luis Vélez de Guevara's *Diablo Cojuelo* (1641), both adopted rather than adapted by Le Sage, and thence turned into English; and Dr Carlos García's graphic account of systematic roguery, *La desordenada condicia de los bienes agenos, y la oposicion y conjuncion de los dos grandes luminares de la tierra* (1619) which came into English as *The Sonne of the Rogue* (1638).

[2] Rowland translated with the French version of Jean Saugrain (1560) before him, and also probably the Spanish text.

they are more entertaining, but of course do not represent Alemán. Mabbe also translated the *Exemplary Novels* of Cervantes (1640). Quevedo's *Sueños* was the first of his books to be translated.[1] Quevedo was a favourite Spanish author after the Restoration, and translations of the *Buscón* and of various groups of his works were frequently appearing. One of the translations of the *Buscón* was by John Davies of Kidwelly (1657), and this hard-working gentleman also published a rendering through the French of *La Garduña de Sevilla*, under the title of *La Pícara* (1665). The *Viaje Entretenido* was not translated, but it gave Scarron the idea for his *Roman Comique*, which appeared in several English versions in the seventeenth century. *La Pícara Justina* was adapted to form part of a set of picaresque stories entitled *The Spanish Libertines* (1707). Of imitations and of the effect of the picaresque spirit upon English writers much will be said in later pages. Many of the translations mentioned date, it will have been noticed, long after what has been specially described as the age of translation. To this later crop belong, of course, the English editions of Cervantes, beginning with Shelton's version of the first part of *Don Quixote*, in 1612. The influence of Cervantes on the English novel was the most penetrating of all, but it came into operation at a much later era.

Translations from French, etc.

Compared with those from the classical languages and from Italian and Spanish, Elizabethan translations from other sources were not of remarkable importance. The language best known to the professional translator was French; but French was used chiefly as a medium through which Italian, Spanish, or Greek and Latin works were rendered into English. Even when the English writer knew his author's tongue, there is often evidence that he had a French version as well as the original text before him. Otherwise, the literature which had contributed most to ours—and was to contribute freely again after the close of the Elizabethan age—had very little to give us at this time in the way of prose fiction. The *Heptameron* was regarded as a model by some of the compilers of story-books—at least by such as gave their collections a dramatic frame; Painter selected some items from this storehouse, and there

[1] In *Visions, or Hel's Kingdome, and the World's Follies and Abuses, strangely displaied by R. C.* [Richard Croshawe]. *Being the first fruits of a reformed life* (1640). There was another version by Roger L'Estrange (1667).

was a translation of the *Heptameron* in 1597 and another in 1654. Persons of literary taste read Rabelais, as allusions make evident. *Gargantua* was entered in the Stationers' Register in 1594 ; but the earliest translation extant, Urquhart's first book of the works, was not printed till 1653. Odd sets of stories, such as Thomas Beard's *Theatre of God's Judgements* (1597)—retailing instances of the divine justice executed on malefactors—or Simon Goulart's *Admirable and Memorable Histories containing the wonders of our time* (1607), were catchpenny articles meant for a certain public, and have no significance in literary history. The old romances of French origin continued to be popular, in a curtailed and simplified form. *Huon of Bordeaux*, *The Four Sons of Aymon*, Caxton's version of Le Fèvre's *Recueil* and, above all, minor sentimental tales like *Paris and Vienne* and *Valentine and Orson*, had a profitable sale as chap-books right on into the next century. Among such was *The True and Admirable History of Patient Grisel*, an interesting French parallel to the ballad-histories of Robin Hood, Guy of Warwick, and other national heroes.

Other popular stories of foreign origin

The plebeian literature of jocularity, sensational legend and crude didactic fable was continually receiving additions from abroad. Tales widely current in Germany and the Low Countries, in Denmark, France and Italy, found their way into print in England, without being adapted to English surroundings—like those that had travelled across by oral transmission or had been gathered in for homiletic or some other use. Versions of and episodes from the history of Reynard the Fox went on being printed as chap-books till after the seventeenth century. Wynkyn de Worde produced two editions of *Robert the Devil*, a French story of a mischievous scamp who repents and becomes a devout servant of Jesus Christ. A more truly diabolical tale is the Danish legend of Friar Rush, who is sent by the prince of darkness to plague the inmates of a monastery, and when he has turned the whole house into a place of strife and debauchery is detected and exorcized by the prior. The fabulous story of Hamlet also came from Denmark, but not at first-hand ; in the printed edition of 1608 *The Hystorie of Hamblet* is translated from Belleforest, who took it from the Latin of Saxo Grammaticus. The legend of Virgil the enchanter grew up in Italy during the early Middle Ages, and spread into France, Germany and the Netherlands. The first English edition of *Virgilius*, the so-called life of Virgil, recounting the marvels he did "by witchcraft and necromancy through the help of the devils of hell," was printed at Antwerp (1518), and there was another edition by Copland half-a-century later. From a Dutch source seems also to have come the first of several versions of the tale of Fortunatus, who is rescued from abject poverty and given an inexhaustible purse, and by the aid of a miraculous hat is enabled to transport himself whithersoever he wills. This very popular wonder-tale was dished up in one of Dekker's plays.[1] Both the German Faust-books were translated, and there were numerous editions, besides abridgements. *The Historie of the Damnable Life, and Deserued Death of Doctor John Faustus* was printed in 1592, five years after the German original and three after Marlowe's play. *The Second Report of Doctor John Faustus, containing his Appearances, and the Deedes of Wagner,* followed in 1594. Of that good old story-book, *The Seven Wise Masters,* more than a score of reprints or new editions saw the light during the Tudor epoch.[2]

What was the effect of the translations on the English novel?

What was the result of all this busy translating on the history of the novel? In considering that question, these levies on foreign popular fiction may as well be left out of account. They went to swell the volume of vernacular literature and supplied some incidents and comic turns to Deloney and other retailers of homely English fiction. They flattered the vulgar palate and kept readers amused and ready for something more. They are, indeed, interesting chiefly as showing what the public liked, then and long afterwards. The jest-book was not so much superseded as absorbed by the novel. This particular comic element has never lost its value as an ingredient in fiction of a higher order. The hoaxes, quips, blunders and drolleries that shook the sides of those who read the jest-books are still in demand. Such tales as those of Mr W. W. Jacobs are only a more craftsmanlike edition of the immemorial merry tales.

It is certainly hard to trace any profound effect upon the

[1] Influenced by the numerous translations from the Spanish, there appeared a thoroughly picaresque version (1676) entitled *The Right, Pleasant, and Variable Tragical History of Fortunatus. Whereby a Young-man may learn how to behave himself in all Worldly Affairs and Casual Chances,* relating the adventures of a youth whose fellow-servants plot against him out of spite at his master's favouritism. He falls into low company, loses all he has, and barely escapes hanging. The magical business of the inexhaustible purse and the wishing-cap follows.

[2] See Volume I., p. 287, and for other jest-books, 292-293.

development of fiction to the influence of the Italian story-tellers, who supplied the Elizabethan translator with the bulk of his material. Such a course of apprenticeship should have been most wholesome for the artificers of the coming novel. The lessons in artistic method ought to have been invaluable. But the lessons seem to have been received at the wrong time, and what the Elizabethans learned was forgotten by the next two or three generations. Those lessons were not being conned at the date, considerably later, when English writers of fiction began to make real progress. Greene and some others tried their hand at *novelle*, with indifferent success ; but with them the genre ceases, except for a few examples in the shape of inset stories. Perhaps the most useful service performed by this group of translators was to have helped on the evolution of a suitable prose. Those, such as Painter, who stuck to their business, and eschewed inordinate disquisition and decorative word-play, did more than they usually get credit for to provide fiction with a plain and workmanlike style. But this was an incidental benefit aside from the question at issue.

That question is not difficult to answer in regard to the importations from Spain. Both picaresque fiction and the mature art and exquisite humour of Cervantes made a lasting impression on the English novel ; but this did not come to pass for a long while yet. There is very little evidence that any English writer set himself to imitate the Spanish picaresque stories before the middle of the seventeenth century, and it was on Fielding and his successors that the mantle of Cervantes descended. They coupled his name, as often as not, with that of Le Sage, through whom rather than directly from the Spanish originals the picaresque tradition made its way into our literature.

Influence of Greek romance

A more drastic influence is assignable to the translation and study of the ancient Greek romances. Sidney and Greene are the writers principally concerned at the time, but the influence was far from ending with the avowed imitators of the ancients. Sidney was an admiring student of Heliodorus, and knew his Achilles Tatius at first-hand ; and he not only borrowed whenever he wished, he also fashioned his art on these models. Greene, too, borrowed from these writers and from Longus ; but he did not take the pains required to make himself a romancer capable of originating similar work. In Sidney's and in Greene's romances, the unexpected situations, the disguises, the mistakes of identity, the suffering and suspense relieved in the end by events that had been long since foreshadowed by oracles—all this, together with the general conception of Fate, Fortune, or Nemesis controlling human destinies, for which Sidney tended to substitute the agency of Providence or even the more rational idea of virtue or character, is the bequest of Greek romance, either directly or through the medium of Boccaccio and his successors. In the manipulation of these romantic elements and in the architectonics of plot, Sidney deliberately sought and achieved an immense complexity. Extreme complication with perfect coherence was the ideal transmitted to later romancers, and realized most completely, and often most immoderately, by the French school in the following century. It became the traditional requirement, so that even such novelists as Marivaux and Richardson, who sought to demonstrate that romance could be found in their own everyday world, or such as Fielding, who wrote against the romantic view of life, could not escape it.[1] In endeavouring to provide a better sort of fiction, they were put upon their mettle to show that it was better in the same respects, and that reality was no poorer in the romantic qualities of surprise and unsuspected complication than the fantastic world imagined by their opponents. Hence the romantic stock-in-trade was incessantly reappearing, in shapes latterly so familiar that the strangeness and unexpectedness which gave it artistic value often made their effect without seeming strange or unexpected.

But even this legacy of antique romance might have gone unclaimed had it not been that French disciples of Sidney and of the ancients set a higher value upon it than did Sidney's countrymen, the legitimate legatees. The Sidneian influence was a French influence by the time it began to react on English novelists. And with

[1] Dr S. L. Wolff: *The Greek Romances in Elizabethan Fiction*, 462-463. Mr Wolff instances Richardson's adoption of the name Pamela, Clarissa's threat of suicide to save her honour, Miss Byron's abduction by Sir Hargrave Pollexfen, etc., as incidents parallel to some in the *Arcadia*. But it is hardly necessary to suppose that Richardson was deliberately borrowing, or was consciously imitating the *Arcadia*. The influence was much more indirect. Things of this kind were traditional in fiction, and he would give as good as could be demanded by the most insatiable reader of romance. Realistic novelists from that day to this fall into two sets: those who have recognized and avoided the romantic pitfalls and those who have tumbled straight in.

this important exception the net result of all the indefatigable work of all the translators was simply this, to have provided a stock of admirable translations. Later ages have produced few indeed to compete with these in literary merit: but their practical effect upon the development of fiction was surprisingly small.

CHAPTER IV

LYLY'S *EUPHUES*

In December 1578 Gabriel Cawood, dwelling in Paul's Churchyard, published *Euphues, the Anatomy of Wit*. It was the first literary work of John Lyly, then aged twenty-five or twenty-six, who had left Oxford three years before under a cloud, and was trying by the avenue of aristocratic patronage to step into some such office as the mastership of the revels. One road to success in this endeavour was to win distinction as an author. Lyly came of a scholarly family, his grandfather being William Lyly the grammarian, friend of Erasmus, More and Colet; an uncle was a canon of Canterbury and the author of several erudite works; his father was registrar of the city and diocese of Canterbury. The book secured him public attention without delay. There had already been four editions when he followed it up, in the spring of 1580, with a second part, *Euphues and his England*. He had meantime added the degree of Master of Arts at Cambridge to that awarded by his own university. He became a favoured dependent and probably the secretary of the Earl of Oxford, son-in-law to his old patron, Burleigh, and, helped perhaps by this influential backing, he brought out his first two plays, *Campaspe* and *Sapho and Phaon*, which were acted before the court. After this success he devoted his talents to the stage, where we need not follow him. He wrote no more fiction, and died in 1606.[1]

Lyly's "Euphues"

Euphues, to speak collectively of the two books which are now usually found in one pair of covers, is a work of considerable importance in literary history; but the degree of its importance requires very careful evaluation. It is often described as the first English novel, or the first novel of manners. If this be taken as meaning that it is the first work that can be regarded as falling within a loose definition of the novel, or as the first to combine a thread of

[1] The best account of Lyly's life and work is *John Lyly: contribution à l'histoire de la Renaissance en Angleterre*, par Albert Feuillerat, 1910.

narrative with a view of life and manners, the description may be accepted for what it is worth. But if it implies that *Euphues* was the pattern and starting-point from which the English novel proceeded to develop, it is far from true. *Euphues* made a great hit, and was widely imitated, both style and story, for ten or a dozen years. Then it went into gradual oblivion, from which it has been resurrected, like a museum specimen, for the edification of modern students. In certain ways it was a forerunner of the novel of manners which came into being a century and a half later; but the novelists of manners hardly knew of its existence, and probably learned nothing from it either directly or indirectly.

Outline of "Euphues." Part I.—"The Anatomy of Wit"

There are two stories in *Euphues*, besides incidental anecdotes, and besides other contents which are by no means tributary to the narrative: there is that of *The Anatomy of Wit*,[1] and there is the sequel, *Euphues and his England*. Let us review them in outline. In the first an educated young Athenian, wishing to see the world, visits Naples, a frivolous and dissolute place, well exemplifying the demoralized state of Italian society, of which it is one main object of the book to give young men a warning. Here, after being greeted with a protracted lecture on the follies of youth from an old man, Eubulus—who might stand for Conscience in a morality play—and replying impatiently at similar length, Euphues falls in with a gallant of his own age, Philautus. With much prolix declamation on the theme of friendship the two enter into bonds of closest amity, and Philautus takes his new acquaintance with him to the house of the lady whom he is courting. Euphues has the ill grace to fall in love, and when his friend's back is turned to woo the lady himself. He cuts out Philautus; but Lucilla speedily jilts him too, and both the swains are left lamenting. There is nothing more in the shape of story.[2] Euphues, disillusioned and penitent, indites a "Cooling Card for Philautus and all Fond Lovers"; this is put into an appendix, with a dissertation "Euphues and his Ephebus," derived through

[1] "Anatomy" means a dissection or exposure—*i.e.* of the empty writing for display, the art for art's sake, and like symptoms of the Italian influence denounced by Ascham. This is the ground of the attack on Oxford.

[2] See p. 42, n., on Dr Wolff's comparison of the general situation with that in "Tito e Gisippo" (*Decameron*, x. 8). There is no inherent inconsistency between the view that Lyly adopted the same situation, finding a converse *dénouement*, and the theory that he had the Prodigal Son theme at the back of his mind, or even converted a play into prose fiction (see p. 61, n. 1).

Erasmus from Plutarch's *De Educatione*; and so, with further letters and addresses, the first book is brought to a conclusion.

In all this there is manifestly very little of the stuff that now goes to the composition of a novel. The thread of story is of the slightest, exciting hardly any interest in itself; the characters are not persons, but merely copy-book headings, and their doings or mishaps appeal neither to our sympathy nor to our sense of humour—except in ways not calculated upon by the author. The story, such as it is, forms a mere pretext for the moralization, which Lyly dispenses in a lecturing style in dialogue and soliloquy, like those in Pettie's tales, or in epistles bearing the signature of the hero. He was evidently doing his best to exploit the widespread taste for moralistic debate; and the story not only fails to hold the modern reader, but is also a very faint reflection of life, either then or in any other age. Lyly found, however, that the public who bought his book preferred even this attenuated measure of fiction to the lectures, and accordingly he constructed the sequel on somewhat better lines.

Part II.—"Euphues and his England"

In *Euphues and his England* the reunited friends leave Italy for these shores. Euphues, by sad experience, has learned wisdom and seriousness, and at an early point relates the edifying story of the hermit Cassander and his headstrong nephew, Callimachus. A much better tale is the one put in the mouth of the venerable Kentishman, Fidus, which follows after some pleasing dialogue. Its moral is the folly of love. But that is not the doctrine enunciated at large in *Euphues and his England*, which is in the main a recantation of the diatribes against women and love between the sexes contained in the *Anatomy*. This second book has a preface addressed to the ladies as well as the gentlemen of England, in which respect it follows Pettie's lead. Philautus is now the central figure. He falls in love with the arrogant Camilla, and the reader's interest is solicited in his sentimental experiences. Philautus is not successful here, but he finds happiness with a lady who has remained heart-whole. After his friend's marriage Euphues returns philosophically to Athens, whence he sends to the Neapolitan ladies his *Glass for Europe*—a panegyric of Elizabeth and the ladies of England. Finally, he retires to a life of meditation at Silexedra.

Though little is made of them, there are dramatic opportunities in the story. Bare as it seems, it is not half so bare of incident as some modern stories which hold us spellbound. But, whilst Lyly gravely anatomizes the thoughts and emotions of men and women in love, he fails to persuade that his men and women are alive or ever were alive. Deloney reveals more knowledge in one little episode—the comedy of Long Meg and Gilian waiting in Tuttle Fields for the same young man, who never comes [1]—than Lyly in any of his expositions of the deceits and pangs of love. But Deloney does not analyse and discuss the moral and sentimental bearings of the case. Still more glaring is the inferiority of Lyly's diagnosis of the love malady to Chaucer's in *Troilus and Cressida*, or even to Lefevre's broader treatment in the *History of Jason*.[2] Of character in the sense of individuality there is more in an average play-bill than in both parts of *Euphues*. Fond editors have discerned character in these abstract figures, forgetting that it was character only in the ethical sense that Lyly was aiming at, and that he devised his story only as a framework for the abstract discussion.

"Euphues" a treatise on education and manners rather than a novel

For the proper way to regard *Euphues* is not as a rudimentary novel, even though some of the stories that resulted from copying his performance did approximate slightly to the species. Looking back we are naturally obsessed by the idea of the novel as a goal towards which earlier forms of literature were tending.[3] But Lyly had his mind on the present, not the future. He essayed to produce a more taking kind of book than those already accessible on the ideals and discipline required for the making of a finished gentleman.

There were a number of grave treatises at the bookshops handling the problem in different ways, among them Sir John Elyot's *Governour* (1531), Hoby's translation of Castiglione (1561), and Ascham's *Scholemaster* (1570)—from which he took the word

[1] See pp. 181-182. [2] See Volume I., pp. 230-233.

[3] M. Abel Chevalley has some interesting remarks on this tendency, which he calls "Messianism," in an article "Le Roman anglais, histoires et destins" (*Vient de Paraître*, juillet, 1925):

"De cette vaste enquête allant des vagissements qu'interroge M. Baker aux tout derniers cris enregistrés par MM. Gould et Starr, quels enseignements tirer? D'abord, *qu'il faut abandonner l'attitude messianique.* L'histoire du roman n'est pas du tout une Marche à l'Étoile orientée vers Richardson et Fielding et, de là, sur les constellations du dernier siècle. Elle n'aboutit pas plus à notre époque que l'Histoire de France à la Troisième République. Bannissons-en l'idée de progrès qui jalonne de faux indicateurs tant d'histoires de la littérature. C'est une série de recommencements. Si, comme on a droit de le croire, la fiction romanesque est un besoin éternel et universel de l'âme humaine, toutes les variétés du roman co-existent, et dans tous les temps y compris le nôtre. Toutes sont également légitimes, et *nécessaires.*"

"euphues" and made it the name of his hero. He proposed to put the aspirant to good manners, sound morals, and a cultivated mind in a setting of real life, and thus to show the trials and conflicts in which he must triumph if he would attain the perfection which he coveted. Thus we have to judge *Euphues* as a book of theory and precept, set forth in an entertaining way, the fiction being only a device for illustrating the teaching and not an object in itself.[1]

Euphuism—Lyly's style: was it assimilated from Guevara?

Euphues has, further, received disproportionate attention from literary historians on account of its remarkable style. That style has been christened euphuism after Lyly's book,[2] although it was not invented by him and had indeed been in use for some time already. The author of *Euphues* practised it more systematically than his predecessors, and gave it the finishing touches; that was his sole claim to the patent. He was the last, rather than the first, of the euphuists. For many years Dr Landmann's theory[3] met with general acceptance, that euphuism was a novel species of rhetoric acquired by Lyly and others from Antonio de Guevara, Archbishop of Mondoñedo and Cadiz, whose most celebrated work[4] was the *Libro del Emperador Marco Aurelio con relox de principes* (1529), a work translated by Lord Berners as *The Golden Boke of Marcus Aurelius* (1534), and by Sir Thomas North as *The Diall of Princes* (1557).[5] Unhappily for this theory, both Berners and North made their translations, not straight from Guevara's Spanish, but from a French rendering in which the distinctive features of Guevara's prose were completely altered.[6] They were both of them apparently unable to

[1] According to Mr J. Dover Wilson ("Euphues and the Prodigal Son" in *The Library*, Oct., 1909), *Euphues and the Anatomy of Wit* is to a large extent an old play cast into narrative form, such play being one of the Prodigal Son dramas that began with the Dutch *Acolastus*. Eubulus and Philautus were characters in this. At all events, Euphues goes out into the world and is tried by its temptations, returning home at last a sadder and wiser man.

[2] Gabriel Harvey was the first to employ the term, in the *Aduertisement for Papp-hatchett*, applying it to Lyly's ridiculous fondness for comparisons drawn from a fabulous natural history (Feuillerat, pp. 472-473).

[3] Set forth in *Der Euphuismus* (1881) and in "Shakspere and Euphuism" (*New Shakspere Society Transactions*, 1880-1885, Pt. II.).

[4] Guevara pretended that the *Libro* was translated from a Greek work that he had discovered at Florence.

[5] Berners rearranged the matter of his original completely, whereas North gave a full and faithful translation.

[6] Mr K. N. Colvile, ed. of *The Diall of Princes*, by Don Anthony de Guevara: being select passages, with introduction and bibliography (The English Scholars' Library, 1919), is strongly against the view that Lyly borrowed from the Spanish work.

read their author in the original, nor is there the slightest reason to suppose that Lyly was acquainted with Castilian or had made any study of Guevara's peculiar variety of *estilo culto*, the artificial, highly ornate diction which was being cultivated at this period by Spanish, Italian, French, and also English men of letters. Sir Sidney Lee remarked, in editing Berners' translation of *Huon of Bordeaux* (1887), that this great translator, in his preface to Froissart, was writing in a style singularly like euphuism in 1524, five years before Guevara's book had appeared in Spain. There was no need for Lyly to read Spanish literature in order to learn euphuism. In the previous chapter it was noted that Fenton and Pettie indulged freely in euphuistic prose before the advent of Lyly's book[1]; and among others whose style had similar characteristics may be named Latimer, Cheke, Gosson, author of *The Schoole of Abuse* (1579),[2] and even Ascham, when he was not expressly maintaining classical dignity and restraint. Between Lyly and Guevara the main analogy was that both wrote to edify and were never tired of moral disquisition, and both cultivated style for its own sake; both, in particular, made inordinate use of alliteration, a favourite ornament of artistic prose at that era.[3] For the rest, Spanish censoriousness and English Puritanism were sufficiently alike to make the parallel seem a close one.

The main characteristics of euphuism

The bibliography of euphuism is immense, criticism of the style beginning with Lyly's contemporaries, who thought it strange and rather absurd. The question of its derivation is now growing clearer. Euphuism did not originate in Spain and was not immediately derived from any foreign source; it was the latest form of a fashion of writing which had long been established in this country, and to which the artifices of Guevara's elaborate diction contributed next to nothing. It would have had a notable place in Tudor literature even had Lyly never written. The special marks of euphuism have now been traced a long way back in the literary use of English.[4]

[1] See above, pp. 26, 30-33.

[2] This was dedicated to Sidney and called forth the *Apologie for Poetrie*, in which they who "cast sugar and spice upon every dish that is served at the table," and other votaries of artificial diction are properly stigmatized. By "Similiter cadences" Sidney apparently means the *schemata*.

[3] Feuillerat, p. 260, n. 3.

[4] See the edition of *Euphues* by Morris William Croll and Harry Clemons (1916).

What are these special marks? Euphuism is a method of prose composition distinguished by the systematic use of certain rhetorical figures, which are figures of sound rather than of sense, principally the three called, in technical language, isocolon, parison, and paromoion. Isocolon means equality of limbs, and applies to that balancing of phrases or clauses by their close correspondence in length and weight on which the monotonous symmetry of euphuism is based. Parison, equality of sound, applies to the answering of word to word in the internal ordering of phrases. Thus, "suspect me of idleness" and "convince me of lightness" are phrases of about the same length, and the contrasted words occur at the same points in the order of the phrases. Paromoion, similarity of sound, includes alliteration, use of the same initial consonant in different words, and assonance, similarity of the terminal sounds; it also covers the repetition of syllables in the internal parts of words. Lyly employs the various forms of paromoion to accentuate the other correspondences. Alliteration is the most obvious device for this purpose, and there is continual use of transverse alliteration.[1] But such kinds of syllabic antithesis as the echoing of "thrift" and "theft," "lightness" and "lewdness," "loving" and "having," "hopeless" and "hapless," and the rhyming of unstressed syllables, as in "dissolute" and "resolute," "nature" and "nurture," or "most contemptible" and "most notable," serve the same end.[2] By this balancing of members having a similar sound scheme the sentence has a symmetrical structure imposed on it analogous to that of verse. The clauses may fall into antithetic pairs like couplets, and by more intricate correspondences a sentence may assume an almost stanzaic form. Sentence may further be articulated into sentence, until a complete paragraph falls into a complicated pattern of interlacing cadences. Antithesis is certainly the most prominent characteristic of euphuism; but the antithesis, let it be repeated, is not so much for the sake of defining and emphasizing meaning as for the pleasure of like but contrasted sounds; and the object that dominates

[1] *E.g.* "Under the colour of wit thou mayest be accounted wise"; "Let thy tune be merry when thy heart is melancholy"; "Bear a pleasant countenance with a pined conscience."

[2] For a careful and lucid summary of the *schemata* used by Lyly, and of their history, see the introduction by Messrs Croll and Clemons, who hold different views on the question from those of M. Feuillerat."

everything is to make language conform to a symmetrical design, and thus attain effects equivalent to those of rhyme and metre.

But, as already observed, it was not these mechanical devices of Lyly's style that struck his contemporaries as something unusual, for they were practising various kinds of *estilo culto* themselves and had no rooted objection to artifices and preciosities. What excited the ridicule of Harvey, Sidney, Nashe, and others, was Lyly's addiction to similes drawn from mythology and ancient learning and all manner of later sources, more particularly the fictitious natural science current in mediæval bestiaries and long-established encyclopædias of knowledge which had not been discarded at the invention of printing.[1] Preachers and orators had from of old delighted in such illustrations, as writers trained in the schools delighted in the *schemata*. Of these far-fetched similes there is little need to quote examples; they have been reproduced in every account of the style until the very word euphuism bores rather than amuses.

The true derivation of the "schemata"

Messrs Croll and Clemons have, perhaps finally, traced the genealogy of the *schemata* or word-schemes which are classified under the heads of isocolon, parison and paromoion. The ultimate source was the Greek orator Gorgias. He and his followers made continual use of the *schemata* as a means of securing rhythmic effect. Not that they made them the mainstay of their rhetoric; they employed them with varying degrees of taste and moderation, Isocrates, in particular, to whom M. Feuillerat would ascribe the chief influence on English imitators,[2] preferring a nobler and more varied rhythm to the monotonous parallelism and repetition of cadence which resulted from the excessive use of the schemes. Through the later sophists the rhetoric of the Gorgianic schools found its way into the schools of imperial Rome, and was adopted by teachers of oratory training men for the Christian Church. Mediæval professors of rhetoric were hardly capable of appreciating the fineness of the Greek oratorical style; but they were readily attracted by such definite and easily imitated devices as isocolon, parison and paromoion, and made these the principal means of attaining stateliness and fervour. The ancients used the word-schemes sparingly; mediæval teachers made them the very basis

[1] For a list of such works see Feuillerat, p. 422.
[2] Feuillerat, pp. 469-470.

of an effective style. Bede in his sermons, Thomas à Kempis, and other writers have been shown to have used these ornaments with the same monotonous persistency and to have woven them into the same intricate patterns as those of the euphuists.[1] From writers in Latin they passed into early English prose. They have been traced in the *Ayenbite of Inwyt*, in Richard Rolle of Hampole and the mystic Walter Hilton, and so on to Fisher and Latimer's sermons, and to the other exponents of a euphuistic style who preceded Lyly.[2] And these peculiar figures are commonly found associated with the peculiar similes which were fastened upon by contemporary critics as the hall-mark of euphuism; the mediæval rhetorician was as fond of the one as of the other. *Estilo culto*, and its sub-variety euphuism, owed next to nothing to the revival of learning; it was something, on the contrary, antipathetic to such humanists as More and Elyot, who inculcated classical standards in prose composition.[3]

Influence of euphuism

The euphuistic fashion of writing, and also of speaking, was cultivated enthusiastically for a few years after Lyly had carried it to the last stage of elaboration; then it was contemptuously abandoned. But the cult was not without its lesson to writers of prose, especially prose fiction. The kind of prose urgently required, even if nobody yet realized the want, was one adapted to the description of everyday reality and the natural expression of thoughts and feelings—a style that would attract little attention to itself, but would form, as it were, a transparent medium between the reader and the life presented. Any disturbance of the stiff and cumbrous prose that was accepted as the regular literary equipage could not fail to

[1] Croll and Clemons, pp. xxxv.-xxxvi. [2] *Ibid.*, lvi.-lviii.

[3] Why the revival of the *schemata* had such a charm for the sixteenth century is well put by Messrs Croll and Clemons (see their introduction, pp. liv. and lx.): "The true explanation of the phenomenon is certainly that now for the first time these figures appeared in an artistic and elaborate use in the vernacular. The novelty consists, not in the figures themselves, but in the fact that they are sounded on a new instrument, and that an art which had been the possession of clerks alone becomes the property of men and women of the world. In the history of fashions there are episodes much stranger than this. . . . The phenomenon was caused by the concurrence of the same elements in the taste of the Renaissance that gave the character of ornateness to nearly all of its art, the same mixture of the classical, the mediæval, and the courtly in the culture of the age that makes the *Orlando Furioso*, for instance, and the *Faerie Queene*, so fantastic and so unclassical. And of the causes that apply particularly to prose-style, the first place must be given, not to the imitation of the classics, but to the novelty of literary prose in the vernacular, and the need of adapting the familiar speech to unaccustomed uses of art and beauty."

be useful. Euphuism certainly did tend to break up the involved, would-be Ciceronian periods of the erudite, and the rhapsodizing, semi-poetic diction inherited from the romancers. In making prose-writing an art, obedient to as many conventions and structural obligations as were imposed on verse, Lyly made an experiment which was instructive to writers who aimed at nothing so artificial. His sentences were true sentences, and not paragraphs clumsily knit into lengths of meandering discourse that came to a halt when nothing more could be hitched on. Such structural punctilio, though so much overdone, was a wholesome reaction against the prevailing formlessness. Affected and unnatural as it was, euphuism came nearer than much of the current literary prose to the direct, pithy and nervous language of spirited conversation.

Summary of the effects of "Euphues" on the novel

Euphues was, in sum, the first English work not composed in verse in which characters, actions and sentiments—sentiments above all—were set forth with the internal unity of a definite attitude of mind and tone of feeling, and with the external unity of a consistent and well-wrought style. Lyly aimed at the coherence of a work of art; and such a style—whether the particular one adopted were the right or the wrong one is another question—was essential to that aim. He was not successful in presenting character; his actions and incidents are not of absorbing interest; the analysis of sentiments—a novelty at the time—does not go very deep. Nevertheless, the effort was in itself an event in literary history, and could not be entirely without consequences. This is Lyly's claim to importance in the annals of fiction; not that *Euphues* was the first novel addressed to women, nor that it inaugurated the literature of the drawing-room. Women had long been the chief readers of romances. This particular form of drawing-room literature was speedily superseded by one of a different stamp, which in turn was ousted by a newer fashion. Its importance, in short, is much the same as that of Sidney's *Arcadia*, which falls next for consideration. Here, again, is a book aiming at artistic coherence of matter and style, and achieving its aim in equal measure; and a book as influential as Lyly's, if not more so, on books to follow.

CHAPTER V

SIDNEY'S *ARCADIA*

Sidney's variety of "estilo culto"

An appropriate style was as essential in Sidney's case as in Lyly's. He, too, considered any kind of imaginative literature, such as romance or novel, as a form of art requiring beauty in the workmanship as much as in the other constituents. But he had no liking for the style of *Euphues*, which was too full of "sugar and spice," of similitudes rifled up from all herbarists and "all stories of beasts, fowls, and fishes," of "similiter cadences," by which he apparently meant the word-schemes, and of far-fetched metaphors.[1] He himself fell into other conceits; but his style was never so far removed as Lyly's from the language natural to man, and his affectations are mainly the result of overwrought feeling trying to find adequate expression. Any style that would have been appropriate to Lyly's book must, further, have been unsuited to Sidney's. In his anatomy of sentiments Lyly struck the attitude of a cold and disillusioned intellectual. His style had to be prosaic, however much it provided attractions rivalling those of verse. Sidney conceived the *Arcadia* as a poem in prose. All creative literature was included by him in the category of poetry.[2] It would have hurt his feelings to have

[1] *Apologie for Poetrie*; see the later sections on the artificial nature of most of the contemporary verse and prose.

[2] "For Xenophon," says he, "who did imitate so excellently as to give us the portraiture of a just Empire under the name of *Cyrus*, made therein an absolute heroicall poem. So did Heliodorus in his sugared invention of that picture of love in *Theagines and Cariclea*. And yet both these writ in prose: which I speak to show, that it is not riming and versing that maketh a Poet, no more than a long gowne maketh an Advocate."

See also his view of the nature of poetry in his account of the poet: "disdayning to be tied to any such subjection (as the natural rules of things), lifted up with the vigor of his owne invention, dooth growe in effect another nature, in making things either better than Nature bringeth forth, or, quite anewe, formes such as never were in Nature, as the *Heroes*, *Demigods*, *Cyclops*, *Chimeras*, *Furies*, and such like: so as hee goeth hand in hand with Nature, not inclosed within the narrow warrant of her guifts, but freely ranging onely within the Zodiack of his owne wit." "Nature never set forth the earth in so rich tapistry, as divers Poets have done, neither with so plesant rivers, fruitful

Sidney's "Arcadia" conceived as a poem

heard Milton's gibe at his "vain amatorious poem,"[1] but he would have accepted the substantive. That he spoke of the *Arcadia* as "a trifle, and that triflingly handled," matters nothing.[2] This was his modesty, whilst there are evidences in plenty that he took unstinted pains to satisfy his craving for harmony in every detail. The harmony required by the ideality and exalted feeling of the *Arcadia* was a harmony not far removed from that of a poem in which imagery, diction and rhythm are the outward expression of all that is within. Sidney himself would have put it that his heroic figures and surpassing inventions must be apparelled in suitable raiment.[3] And, except

trees, sweet smelling flowers, nor whatsoever els may make the too much loved earth more lovely. Her world is brasen, the Poets only deliver a golden" (*Ibid.*). This agrees with Bacon's account of Poesy: "Poesy is a part of learning in measure of words for the most part restrained, but in all other points extremely licensed, and doth truly refer to the imagination, which, not being tied to the laws of matter, may at pleasure join that which nature hath severed, and sever that which nature hath joined; and so make unlawful matches and divorces of things: *Pictoribus atque poetis*, etc. It is taken in two senses, in respect of words and matter. In the first sense it is but a character of style, and belongeth to arts of speech, and is not pertinent for the present. In the later it is (as hath been said) one of the principal portions of learning, and is nothing else but feigned history, which may be styled as well in prose as in verse.

"The use of this feigned history hath been to give some shadow of satisfaction to the mind of man in those points wherein the nature of things doth deny it, the world being in proportion inferior to the soul; by reason whereof there is, agreeable to the spirit of man, a more ample greatness, a more exact goodness, and a more absolute variety, than can be found in the nature of things. Therefore, because the acts or events of true history have not that magnitude which satisfieth the mind of man, poesy feigneth acts and events greater and more heroical. Because true history propoundeth the successes and issues of actions not so agreeable to the merits of virtue and vice, therefore poesy feigns them more just in retribution, and more according to revealed providence. Because true history representeth actions and events more ordinary and less interchanged, therefore poesy endueth them with more rareness, and more unexpected and alternative variations. So as it appeareth that poesy serveth and conferreth to magnanimity, morality, and to delectation. And therefore it was ever thought to have some participation of divineness, because it doth raise and erect the mind, by submitting the shows of things to the desires of the mind; whereas reason doth buckle and bow the mind unto the nature of things. And we see that by these insinuations and congruities with man's nature and pleasure, joined also with the agreement and consort it hath with music, it hath had access and estimation in rude times and barbarous regions, where other learning stood excluded" (*Advancement of Learning*, Bk. II. 4).

[1] After this backhander, Milton admits that it is "a book in that kind full of worth and wit" (*Eikonoklastes*, c. i.).

[2] He said this of the old *Arcadia*, see below, p. 89.

[3] "The greatest part of poets have apparelled their poetical inventions in that numberous kind of writing which is called verse. Indeed but apparelled, verse being but an ornament and no cause to poetry" (*Apologie*). He seems to have regarded, not verse alone, but diction and metaphor as mere decoration, and thought that by making his prose ornamental he made it poetical (*Apologie for Poetrie*).

that it would be devoid of the ornament of metre, the raiment would not be very different from that used by the poet to clothe his creations. Hence, instead of the incessant logic-chopping and laboured distinctions of meaning which characterize the style of *Euphues*, the *Arcadia* affects the language of sensuous description. Avoiding the stiff and formal, its style is loose and flowing. But, in spite of his protest against exuberant imagery and tedious similitudes, Sidney indulges in tropes and conceits that are not less absurd. He shuns "similiter cadences," but he over-modulates the emotional parts of his narrative and dialogue, and attains an artificial and cloying sweetness much oftener than pathos or beauty. Thus the euphuistic and the arcadian styles are different yet parallel varieties of the *estilo culto* which resulted from excessive labour on the externals and a misconception of the inner problem of style.

The passage describing the death of Parthenia, who, disguised as the Knight of the Tomb, had been mortally wounded by Amphialus, may be taken as a not unfair specimen of Sidney's prose when he is studying most to write like a poet yet remains tolerably free from the antithetical word-play to which he was prone in his more elevated passages.

But the headpiece was no sooner off, but that there fell about the shoulders of the overcome knight the treasure of fair golden hair, which with the face, soon known by the badge of excellency, witnessed that it was Parthenia, the unfortunately virtuous wife of Argalus; her beauty then, even in despite of the passed sorrow, or coming death, assuring all beholders that it was nothing short of perfection. For her exceeding fair eyes having with continual weeping gotten a little redness about them; her roundy, sweetly swelling lips a little trembling, as though they kissed her neighbour death; in her cheeks, the whiteness striving, by little and little, to get upon the rosiness of them; her neck—a neck indeed of alabaster—displaying the wound which with most dainty blood laboured to crown his own beauties; so as here was a river of purest red, there an island of perfectest white, each giving lustre to the other, with the sweet countenance, God knows, full of an unaffected languishing: though these things, to a grossly conceiving sense, might seem disgraces, yet indeed were they but apparelling beauty in a new fashion, which all looking upon through the spectacles of pity, did even increase the lines of her natural fairness, so as Amphialus was astonished with grief, compassion, and shame, detesting his fortune that made him unfortunate in victory." [1]

Ancient parallels to the style of Lyly and Sidney

The style of the ancient romancers furnishes a remarkable parallel to the euphuism and the arcadianism of the Elizabethans, for they in like manner endeavoured to evolve a kind of prose that would have charms akin, or at any rate equivalent, to those of poetic diction. Heliodorus borrowed unusual words, picturesque phrases, and musical cadences from the classic poets. Sidney modelled his plot, and in large part fashioned his style, upon the *Ethiopica*. The style of Apuleius yields many analogies to the special tricks of euphuism: the reiterated antitheses, the word-jingles, the semi-metrical cadences, the strained alliterations. But, on the whole, it is yet nearer to that of Sidney. Phrases of the same mintage as "Sine pretio pretiosae," "Amores amore coerceas," "Atra atria Proserpinæ," are common in the *Arcadia*. The scholiasts used to arrange the prose of Apuleius in iambic measures, and might have applied a similar test to Sidney's with equal propriety. The involved, musical periods, the unrestrained sensuousness, the general artificiality, are features common to both. Take such exaggerated phrase-making as these of Apuleius: "Deus deum magnorum potior et maiorum summus et summorum maximus et maximorum regnator Osiris"; or alliterations like "Quin sumis potius loco congruentes luctus et lacrimas," and "Verae Veneris vehementer incendit animos" [2]; there is no need to look far in either *Euphues* or the *Arcadia* to find the counterpart of these conceits; and, on the other hand, the Latin novelist might easily, in an abandoned moment, have written such a sentence as Sidney's "Exceedingly sorry for Pamela, but exceedingly exceeding that exceedingness in fear for Philoclea." [3]

[1] *Arcadia*, ed. E. A. Baker, 1923, pp. 373-374.

[2] *Metamorphoses*, xi. 30.

[3] It is worth while to compare the following passages from the *Metamorphoses* with the prose of Lyly, of Sidney, and of the Elizabethan translator of the *Hypnerotomachia*:

"Sub extrema saxi margine poma et uuae faberrime politae dependent, quas ars aemula naturae ueritati similes explicuit. Putes ad cibum inde quaedam, cum mustulentus autumnus maturum colorem adflauerit, posse decerpi et si fontem, qui sub deae uestigio decurrens in lenem uibratur undam, pronus aspexeris, credes illos marmore pendentes racemos inter cetera ueritatis nec agitationis officio carere" (*Metamorphoses*, ii. 4).

("Down the extreme margin of the rock hung apples and grapes, exquisitely

In the *Arcadia* Sidney evolved a composite form of romance from his enthusiastic study of three very different models. In wedding the chivalric style of the *Amadís* to Italian pastoral—as exemplified in the *Arcadia* of Sannazaro—he had in some sort a predecessor in the Portuguese Montemayor; Montemayor had

Composition of the "Arcadia"—Sidney's debts to Amadisian romance, to the pastoral, and to Heliodorus

finished, which art in rivalry with nature had wrought to the likeness of truth. You would have thought they might be plucked for eating, when autumn, full of new wine, had breathed into them the hues of maturity. And if, stooping down, you had regarded the spring, which, running down beneath the feet of the goddess, was shaken into gentle ripples, you would have thought that those marble clusters hanging among the rest were not devoid even of motion among the other attributes of reality.")

"Iamque proximas ciuitates et attiguas regiones fama persuaserat deam, quam caerulum profundum pelagi peperit et ros spumantium fluctuum educauit, iam numinis sui passim tributa uenia in mediis conuersari populi coetibus, uel certe rursum nouo caelestium stillarum germine non maria sed terras Venerem aliam uirginali flore praeditam pullulasse. Sic immensum procedit in dies opinio, sic insulas iam proxumas et terrae plusculum prouinciasque plurimas fama porrecta peruagatur. Iam multi mortalium longis itineribus atque altissimis maris meatibus ad saeculi specimen gloriosum confluebant. Paphon nemo, Cnidon nemo ac ne ipsa quidem Cythera ad conspectum deae Veneris nauigabant. Sacra diae pretereuntur, templa deformantur, puluinaria spernunter, caerimoniae negleguntur, incoronata simulacra et arae uiduae frigido cinere foedatae. Puellae supplicatur et in humanis uultibus deae tantae numina placantur, et in matutino progressu uirginis uictimis et epulis Veneris absentis nomen propitiatur, eamque per plateas commeantem populi frequenter floribus sertis et solutis adprecantur" (*Ibid.*, iv. 28).

("And now the tidings had spread to neighbouring cities and adjoining regions that the goddess, brought forth in the blue depths of ocean and reared in the spray or the spuming billows, scattering abroad the grace of her divinity, had come to dwell in the midst of mortals, or at least that the earth, and not the ocean, impregnated anew with heavenly dew, had brought forth another Venus, endued with the bloom of virginity. Thus rumour waxed stronger every day; thus fame travelled afar over neighbouring islands, a great part of the continent, and provinces innumerable. Many were the mortals who, journeying afar and voyaging over the deepest seas, flowed together to behold this matchless glory of the age. None set sail for Paphos, none for Cnidon, or even for Cythera itself, to have sight of the goddess Venus. The rites of the deity were forgotten, her temples dishonoured, her couches trampled under foot, her ceremonies neglected, her images unchapleted, and her desolate altars defiled with frigid embers. To the maiden supplications were addressed, and the majesty of the mighty goddess was adored beneath a human form. In the virgin's morning walk, the name of the absent Venus was propitiated with victims and banquets, and the people, as she passed along the streets, worshipped her in crowds with garlands and scattered flowers.")

"Gemens ac fremens indignatione, 'per ego te' inquit 'maternae caritatis foedera deprecor, per tuae sagittae dulcia uulnera, per flammae istius mellitas uredines, uindictam tuae parenti sed plenam tribue et in pulchritudinem contumacem seueriter uindica idque unum et prae omnibus unicum uolens effice" (*Ibid.*, iv. 31).

("Groaning and raging with indignation she said, "I conjure thee by the bonds of maternal love, by the sweet wounds of thy darts, and by the honeyed pangs of thy fires, vouchsafe vengeance, and that abundantly, to thy parent, and chastise this insolent beauty grievously; and this one thing, also, and above all things else, obediently perform.")

at any rate affianced the two in his *Diana*, which was well known to Sidney, who turned certain of its lyrics into English. The Portuguese is not mentioned in his *Apologie for Poetrie*, which has divers outbursts of admiration for both Sannazaro and the *Amadís*, and more fervid tributes to the *Ethiopica* of Heliodorus. Perhaps Montemayor was too modern to be coupled with names that he held to be of the status of classics. Heliodorus was his third and ultimate model. Sidney wove and rewove the multiple threads of his story into an intricate web, in imitation of the elaborate epical scheme of the *Ethiopica*. The result was the most complicated plot in English fiction, and at the same time one so minutely and accurately worked out that there are no loose ends.[1]

Origins of pastoralism

The pastoral idea was nothing new in English literature. Spenser had recently published his *Shepherd's Calendar*, which no one appreciated better than Sidney. Long before the Renaissance the *pastourelle* had been a favourite form with French poets, and had had English imitators. But the Italian mixture of prose narrative and metrical eclogues, in which sophisticated people were dressed up as shepherds and herdsmen, talked sentiment in poetical language, and lived an artificial kind of simple life, was of recent origin. Theocritus and Virgil were the original founts of pastoralism. Virgil had drawn freely from the Sicilian poet, whom the earlier modern pastoralists did not know; to them the influence was transmitted through the channel of his *Eclogues*, in which the idyll had become an allegory and even a *roman à clef*, and the pure breath of the woods and fields had been blended with personal, political and social interests.[2]

Boccaccio's "Ameto"

In the first modern example, Boccaccio's *Ameto* (1341)—a rambling prose narrative with songs and hymns interspersed—the philosophic intention is something akin to the lofty didacticism of Dante. The idea implied is of humanity chastened and refined by love and ascending by virtue and devotion to knowledge of the divine. But this tends to be submerged in the more earthly view

[1] Wolff discovers one inconsistency in Bk. II., where Leonatus speaks of this country as Paphlagonia, instead of Galatia, Sidney or the printer having failed to alter the name in the change from the old version to the new (*Arcadia*, ed. E. A. Baker, p. 171; see Wolff, p. 353, n. 33).

[2] See W. W. Greg, *Pastoral Poetry and Pastoral Drama* (1906), for the origins and the modern development of pastoralism.

of life that was to characterize the *Decameron*, a view foreshadowed in some of the inset stories. Boccaccio imagines his incidents to have happened long ago amid the hills and woods in the neighbourhood of Florence, where the hunter Ameto is initiated by the nymphs into the service of the celestial Venus, and is privileged to hear stories told and hymns sung, expounding now pagan myth and now Christian verity. True to the Virgilian precedent, Boccaccio hints somewhat vaguely at more personal meanings to be read through the allegory.[1] Fiammetta comes into the story, with her lover Caleone, who no doubt is the author himself.

Sannazaro's "Arcadia"

Sannazaro in his *Arcadia* (1502) used a more formal alternation of prose and verse, a dozen eclogues being each introduced by a prose recital of the incidents. He likewise followed tradition in bringing his friends on the scene masquerading as shepherds, and recorded experiences of his own for the benefit of such as could read hidden meanings. Jacopo Sannazaro was a Neapolitan of Spanish descent who, writing in an age of disillusionment, when the bright hopes kindled by the Renaissance had faded and he and his countrymen were but the more acutely sensible of their political and spiritual bondage, turned for diversion and refreshment to the picturing of an untrammelled existence in the lap of nature, where he might enjoy, at least in fancy, the raptures of truth and virtue and of a pure and refined love. Virgil was the favoured classic poet at this period. From the *Eclogues*, and to a less extent from the *Æneid*, Sannazaro culled many little details of pastoral lore, fragments of ancient myth and magic, modes of artistic procedure. He showed the same devotion as his contemporary Mantuanus, as the poet Johannes Baptista Spagnuolo called himself after his countryman Virgil. The *Arcadia*, which took both its title and its fanciful setting from Virgil's *Eclogues*,[2] was actually finished in 1489; Mantuan's *Eclogues*, a close imitation of Virgil's, appeared in 1498. Both were enormously popular. In England the latter was widely adopted as a school-book, and nine of the ten eclogues were translated by George Turberville (1567). Sannazaro and

[1] F. M. Warren: *A History of the Novel previous to the Seventeenth Century* (1908), pp. 200-236—"The Italian Pastoral."

[2] *Eclogues*, 5 and 10.

his contemporaries were not yet acquainted with the one prose pastoral of antiquity, the *Daphnis and Chloe* of Longus. This, the most idyllic of the Greek erotic romances, had been given a conventional rustic setting in the isle of Lesbos. Except in the outdoor staging, however, there was nothing here of either Theocritus or Virgil, but a good deal of the old Milesian ribaldry, draped in the transparent muslin of a factitious innocence. No translation of this seductive tale into a modern language appeared before the French version of Amyot (1559).

Pastoralism as an expression of contemporary ennui

The scene of Sannazaro's pastoral is neither the real Arcadia nor an Italy idealized. Rather is it the tame wilderness which a jaded citizen's fancy conjured up out of his longing for the opposite to life in town. The shepherd-hero is a townsman, whose boredom with existence is figured as the melancholy born of unrequited love. He wanders away to mingle with the rustics of Mount Partenio, joins in their games and festivities, hearkens to the tale of their hapless loves, assists in the sacrifices to their goddess Pales and in the more mysterious rites of Pan, and eventually, after burying and bewailing his dearest friend, is led home by a nymph through marvellous submarine caverns, to Naples, comforted and inspired. It is a series of pictures rather than a story, the colours appropriated from ancient canvases. And, either with or without a unifying plot, this was to be the general character of the pastoral. It was to live through its rural background ; woods and fields and sorrowful or rejoicing villagers were to be the pipe on which the lover and idealist discoursed his sentimental music. The sense of an intimate communion with nature was beyond the grasp of any man in that age. Pastoralism was based on what modern criticism has called the pathetic fallacy. Nature offered sensuous delights ; nature also responded to man's joys and sorrows. Willows wept, woods frowned, flowers and fields smiled, and the seasons were cheerful or dejected, all in harmony with the poet's moods. The best relief for the ills and disappointments of life was to sojourn with mind at ease amid luxuriant valleys, lakes and streams. Nature to the pastoral romancer was an extended garden, a fenceless pleasance, uncultivated but not wild, diversified but not rugged, with countless acres of greensward never touched by scythe but smooth as velvet from browsing sheep. There must be flowers and fruit-trees, tame animals and friendly birds, rivers for bathing and waterfalls for music, and weather that never interfered with rustic festivals or poetic contests. In the pastoral the weary spirit of the Renaissance took its rest-cure.[1]

The Spanish pastorals

Italian exponents of pastoralism after Sannazaro are too many to enumerate. The romance was followed by the pastoral drama, this about the time when Sidney was writing. Tasso's *Aminta* was simple and unimpassioned; Guarini's *Pastor Fido*, artificial and full of conceits. These incited Fletcher to write his *Faithful Shepherdess* (1607). Meanwhile Spain had been captivated by the pastoral idea, and, not content to imitate Italy, was engaged in naturalizing it in what proved a most congenial environment.[2] From the indigenous *auto* to the dramatic pastoral was an easy transition. Encina translated and also imitated Virgil's *Eclogues*. But the man who introduced the new Italian mode was Garcilaso de la Vega, who wrote several poems in which a pastoral story (*c.* 1526), animated with sincere emotion, was furnished with a veritable Spanish setting. For Spain was a land of flocks and herds, and fully as picturesque as Arcadia. The Portuguese Francisco Sà de Miranda took up the challenge with his pastoral *Fabula do Mondego*, written in Castilian. His compatriot, Bernardim Ribeiro, kept to his own language, writing first poems in the eclectic style of Encina and Garcilaso, and then a romance in prose and verse—his *Menina e Moça* (printed 1554), in which knight-errantry and adventure of the Amadisian stamp outbalance the incidents appropriate to the pastoral. But, true to the established tradition, his knights masquerade as neatherds; he provides attractive natural scenery, and adopts from his predecessors the trick of covert personal allusion. Narbinder, especially when he changed his name to Bimnarder, is unmistakably Bernardim himself; Aonia stands for the woman he loved, and other personages in the story were no doubt easily identified by his contemporaries. The story was never finished.

Montemayor's "Diana"

Thus the pastoral had been fully acclimatized and engrafted on a native stock, and trained to express the emotional temperament of the Peninsula, before Montemayor wrote his *Diana*—the most successful production of all this group, and the only one that

[1] Warren, pp. 200-236.

[2] Greg, pp. 53-61.

either had any deep influence at home or was widely read beyond the Pyrenees. Jorge de Montemôr, or Montemayor, was another Portuguese ; but he wrote his book in Castilian, except that a few poems and other passages are in his native tongue. The *Diana* (*c.* 1559-1560) is an imaginative version of the writer's own unhappy love-story ; the beautiful shepherdess Diana is the lady whom he loved and lost, the mournful Sireno is himself. He roams the woods beneath the mountains of Leon with another shepherd, his former rival, now his partner in musical complaints of the fickle Diana, who has taken another mate. The plot is very intricate. The web of love at cross-purposes, in which several pairs of swains and shepherdesses are enmeshed, is complicated by disguises and changes of name, with the consequent mistakes of sex, which were to be exploited later by Sidney in the *Arcadia*, and with extended episodes connected with or merely attached to the original thread. Witchcraft, spells and wonder-working potions sustain the time-worn tradition of magic. Savage men, more in keeping with forests and sierras, take the place of satyrs, and threatening nymphs with ravishment are struck down by the arrows of the doughty shepherdess Felismena. This fair creature was to Montemayor's readers the most compelling figure in the tale. She is reminiscent of classical story in her trouble with Venus for her mother's criticism of the judgment of Paris ; but her passion for Don Felix, and her dressing up as a page and carrying messages to his mistress Celia, are of the very essence of romance. This piece of plot-business had been used by Bandello and Cinthio, and was to be employed by Shakespeare in *Twelfth Night* and *Two Gentlemen of Verona*. In the latter play he was probably indebted to Montemayor.

Infusion of chivalric romance

It is in an episode of the Moorish wars related by Felismena, the well-known story of the last of the Abencerrages, that the martial strain of Amadisian romance becomes dominant, and this may have come from another pen than Montemayor's. But the numerous escapes and adventures, the suspense and surprises, the oracles and enchantments, together with the high-flown gallantry of the love passages, are more in the fashion of Spain than of the Italian pastoral. Montemayor did not write his promised sequel, which would have shown Sireno at length rewarded for his sufferings and his mistress duly chastened. In 1564, however, within three years of his death, two continuations were put on the market, by Alonzo Pérez and Gaspar Gil Polo respectively, both of which were included in the French translation and the English one by Bartholomew Yong, finished in 1583 but not published till 1598. That of Pérez was a pedantic and inconsequent farrago; the other, which Gil Polo entitled *Diana Enamorada*, was not an unworthy sequel to Montemayor's inconclusive story. It is not too long. With a few digressions and poetical flourishes it tells how Sireno is brought back to his allegiance, and, all obstacles removed, is united at last to his mistress.

Later Spanish pastorals and d'Urfé's "Astrée,"

These were not the last attempts to carry on the story, and very far from the last of the Spanish pastoral or pastoral-chivalric romances. The whole species was reduced to the terms of Christian devotion by a monk, Bartolomé Ponce, in his *Clara Diana á lo divino* (1599) By that time Honoré d'Urfé was writing his *Astrée*[1] and Sidney's *Arcadia* was going into its fourth edition.[2] These were the two most famous offspring of the *Diana*. Sidney had imitators, who were without a spark of genius; but the *Astrée* became the starting-point of a new kind of sentimental fiction which was to fascinate the whole of Europe and to have more influence in English literature than even its own *Arcadia*.[3]

The two forms of Sidney's "Arcadia"

Sidney's *Arcadia* was published in 1590, four years after his death. What was the date of its composition? Until 1907, when some long-forgotten facts came to light, it was generally supposed that he wrote the romance whilst he was in retirement at Wilton, in 1580, banished from the court owing to his determined opposition to the project of marriage between Elizabeth and the Duke of Anjou.[4] That he wrote it as a holiday task for the pleasure of his sister, the famous Countess of Pembroke, there is no doubt; we have his own word for it. Further, it is probably safe to say that he was actuated by a sense of disappointment with the way affairs were tending and of disillusionment towards the pomps and frivolities of court life and the brutal passions and unscrupulous ambitions that lurked beneath the glittering surface. The *Arcadia* depicts life as a

[1] He sketched out the story in his youth, and the first part (printed 1607) had been circulated in manuscript long before it was published (Reure, p. 204).

[2] It describes itself erroneously as the third edition.

[3] Warren, c. 8-9, pp. 237-283.

[4] See, *e.g.*, J. A. Symonds: *Sidney* (English Men of Letters), pp. 76-81.

glowing spirit, such as Sidney's, would have it lived. But that the occasion was his temporary exile, and the date 1580, is now hardly credible.

In 1907 Mr Bertram Dobell made the startling discovery that the *Arcadia*, in the form we now have it, the *Arcadia* in five books, which was published with the Countess of Pembroke's authority in 1593—the previous edition of 1590 containing only three books—is not the identical *Arcadia* which was handed about among Sidney's friends in 1580 or soon afterwards, but a new work, completely recast and rewritten, and differing from the other in many important particulars. Sidney's friend and biographer, Fulke Greville (Lord Brooke), called the early version the old *Arcadia*, and spoke of the many copies of it circulating in manuscript as unsuitable for printing, since a corrected version of the book had been left in trust with him.[1] This old *Arcadia* was written probably between 1578 and 1580. At some later date, before his death in 1586, Sidney undertook the formidable task of altering it from beginning to end, and got as far as the point, two-thirds of the way through the third book, where the reader is now told that the story has had to be continued from the author's papers.[2] This altered portion formed the edition of 1590, the remainder of the work, as it was published in 1593, being made up from the old *Arcadia*, with a few explanatory words to fill the gap. The later continuations by Sir William Alexander and Richard Beling may be ignored.

The Old "Arcadia"

The *Arcadia* as the young Sidney first wrote it [3] was a complicated story, but it was narrated in a straightforward manner ; that is, in the chronological order of the incidents. In the new form all this is changed. Chronology is continually inverted. The reader is plunged into the middle of the story, and is left to guess what has preceded. At various points in the sequence of events the chief characters relate their past history to their friends, such a relation being in itself an incident in the story, and the element of suspense being kept up by various interruptions, so that the reader, like

The New "Arcadia"

[1] B. Dobell: "New Light on Sidney's *Arcadia*" (*Quarterly Review*, vol. 211, July 1909). A succinct account is given by S. L. Wolff (*The Greek Romances in Elizabethan Fiction*, pp. 344-366).

[2] *Arcadia*, ed. E. A. Baker, 1907, p. 451.

[3] *The Countess of Pembroke's* Arcadia, *being the original version now for the first time printed*, ed. A. Feuillerat, Cambridge, 1926.

the persons in the story, is kept waiting for an account of what eventually happened, even when this is necessary to explain the existing situation. Large episodes are inserted either as part of these narratives or as expansions of the main plot. All this ingenuity makes the various threads of events very difficult to unravel; it seems to put obstacles wantonly in the reader's path. Nevertheless, those who persevere in solving the puzzle will be filled with admiration for Sidney's ingenuity and thoroughness, if not for his judgment. His courtly readers manifestly experienced as much enjoyment in following the intricacies of his design, and finding them all brought to a point where order was evolved out of utter perplexity, as the devotees of La Calprenède and Mlle de Scudéry, at a later date, experienced in the prolixities and hypercritical analysis of sentiment in those still more protracted stories.

The plot

Only the barest outline of the main story will be offered here.[1] At the opening of the *Arcadia*, in its final shape, two shepherds on the coast of Laconia help a man out of the waves who has escaped from a burning ship. This is Musidorus, prince of Thessaly, whose cousin, Pyrocles, prince of Macedonia, is still aboard the wreck. Before they can rescue Pyrocles he is carried off in front of their eyes by pirates. Thus we are introduced to the two heroes of the story, two cousins and comrades who are bound to each other by ties of the closest affection, and have already shared adventures and heroic achievements that are to be afterwards related as subordinate but by no means unimportant episodes. Musidorus is taken on a two days' journey into Arcadia, where he is entertained, under the assumed name of Palladius, by a wealthy gentleman, Kalander. Intelligence arriving that Clitophon, the son of his host, has been captured by the Helots, who are in revolt against the Laconians, Musidorus joins the rescue expedition, and by a stratagem gets within the walls of the city. A hand-to-hand conflict is waged in the market-place between Helots and Arcadians, and Musidorus finds himself pitted against the enemy's leader. His helmet is struck off; whereupon his adversary flings down his sword, crying: "What! hath Palladius forgotten the voice of Daiphantus?"—this

[1] The *Arcadia* is analysed at great length, the chronology of the main plot and of all the episodes being clearly determined, by S. L. Wolff (*Greek Romances*, c. 2).

was the name assumed by Pyrocles when Musidorus took that of Palladius. Clitophon is released; they all go back to Arcadia; and now the central matter of the whole story is unfolded, only in part, however, for much that is needed to make the action intelligible is kept back for a long time yet. Pyrocles has fallen in love, and confesses it to Musidorus, who rallies him on his weakness but soon finds himself in the same plight.

The objects of their passion are two princesses, daughters of the King of Arcadia, the aged Basilius, and of his young and beautiful wife, Gynecia. Basilius has recently been filled with alarm by the obscure threats of an oracle, the terms of which are not revealed to the reader till half-way through the third book. To avoid the misfortunes foreshadowed, the panic-stricken king leaves his palace, and betakes himself with his queen and younger daughter, Philoclea, to a rustic lodge in the forest, placing the elder daughter, Pamela, in a neighbouring lodge under the guardianship of a shepherd, Dametas, and his grotesque wife and daughter, Miso and Mopsa. To gain access to the young ladies, Musidorus and Pyrocles disguise themselves, the one as Dorus, a shepherd, the other as the Amazon, Zelmane. The device is not without success. Zelmane soon has the honour of slaying a lion that attacks his mistress, Philoclea; Dorus distinguishes himself by killing a bear and saving the life of Pamela. Not till a later stage in the evolution of the story is the inner meaning of this incident disclosed: bear and lion were let loose by the sister-in-law of Basilius, Cecropia, Queen of Argos, who had regarded herself, before the birth of Pamela and Philoclea, as entitled to the succession of his throne, and sticks at no artifice for making away with the young princesses. She is now intent on securing the kingdom of Arcadia for her son, Amphialus, who is enamoured of Philoclea. Cecropia stirs up rebellion among the subjects of Basilius, incidentally affording further opportunities for Zelmane and Dorus to show their valour and address.

Cecropia

But the chief episode in which Cecropia is the prime mover is that which begins with her treacherous capture of the two princesses and Zelmane. This, which did not appear in the old *Arcadia*, is romance in the Amadisian style from beginning to end. The castle is besieged by Basilius. Outside, a furious succession of battles and duels proceeds; inside, the queen is trying by fair means and foul to bend the captives to her will. But Amphialus is a chivalrous prince, and whilst he remains unwounded his mother has to work cautiously. He issues a general challenge, making many champions bite the dust, among others slaying Argalus, the devoted husband of Parthenia. The last scenes of their pathetic history, than which none seemed more affecting to Sidney's admirers, thus come into this episode. The widowed Parthenia rides into the lists as the Knight of the Tomb, challenges Amphialus, and falls mortally wounded, her sex being discovered before she dies. Her slayer is overcome with remorse, but is summoned to single combat with the Forsaken Knight, none other than Musidorus. Both are sorely wounded, and Cecropia avails herself of her son's disablement to employ her vilest arts in torturing and intimidating the prisoners. She reduces Zelmane and Philoclea well-nigh to despair by a make-believe execution of Pamela. Zelmane is made to see Philoclea's head in a bowl swimming with blood. These tragic shows are contrived by methods that would have suited Mrs Radcliffe : they are Sidney's substitutes for the prodigies and enchantments of the *Amadis*. Nor, it must not be overlooked, could he dispense with the machinery of oracles and prophetic dreams. Cecropia's foul play is at length detected by her son, who is about to kill himself before her face, when she falls dead.

But it is time for the oracle, which is the origin of and the key to all these bewildering events, since it led Basilius into a foolish attempt to evade the inevitable. It ran as follows :

The dénouement

Thy elder care shall from thy careful face
By princely mean be stolen, and yet not lost ;
Thy younger shall with nature's bliss embrace
An uncouth love, which nature hateth most ;
Both they themselves unto such two shall wed,
Who at thy bier, as at a bar, shall plead ;
Why thee, a living man, they had made dead.
In thy own seat a foreign state shall sit ;
And ere that all these blows thy head do hit,
Thou with thy wife adultery shall commit.

The first two lines are fulfilled by the elopement of Pamela and Musidorus ; the second two by Philoclea's love for the supposed Amazon. The rest of the prophecy is accomplished in due course. Zelmane excites a guilty passion in two breasts. Basilius falls in love with the supposed woman ; his wife, Gynecia, sees through the disguise and becomes madly enamoured of her daughter's suitor. Zelmane, to escape them both, makes an assignation with Gynecia in a cavern, and promises to meet Basilius in the same place. Basilius goes, finds his wife there, and they both have to make the best of a bad business. Thus the prophecy of the last line comes to pass, and the other predictions are soon made good. Gynecia had prepared a love-potion for Pyrocles ; it is drunk by the amorous king, who drops down apparently dead. This pregnant situation, with some rude buffoonery at the expense of Mopsa—whom Musidorus has had to court in prosecution of his clandestine suit—forms the main subject of the fourth and fifth books, and stands as it did in the old *Arcadia*. The eloping lovers, Musidorus and Pamela, are captured ; Pyrocles and Philoclea are also arrested on the charge of an unlawful intrigue. Gynecia is accused of poisoning her husband. Everything is in chaos. At this juncture, Evarchus, King of Macedon, who is the father of Pyrocles and uncle of Musidorus, arrives on a visit to Basilius. He is unanimously chosen arbiter and, with the king's body on a bier before him, takes his seat on his kinsman's throne. After a long and dramatic trial all the accused are sentenced, and the two princes are being led away to execution, when the supposed corpse is seen to stir. Basilius revives from his swoon. He declares that the oracle has been fulfilled in every particular, and confesses his errors ; he and Gynecia forgive each other and vow to be loyal for the future ; the lovers are made happy.

Sidney may have been prompted by the success of *Euphues* to write the *Arcadia* ; Lyly's foppish sentimentality and wordy philosophizing may have moved him to sound a romantic counterblast. If so, he not only showed the advantages of having a story to tell—in which respect his rival was out of the running altogether—he even beat Lyly, in another respect, on his own ground. It is unfair to judge *Euphues* as a novel ; yet it does attempt one thing which is legitimately expected of the novel—to bring out the relation between character and conduct. Sidney, a romancer, is more concerned with things that happen, and the interesting ways in which they happen, than with aspects of human nature. Yet the significance of character as a chief agent in man's destiny is never

Sidney's interest in character

absent from his mind. And in the part of the action centring in Gynecia and her rivalry with her doting husband and her trustful daughter for the affection of Zelmane there is effective drama of a kind that has often been made the groundwork of an interesting novel. The love passages, too, between the two heroes and the young princesses, show the play of character as well as the shy movements of feeling typical of a girlish heart.

Sidney's portraiture of character was only of that minor order which presents types, recognizable examples of general human qualities—that is, he does much the same as Lyly without any parade of mental analysis or expatiation on fine shades of sentiment. The principal figures in his story are clearly distinguished from each other; they are not mere puppets, even though their individuality consists merely of such differences of traits as that Philoclea is tender and yielding, Pamela strong-minded and majestic, Musidorus a self-reliant and resourceful man of action, and Pyrocles of a finer temperament, more spirited and highly strung. No less than eighty-eight named persons have been counted in the *Arcadia*[1]; many of these are names and nothing more, but a considerable number are carefully distinguished by some well-marked propensity. By far the strongest and the only one of any complexity is the passionate Gynecia, "a woman," as Kalander describes her at the outset, "of great wit, and in truth of more princely virtues than her husband; of most unspotted chastity, but of so working a mind and so vehement spirits that a man may say, it was happy she took a good course for otherwise it would have been terrible." The course she subsequently takes, on which she is forcibly arrested by the adventure in the cave, corroborates this judgment. She has in her the makings of a tragedy queen, and her counterpart, if not her like, is to be found more than once in Elizabethan drama. Even in the Sidneian rhetoric of a soliloquy she is impressive:

But the great and wretched lady Gynecia, possessed with those devils of love and jealousy, did rid herself from her tedious husband; and taking nobody with her, going toward them; "O jealousy," said she, "the frenzy of wise folks, the well-wishing spite, and unkind carefulness, the self-punishment for others' faults, and self-

[1] Wolff, p. 330.

misery in others' happiness, the cousin of envy, daughter of love, and mother of hate, how could'st thou so quietly get thee a seat in the unquiet heart of Gynecia! Gynecia," said she sighing, "thought wise and once virtuous! alas! it is thy breeder's power which plants thee there: it is the flaming agony of affection, that works the chilling access of thy fever, in such sort, that nature gives place; the growing of my daughter seems the decay of myself; the blessings of a mother turn to the curses of a competitor; and the fair image of Philoclea appears more horrible in my sight than the image of death."[1]

The idea of destiny as influenced by character

Strength of character as a moral force has its due place in Sidney's conception of life, and is a potent factor in the determination of events. Chance and fortune are words that he uses only as the familiar counters of discourse, without giving them any such special significance as they had in Greek romance and later. More than once he points out that what appears to be accident has its real causation in human strength or weakness. In this there is nothing inconsistent with the sense of a divinity watching over man's affairs, expressed in the oracle and its plenary accomplishment. He takes for granted the existence of a higher power dealing out justice and performing chastisement—a power that may save the deserving from the consequences of their errors, if they submit to its authority. Instead of showing resignation and endurance, Basilius runs away from his destiny, and not only has to put up with the mishaps that are in store for him, but is made ridiculous into the bargain. Each man is responsible for his own character. As the *Apologie for Poetrie*[2] clearly teaches, he should acquire the virtues of courage, patience, fortitude, and the rest; then, whatever happens, he will be able to rise superior to mere circumstance.

The *Arcadia*, in truth, is the ethical theory implied in the *Apologie* set forth in action. "The ending end of all earthly learning being vertuous action, those skills that most serve to bring forth that have a most just title to be princes over all the rest." Of such skills poetry is the most princely, philosophy dealing only

[1] *Arcadia*, Bk. II., p. 253. Wolff points out that Sidney's Gynecia is a study from Melitta, in the romance of Achilles Tatius, the young widow of Ephesus who induces Clitophon to marry her and then learns that she was not a widow.

[2] The *Apologie* was written about 1580 or 1581—that is, about the same time as, or more probably a little later than, the old *Arcadia*.

in abstractions, and history being tied down to fact: "the one giveth the precept, and the other the example." "Now doth the peerless poet perform both: for whatsoever the philosopher saith should be done, he giveth a perfect picture of it in some one, by whom he presupposeth it was done."

Tullie taketh much pains, and many times not without poetical helps, to make us know the force love of our country hath in us. Let us but hear old Anchises speaking in the midst of Troy's flames, or see Ulysses, in the fullness of all Calypso's delights, bewail his absence from barren and beggarly Ithaca. Anger, the Stoics say, was a short madness: let but Sophocles bring Ajax on a stage, killing and whipping sheep and oxen, thinking them the army of Greeks with their chieftains Agamemnon and Menelaus: and tell me if you have not a more familiar insight into anger, than finding in the schoolmen his genius and difference? See whether wisdom and temperance in Ulysses and Diomedes, valour in Achilles, friendship in Nisus and Euryalus, even to an ignorant man, carry not an apparent shining; and contrarily, the remorse of conscience in Œdipus, the soon repenting pride of Agamemnon, the self-devouring cruelty in his father Atreus, the violence of ambition in the two Theban brothers, the sour-sweetness of revenge in Medea; and, to fall lower, the Terentian Gnato, and our Chaucer's Pandar, so expressed, that we now use their names to signify their trades. And finally, all virtues, vices, and passions, so in their own natural seats laid to the view, that we seem not to hear of them, but clearly to see through them. But even in the most excellent determination of goodness, what philosopher's counsel can so readily direct a prince, as the feigned Cyrus in Xenophon? or a virtuous man in all fortunes, as Aeneas in Virgil? or a whole commonwealth, as the way of Sir Thomas More's Eutopia?[1]

In the *Amadís* Spain had bodied forth its ideals of heroism, devotion and knightly honour. Sidney, in his imaginary Arcadia—without the lewdness that tarnished the Amadisian picture of life—expressed with ingenuous confidence his cherished ideals of virtue, heroic energy and chivalrous love. His own life, it has been eloquently said, was "a true poem, a composition, and pattern of the best and honourablest things." The perfection that he and a few like him yearned to realize, amid the manifold hindrances and temptations of Elizabethan society, was depicted with inspiring

[1] *An Apologie for Poetrie*, ed. E. S. Shuckburgh, 1891, pp. 18-19.

enthusiasm in the lives and loves of Pyrocles and Musidorus, Pamela and Philoclea.

Sidney's pastoralism

The pastoral element in the book is outweighed by the element of heroic deeds and exciting adventure. Yet a pastoral episode is the starting-point of the action, and it is the pastoral idea that provides the background of beauty to the lofty visions of moral excellence shown on the stage. There is a closer similarity to Sannazaro and Montemayor in the old *Arcadia*, in which the eclogues forming the latter part of each book are a larger item. Much of the incidental matter afterwards expanded into important episodes was originally relegated to the eclogues. Few of these metrical pieces are readable now, except to those who are curious about the attempts of Sidney and other members of the Areopagus to Anglicize classical and other exotic forms of verse. But the pastoral setting is enchantingly laid out, in spite of several too fulsome descriptions in the style of the English *Hypnerotomachia*. Here is a glimpse of Arcadia :

It was indeed a place of delight ; for through the midst of it there ran a sweet brook which did both hold the eye open with her azure streams, and yet seek to close the eye with the purling noise it made upon the pebble stones it ran over ; the field itself being set in some places with roses, and in all the rest constantly preserving a flourishing green : the roses added such a ruddy show unto it, as though the field were bashful at his own beauty : about it, as if it had been to enclose a theatre, grew such sort of trees as either excellency of fruit, stateliness of growth, continual greenness, or poetical fancies, have made at any time famous. In most part of which there had been framed by art such pleasant arbours that, one answering another, they became a gallery aloft from tree to tree almost round about, which below gave a perfect shadow ; a pleasant refuge then from the choleric look of Phœbus.[1]

Still better, and more famous, is this vignette of the river Ladon :

It ran upon so fine and delicate a ground, as one could not easily judge whether the river did more wash the gravel, or the gravel did purify the river ; the river not running forth right, but almost continually winding, as if the lower streams would return to their spring, or that the river had a delight to play with itself. The banks of either

[1] *Arcadia*, p. 92.

side seeming arms of the loving earth that fain would embrace it, and the river a wanton nymph which still would slip from it; either side of the bank being fringed with most beautiful trees, which resisted the sun's darts from overmuch piercing the natural coldness of the river. There was among the rest a goodly cypress, who, bowing her fair head over the water, it seemed she looked into it, and dressed her green locks by that running river.[1]

Indebtedness to Spanish chivalric romance

Sidney's direct loans from the *Amadís* include such suggestions for episodes as that of a young man falling in love with the picture of a lady and entering her service disguised as a woman; of a king and queen falling in love with him, like Basilius and Gynecia; the affairs of Phalantis and Artesia and of Pamphilus and Dido.[2] Sidney borrowed from the *Amadís* even such an important name as Cleophila, that of the Amazon, in the old *Arcadia*, altered to Zelmane in the new. Beginning as a pastoral, the *Arcadia* speedily changes into a romance of the Spanish type. But it levies just as freely from Heliodorus and Achilles Tatius; and, outweighing all his numerous obligations on the score of borrowed incidents and motives, devices, such as oracles fulfilled, and inextricable dilemmas solved by sudden disclosures, there is Sidney's supreme debt to Heliodorus for his vast and complicated structural scheme.[3]

[1] *Arcadia*, p. 178.

[2] The details of Sidney's indebtedness are regularly scheduled by W. V. Moody (*Inquiry into the Sources of Sidney's Arcadia*, cited by Wolff) and S. L. Wolff (*Greek Romances in Elizabethan Prose Fiction*, c. 2). Dr Wolff writes: "Its material—*motif*, situation, incident, episode—comes chiefly from the 'Amadis' and the Greek Romances; the material it gets from the former being fitted into the frame of the latter. For its actuating force is the will of the gods, working itself out partly through the agency of Fortune, partly through the agency of human personality—'Virtue.' And this dominant force shapes the frame of the story into the monumental form which Heliodorus applied to prose romance" (p. 328).

[3] A. J. Tieje, in "The Expressed aim of the long prose fiction" (*Journal of Germanic and English Philology*, xi., 1912, p. 411), says: "It is inexact for Baker to write in the preface to his edition (1907) of Sidney's *Arcadia*: 'The pastoral novel and the Amadis cycle of romances were the two direct progenitors of Sidney's *Arcadia*, in which the spirit of knightly heroism and the idyllic atmosphere of a sentimental Utopia are blended in fairly equal parts,' and for Raleigh to speak of the true love of the chivalric romances *degenerating* to gallantry in the romances of the seventeenth century. For in the Amadisian and the Palmerin cycles reigns a care-free licentiousness." I have no wish to endorse Raleigh's remark without careful qualification; but I cannot see the inexactness in my own statement. Perhaps Dr Tieje is a little too much obsessed with the puritanical view, and thinks that knightly ideals of heroism and honour cannot be presented in a book that also presents examples of frailty and licence in sexual affairs. But, to take only one instance,

Later editions and imitations of the "Arcadia"

The *Arcadia* was read with delight and admiration long after *Euphues* had been discarded as a tiresome piece of affectation. By 1600 there had been four editions; the seventeenth century saw fourteen. An edition in three volumes, wrongly described as the fourteenth, appeared in 1725, and was reprinted at Dublin in 1739,[1] from which date until 1907 only abridgements were printed. Mrs Stanley published a modernized version in 1725, and this was perhaps the form in which Richardson made the acquaintance of Sidney's romance.[2] The various continuations and supplements need only be mentioned, as testimony to the influence of the book; they include Alexander's addition to the third book (1623), Beling's sixth book (1624), Gervase Markham's *English Arcadia* (1607-1613), and *A Continuation of Sir Philip Sidney's Arcadia, wherein is handled the Loves of Amphialus and Helena, Queen of Corinth, Prince Plangus and Erona*, by Anne Weamys (1651). Francis Quarles took the most pathetic of Sidney's episodes and made a poem out of it, in *Argalus and Parthenia* (1627); the same story was dished up in a number of chap-book editions about the end of the seventeenth century.

John Day, in *The Ile of Guls*, Beaumont and Fletcher, Shirley, perhaps Webster, and certainly Shakespeare, cut fragments of material from the *Arcadia*. Besides what has already been mentioned, Shakespeare was in Sidney's debt for the episode of the King of Paphlagonia (Galatia in the old *Arcadia*), which formed the basis of his underplot of Gloucester and his two sons in *King Lear*. The primary source was the *Ethiopica*,[3] but the story was ultimately transformed out of all knowledge. Thoroughly taken in by the

these are found together in Malory's *Morte Darthur*, which Ascham puritanically condemned. The *Arcadia* was as much the offspring of the Amadis cycle as the *Morte Darthur* was of the mediæval *roman d'aventure*, and that of the *chanson de geste*, all of which express the spirit of knightly heroism and, the later romances especially, the licentiousness which, Dr Tieje seems to think, cannot exist in the same society.

[1] This reprint is not enumerated in Esdaile, who enables us to observe the confusion in the numbering of editions, nor in Dr Sommer's bibliographical introduction to his photo-lithographic reproduction of the first edition (1891). See introduction to *Arcadia* (1907) for a brief account of these.

[2] Richardson adopted the name of his first heroine from Sidney (changing the stress from the second to the first syllable, probably not observing how it should be pronounced) as a sort of play upon names. His housemaid, Pamela, was an imprisoned virgin; so he playfully gave her the name of an illustrious captive—in person and circumstances how different!

[3] Wolff, pp. 312-313.

pretended devotion of his bastard son, the deluded king drives out Leonatus, the heir. He is deposed and blinded by the bastard, and when the faithful Leonatus returns to succour him begs to be led to the top of a high crag that he may cast himself down and die. Several fine touches in the story are Sidney's. Shakespeare took these over, including the storm, and added new features. So much for Sidney's unintended contributions to the romantic drama, the lawlessness of which, in its infancy, offended him.[1] His influence on other romancers and story-writers will be considered next.

[1] See his diatribes against its disregard for the unities (*Apologie for Poetrie*).

CHAPTER VI

EUPHUISM AND ARCADIANISM—ROBERT GREENE

Imitators of Lyly and Sidney

THE appearance within a brief space of time of two such notable books as *Euphues* and the *Arcadia* was a great incentive to other writers, and a number of able and educated young men were awaiting just such a lead. Greene, Lodge and Nashe in another age would have been successful journalists; such men as Dickenson and Melbancke would probably have failed to make a living out of the same profession. Warner, like Gascoigne, was a poet trying his hand at the prose fiction of his day. Lyly and Sidney had more in them than any of these young fellows had, hence their greater influence. Lyly dazzled everyone with his showy style, the trick of which was easily learned. But quite as many were captivated by the glamour of Sidney's pastoralism, the sentimental rhetoric of his love scenes, and his dexterous handling of complicated adventures. The first and chief of these imitators—imitators now of one or the other and now of both—was Greene, who has been described, perhaps correctly, as the most prolific of all the Elizabethan men of letters,[1] and was also the first Englishman to win a livelihood by writing for immediate sale to the public.

Robert Greene

Robert Greene is an interesting case in literary history rather than a writer of literary importance. He had no genius, either in the general or in the special sense of the term; there is not a single work from his pen the loss of which would leave a distressing gap, nor is it likely that there would have been had he lived considerably beyond his brief allotment of thirty-four years. And yet, to wind up the list of his undeserving claims to distinction, Greene, in these days of doctorial theses and monographs in the learned periodicals,

[1] J. C. Jordan: *Robert Greene*, p. 6. Greene's writings take up thirteen out of the fifteen volumes in Grosart's edition of his *Complete Works*.

has been the object of the minutest critical investigation. The amount of intellectual energy and acumen—and of intellectual dullness—expended on this man's very second-rate work would have sufficed to set up a whole establishment of Greenes, and would have astonished the writer himself, who, according to his friend Nashe, "made no account of winning credit by his works . . . his only care was to have a spell in his purse to conjure up a good cup of wine with at all times."[1] He was, in short, a journalist, always living from hand to mouth in the literal and also in the literary sense; prepared to "yark up a pamphlet" in a night and a day just "as well as in seven year,"[2] and to make further capital out of any idea, motive or plot that had proved lucrative in other hands. This was not the way to produce literature; and Greene would be remembered, if at all, solely as an expert bookseller's hack but for his having fortuitously struck out a fertile line in his cautionary pamphlets on cony-catching, so making a contribution to the beginnings of realism. His other work, apart from his journeyman productions for the stage, consists of moral stories or collections of pieces in the euphuistic style, and of pastorals and romances after the manner of Sidney. He never attempted anything on a large scale; and while, like Sidney, he borrowed freely from the Greek romances, he did not try for the same amplitude and complexity, but kept as a rule to the brevity of the Italian *novella*.

Greene's life

The facts that we have of Greene's life could all be put into a short paragraph, and are familiar to most people. Besides the facts we have what is worth more, touches of kindly observation from his intimates, not to mention the unfriendly statements from other quarters which put them on his defence. Between the two we can compose a fair likeness of the man. Born in 1558, he left Cambridge in 1583 with the degree of Master of Arts, obtaining the same distinction a few years later from Oxford. At Cambridge he had probably read *Euphues*, and perhaps the *Arcadia*, of which there were copies going about.[3] In the first blush of his enthusiasm for Lyly he wrote his prentice work, *Mamillia*, of which the first part was entered in the Stationers' Register in 1580, but not published

[1] "Four Letters Confuted" (*Works of Thomas Nashe*, ed. R. B. McKerrow, i., p. 287).

[2] *Ibid.*

[3] See p. 93, n. 2.

till 1583, and the second did not appear till 1593, the year after his death. And now for a dozen years, down to the last hours on his deathbed, Greene was hard at it with his pen, soon finding a steady demand for anything he wrote. "Glad was that printer," says Nashe, "that might be so blest to pay him dear for the very dregs of his wit." [1]

Not long after quitting Cambridge Greene married. His wife was the daughter of a Lincolnshire gentleman, and had a portion, which Greene quickly ran through, and then left her, a child being born after they had parted. His conduct towards the poor woman is the heaviest article of his *Repentance*, in which, as he lay dying, Greene reviewed his wasted life as a warning to ill-doers. He avers that he was first led astray by dissolute comrades at the university, and that he went with some of them into Spain and Italy, "in which places I saw and practised such villainy as is abominable to declare." But it would not be inexcusable to wonder whether this alleged tour, and the alleged profligacy also, were not a fictitious touch of the inveterate romancer. His stories are often laid in foreign parts, yet never show any sign of first-hand acquaintance with the places mentioned.[2] Greene was his own favourite subject. His own iniquities, which he obviously depicted in the darkest colours they would bear, were exactly the right stuff for readers who revelled in pictures of vice and depravity, and could not have these too lurid, albeit they expected a moral postscript at the end, or, still better, a sermon in the orthodox Puritan style. It is not suggested that Greene's warnings and repentances were a sham ; but they were assuredly what the modern journalist would call a "stunt." In *Greene's Vision*, for example, he describes in solemn terms a shock of insight and remorse that came to him in church at his birthplace, Norwich, and how he determined on the spot to amend his ways ; but there are accompanying facts which raise more than a suspicion that the incident described was merely a literary device to prepare his readers for a change of tone in his fiction. Greene was not insincere ; nor, on the other hand, was he a John Bunyan. He was a weak and emotional man, easily influenced, with little more depth of character than that

[1] See p. 93, n. 2.

[2] The point is discussed by Jordan (pp. 77, n.), where one passage is quoted that might be the exception proving the rule. See also Wolff: "Greene and the Renaissance" (*Englische Studien*, vol. 37, 1906-1907, pp. 365-366).

with which he endows his Philadors, Francescos, and Robertos. His life was squalid rather than tragic ; and through some tender and idyllic passages in his works, as well as from the testimony of his friends, one may discern much in it that merits compassion, if not esteem.

"Mamillia," a euphuistic story, with a romantic sequel

His first love-pamphlet, *Mamillia : a Mirrour or Looking-glasse for the Ladies of Englande*, is not only composed throughout in the style of *Euphues* ; it actually takes Lyly's initial situation and reverses it. The theme is man's fickleness contrasted with the unquenchable devotion of the woman who loves. This lesson is elaborated, not only in the incidents, but in the regular euphuistic manner—in numerous harangues, debates and didactic epistles. Mamillia arrives at Padua from Venice, and is courted by Pharicles, who before long finds himself hopelessly enamoured of her cousin, Publia. Pledged to both ladies at once, and unable to make up his mind between their rival attractions, the vacillating lover takes himself off to Spain, and assumes the habit of a palmer. When Greene resumed the story he had fallen a victim to the blandishments of Greek romance, no doubt being under the spell of Sidney's *Arcadia*.[1] Hence in *Mamillia : the Seconde Parte of the Tryumphe of Pallas*, the tale runs off on romantic excursions. The faithful Publia has died in a convent, leaving her fortune to the recreant lover. Mamillia's father also is dead, and has left her his large possessions, but on the awkward condition that she shall not marry Pharicles. That unstable person, meanwhile, is in prison at Saragossa, lying condemned to death on a trumped-up charge, through the malice of a courtesan whose advances he had repulsed. The devoted heroine comes to the rescue and marries him, and the impressionable senators at Padua set aside her father's will to reward her matchless constancy.

"The Myrrour of Modestie"

Early in the year following the first part of *Mamillia*, Greene published a version of the story of Susannah and the elders, entitled *The Myrrour of Modestie* (1584).[2] Of this pamphlet there seems

[1] Jordan has a note (p. 32): "Sidney's *Arcadia* with its minute and keen analysis of character was written before 1585, but there is no way of knowing whether Greene had read it." Yet he himself adduces plenty of evidence that Greene must have read and been deeply influenced by it, and probably some time before 1585.

[2] *Complete Works*, ed. A. Grosart, ii.

to have been no further edition. The motive of the Prodigal Son comes more than once into *Mamillia*, in the reflections of Pharicles on the dangers he may incur from vicious associates, and in sundry pieces of advice tendered to the heroine. The earlier portion of the next story, *Gwydonius : the Carde of Fancie* (1584),[1] is based on the same motive ; the young prince of Mytilene behaves riotously at Alexandria and is thrown into prison, in the time before he meets the lady whom he is destined to love. All the rest is romance, of the kind derived from Heliodorus and Achilles Tatius through the medium of Sidney, full of caprices of fortune, wild complications and melodramatic disentanglements. Gwydonius finds himself in the dilemma of having to serve against his own father for the father of his mistress, or evade the obligation to join the army by taking flight. Denounced as a spy, he is imprisoned, and after other unexpected predicaments he is called upon to array himself in the armour of another knight and fight in a single combat which will decide the issue of the war. The hostile champion is his father. Gwydonius saves the situation from becoming too painful for Greene's readers by rushing in and disarming his opponent, and then revealing his identity.

"Gwydonius," romance in the traditional style

"Arbasto"

Equally far from all likeness to reality is *Arbasto : the Anatomie of Fortune* (1584),[2] from which it is difficult to extract any weightier theory of life than that we must ever beware of the whims and spitefulness of fortune, as the title admonishes, although the tale itself is but a chronicle of weakness and folly. Greene puts his querulous story in the mouth of an old king living as a hermit. Arbasto had been infatuated with the daughter of a rival king, and she had rejected his advances. But her sister loved him devotedly, and was instrumental in his escape from captivity. He married her in recompense ; but when she discovered that he was still hankering after her froward sister she died of grief. Then the haughty princess began to come round ; but it was too late, Arbasto had changed his mind, and she too died broken-hearted. At this point—and not too early for the fickle monarch's deserts, though Greene does not regard it as his nemesis—a treacherous noble seizes the crown, and Arbasto retires into exile.

[1] *Complete Works*, ed. A. Grosart, iv.

[2] *Ibid.*, iii.

In *Morando: the Tritameron of Love* (1584),[1] Greene is at his most didactic. Morando and his guests, a lady and her three daughters and three young men, discourse of love and tell each other apposite tales, this felicitous setting being rounded off with a betrothal. *Planetomachia* has a more pretentious framework, the seven planets being represented as debating together on their relative power over the fates of lovers. It is chiefly interesting for the first story, "Venus Tragedie," which is Greene's closest approximation to the Italian *novella*. Rodento, Count Coelio's son, has received encouragement from Pasylla, daughter of the bitterly hostile Valdracko, Duke of Ferrara. Valdracko discovers the intrigue, and contrives a ghastly revenge. Hopelessly weak in his grasp of character, Greene scamps his work at the crucial passages, and fails to give any adequate account of motive. This is how he presents Valdracko's state of mind on the detection of his daughter's amour:

"Planetomachia" and the tale of Valdracko

But Fortune who knoweth no mean, seeing Rodento beginning to climb unto happiness, thought to lift him up to the skies, that she might with more violence push him down lower than hell, and to bring this to pass she thus laid her platform. It fortuned that within few days Pasylla and her cousin Pandina being walking together in the garden, Valdracko thinking his daughter had been in her closet, went up to speak to her, but finding the door unshut, which Pandina by forgetfulness had left open and none within, stepped into the closet, and began to rifle among the loose papers which were lying on the board, and at last by unhappy luck, light on the letter which Rodento sent to Pasylla; which after he had thoroughly perused, and perceived by the contents the sum of his suit, he searched further, and found the copy of his daughter's answer, containing so mild a repulse, and so friendly denials, that he was pained with strange and uncertain thoughts, thinking if he should with rigour reprove his daughter's folly, it were but to make her over fervent in affection: knowing that women fly frowardly from those things whereunto they are persuaded, and wilfully attempt those actions, from which with sensible reasons they are forewarned. To forbid Rodento to prosecute his suit, was to stop swift streams with a sword, and to stay the blasts of the wind with a veil of silk, so that he was doubtful what to do: yet in this resolute: rather than his enemy should triumph in obtaining his purpose, to prevent his pretence with the untimely death of his own

[1] *Complete Works*, ed. A. Grosart, iii.

daughter. Being in this quandary he laid down the letters and went to his bedchamber, where being solitary, surcharged with melancholy dumps, he fell to sundry strange devises: at last after he had leaned a while on his elbow, he determined to colour his secret grief with the baleful shadow of despite, and now to repay his old hate with a speedy and bloody revenge, hoping under the pretensed colour of friendship not only to procure his own gain and good fortune, but also utterly to subvert and extinguish the whole house and family of the Conte Coelio.[1]

Valdracko pretends to be reconciled to Coelio, and consents to the marriage of their children. But before this takes place he has Coelio murdered, and when the bravo who has done the deed is captured he silences him by having his tongue cut out and then puts him to death. Not long after, Rodento and Pasylla are married, with great rejoicings, in which Valdracko affects to join. But before many weeks pass the villainous duke has his son-in-law poisoned. So moving is Pasylla's grief that the poisoner suborned by Valdracko confesses. Pasylla watches her opportunity, and one day when her father is asleep she binds him in his bed, then wakes him up and, taxing him with his crimes, stabs him and then kills herself with the same sword. It is a piece in the most blood-curdling manner of Bandello and Cinthio, and one entirely to the taste of audiences who supped on horrors in the plays of Marlowe and Kyd.

"Penelope's Web"—the tale of Barmenissa

In *Penelope's Web* (1587) the stories are told by Penelope and her handmaids, whilst she is engaged by night in unravelling the work done by day as a pretext for keeping her suitors at arm's length. Each tale is to illustrate one of the special virtues of women, as chastity, obedience, silence. Barmenissa, in Penelope's tale, may be a pleasing figure to readers who find delight in patient Griseldas: she exemplifies unconditional and unquestioning obedience. Barmenissa is the wife of Saladin, Emperor of Egypt, who unhappily falls a prey to the courtesan Olynda and repudiates his lawful wife. The Egyptian lords conspire to vindicate her cause and expel the intruder. At first, Barmenissa is pleased with their loyalty, and soliloquizes thus:

Now Barmenissa, thou seest that delay in revenge is the best physick; that the Gods are just, and have taken thy quarrel as

[1] *Complete Works*, ed. A. Grosart, v., pp. 81-83.

advocates of thine injury : now shalt thou see wrong overruled with patience, and the ruin of thine enemy with the safety of thine own honour : time is the discoverer of mishap, and Fortune never ceaseth to stretch her strings till they crack : shame is the end of treachery, and dishonour ever foreruns repentance. Olynda hath soared with Icarus, and is like to fall with Phaeton : sooner are bruises caught by reaching too high than by stooping too low : Fortune grudgeth not at them which fall, but Envy bites them which climb : now shall the lords of Egypt by revenging thine enemy work thy content."[1]

But, she goes on to reflect, content does not lie in revenge ; and, after all, the iniquitous usurpation of her queenly rights by Olynda redounds to her own glory. And, admitting no exception to the rule of passive obedience, Greene brings her to the conclusion that it is better to give her well-meaning friends away than thwart the most trifling desire of her husband and sovereign. So she makes up her mind to reveal the conspiracy, and accosts her wicked rival with magnanimity. Olynda is thoroughly alarmed when she hears what is in the wind. Saladin, already disquieted by remorse, apprehends the conspirators, but at the same time puts Olynda to a sudden test of her loyalty and affection. He offers to grant three requests, and waits to see what she will ask. The brazen huzzy demands that the obnoxious peers should be executed, the king's son disinherited, and the queen banished. This is too much for Saladin.

Which when the emperor had thoroughly weighed with himself, noting the injurious mind of an insolent concubine, he fell into such hate against her for her presumption, that he burst forth into these terms. I see well, as the distressed estate of poverty is intolerable for want, so presumption of an insolent person is not to be suffered for pride : thoughts above measure are either cut short by time or fortune : they which gaze at a star stumble at a stone : the Cimbrians looked so long at the sun that they were blind : and such as are born beggars make majesty a mark to gaze at : sith that in presuming with Phaeton, they fall with Icarus : and that in desiring with Tarquin to be counted more than Gods, they prove in the end with Polycrates to be worse than men. I speak this, Olynda, for that I see the glory of a crown hath made thee unworthy of a crown, and dignity that ought to metamorphize men into virtuous resolutions, hath made thee a very mirror of vicious affections.[2]

[1] *Complete Works*, v., p. 168. [2] *Ibid.*, p. 176.

Olynda receives her deserts, and the much-enduring queen is restored to her place and dignities.

Greene's euphuistic style

Incidentally the reader will have noticed how slavishly Greene adopts the euphuistic mannerisms. We rarely fail, in his stories and those of his fellows, to meet some person who soars with Icarus to fall like Phaeton, and to be reminded that it is better "to peck at the stars with the young eagles, than to prey on dead carcasses with the vultures." All the metaphors and fantastic similes of Pettie and Lyly are repeated as if they were the only current coin. And as a follower of Sidney, Greene is just as easy-going and unoriginal, just as perfunctory. A fair illustration of his carelessness, sheer impudence in an educated man providing literature for the uneducated, is the way he plays ducks and drakes with chronology. Penelope is well read in the household stories of a period still in the distant future. She quotes Plato and Aristotle; she knows all about Roman history, and is as ready to find comparisons when she wants them from the Middle Ages as from ancient times. So long as he could carry the uncritical reader along, Greene was troubled with no scruples about historical fact, geographical accuracy, or more than the faintest show of verisimilitude. The shoddy character of his plot-work will be more apparent when we return to his romances.

The didactic nature of Greene's framework stories

There are still a few of his framework stories to be mentioned: fourteen out of his twenty-three works of fiction or works containing fiction take this form.[1] *Euphues his Censure to Philautus* (1587)[2] is the account of a philosophical combat between Hector and Achilles, upon "the virtues necessary to be incident to every gentleman . . . especially debated to discover the perfection of a soldier." Thus it comes into line with famous works by Guevara, Castiglione, Roger Ascham, Lyly himself, and many other writers of this era who were interested in the ideal aims of education and culture. It is an ethical treatise, illustrated by imaginary instances. But so were all Greene's framework stories, the philosophic exposition being usually put in the framing, just as Painter, Pettie, Fenton, and the rest put theirs mainly into their prefaces and perorations. Here, Andromache and Polyxena, Cressida, Briseis and Iphigenia are introduced; Hector telling an Egyptian story

[1] Wolff: *Eng. Stud.*, 37, p. 367, n.

[2] *Complete Works*, vi.

is followed by Achilles, Priam as umpire summing up the debate. This pamphlet is supposed to be written by Euphues in his hermitage at Silexedra, and, like Lyly's book, is a patchwork of ideas and aphorisms from Cicero, Plato, Plutarch, Castiglione, and the other authorities from whom the Elizabethans loved to quote precepts on the art of living.

In *Perimedes the Blacke-Smith* [1] (1588) Greene attempted a picture of homely life and contentment with little, in the evening talks of a poor blacksmith in Memphis and his wife, and the stories with which they amuse each other, mostly from Boccaccio. Alcida, in the novel—licensed in 1588, but of which no edition is known earlier than that of 1617—entitled *Alcida, Greene's Metamorphosis*,[2] is an old woman whom a shipwrecked man meets with on the coast of Africa. She relates the history of her three daughters. These young women are a terrible warning against the three vices of pride, inconstancy and proneness to gossip, for indulgence in which they were severally transformed to a statue, a chameleon and a rose-bush, their aged mother herself weeping so profusely that she was turned into a well of tears.

One of Greene's most popular effusions was the mixture of sentimental philosophy, pseudo-history and pastoralism which he called *Ciceronis Amor: Tullie's Love* [3] (1589). Not from the historians, but out of incidents culled from romance and legend, he constructed a chequered love-chronicle, and adorned it with letters and orations in what was supposed to be the Ciceronian style, some passages, for greater effect, being put in Latin as well as English. This was followed by *Orpharion* [4] (1590), a fantastic dream-story, in which the ghosts of Orpheus and Arion appear, and sing the woes of Eurydice and other ladies.

The "Farewell to Follie" and a "Vision"

But Greene seems to mean more seriously in his next two pieces, his *Farewell to Follie* [5] (1591) and *Greene's Vision*, which he is said to have finished on his death-bed, leaving it to be published with other posthumous work in 1592, though some of the contents may have been written a year or two earlier.[6] In the *Vision* he relates how, at the time he had been charged with the authorship of that

[1] *Complete Works*, vii. [2] *Ibid.*, ix. [3] *Ibid.*, vii. [4] *Ibid.*, xii.
[5] *Ibid.*, ix. [6] The question is discussed by Jordan, pp. 169-172.

licentious pamphlet, *The Cobbler of Canterbury*,[1] he was deeply oppressed one day with the thought of his misspent life, and prayed to be delivered from his follies; in which state of mind he saw two old men approach.[2] They were Chaucer and Gower, and he asked for their verdict on his writings. Chaucer approved of his merry way of telling a tale, and presently tickled his sense of humour with the anecdote of Tomkins. Gower dissuaded him from writing any more love-pamphlets, telling the moral tale of Vandermast of Antwerp and his wife, as an antidote to Chaucer's. Then Solomon comes on the scene, siding with Gower, and exhorts Greene to become a divine.[3] From this date, Greene asserts, he renounced his wanton old courses and wrote strictly for the betterment of his fellows. Instead of the motto prefixed to his former books, *Omne tulit punctum qui miscuit utile dulci*,[4] he now adopted the device *Sero sed serio*,[5] which was presently to be discarded for a third, *Nascimur pro patria*.[6] Under the new watchword, *Sero sed serio*, he writes one of his histories of a prodigal son, *Greene's Mourning Garment*, and follows it up with two of like complexion, *Greene's Never too Late*, and its sequel, *Francesco's Fortunes*. The *Farewell to Follie* (1591), designed, so the sub-title announces, as a call to repentance, is a dialogue, with the usual intermixture of tales, which is carried on between seven young gentlemen and ladies staying at a villa near Florence, on the themes of pride, lust and gluttony. The conversation breaks off when they all go in to dinner; and there can be little doubt that Greene, as Henry Morley suggested, meant to write a second part in which the other four in the company would have gone to the end of the catalogue of the seven deadly sins.[7]

[1] *The Cobler of Canterburie, or an Inuectiue against Tarltons Newes out of Purgatorie* (1590), was a jest-book composed of scurrilous tales from Boccaccio, Ser Giovanni, etc. It was afterwards republished (altered somewhat) as *The Tincker of Turvey, his merry Pastime in his passing from Billingsgate to Graues-End* (1630).

[2] *Greene's Vision* (*Works*, xii.): "After I was burdened with the penning of the Cobbler of Canterbury, I waxed passing melancholy as grieving that either I should be wrong with envy, or wronged with suspicion."

[3] Grosart shows reason for believing that Greene was Vicar of Tollesbury, Essex, for a year and a half (1584-1586), see introduction to *Complete Works*, vol. i., lxix.

[4] "He has gained everything who has mingled the useful with the pleasant."

[5] "Late in the day, but serious at last."

[6] "We are born for our country's weal."

[7] *English Writers*, x., pp. 94-95.

The tale of Tomkins

Chaucer's story of Tomkins the Wheelwright might have been filched from *The Canterbury Tales* and put into prose. It is like those broadly humorous tales of his that are nearly related to the *fabliaux*. Tomkins, who lives at Grantchester, is jealous of his wife, who had been a dairymaid and still sells cream in Cambridge. She and a scholar who is one of her admirers hatch a scheme to reform him. This young fellow meets him going to Cambridge, and asks where he lives. When he replies at Grantchester, the scholar asks if he happens to know Tomkins, and informs him that Tomkins is the most famous cuckold in the country. This statement he offers to prove when Kate is in town. Next day the jealous husband sends Kate to market, pretending to be ill. But he joins his informant, and is taken to a college window where he sees Kate sitting on a man's knee eating cherries. Not wishing to be recognized as the deluded husband, he goes off with his companion to drink. A drug is put in his drink, and they take him home sound asleep and place him in his own bed. When he awakes, furious with rage at his wife, she and her mother persuade him that he has been ill and delirious, and that it was all a dream. Thus he is made to disbelieve the evidence of his own eyes, and to think his jealousy an idle fancy.

The tale of Roberto

Roberto's tale, in *Greene's Groats-Worth of Witte*,[1] recounts a lover's stratagem with the same unfeeling kind of humour. A young farmer is about to be married to a lady who has been much courted by lovers of her own station. After the ceremony, one of her disappointed suitors takes him aside and pretends that she is carrying on an intrigue and intends to elope with another man that night. He offers to bring the injured husband to the spot, so that he may impersonate the seducer and bring the woman to her senses. The bridegroom accordingly slips away after the festivities, and is conducted to the supposed place of assignation. There he is led to a chamber, and in the dark finds, as he thinks, his wife. In a few minutes there is a loud knocking at the door, and the astonished bridegroom sees the lady's father outside wanting to know what he is doing here. The woman he has been embracing is an old flame whose mother is in the plot to betray him. Caught, apparently, in the very act, he can think of no excuse to satisfy the indignant bride.

[1] Reprinted in Bodley Head Quartos, vi., 1923.

She throws him over in favour of his astute rival, and the poor farmer has to marry the wench who had tricked him. Both this and the previous tale seem to be Greene's own invention. They are identical in their coarse humour and total disregard of morality with a large proportion of the tales that had been told, in church and elsewhere, from when the *Gesta Romanorum* and the *Alphabet of Tales* were in regular request to Greene's own time, when the jest-book was in everyone's hands.[1] Were they Greene's contributions to the same stock, or was he trying his hand at *novelle* in the style of Boccaccio? Since the genre was as old as the *fabliaux*—nay, as the Milesian tales—and both the English and the Italian stories were derived from the same original patterns, and often used the same motives and plots, the question is possibly insoluble and probably futile.[2]

"Pandosto: The Triumph of Time"

A large number of the stories in Greene's moral collections are miniature romances: let us now cast an eye on some others, not quite so undersized, that were published separately. They are an improvement on *Mamillia*, *Gwydonius*, and *Arbasto*; Greene was gaining in dexterity. The best is certainly *Pandosto: The Triumph of Time* (1588), which was frequently republished right down to the middle of the eighteenth century, and in the later editions was usually entitled *Dorastus and Fawnia.* It is the story which Shakespeare altered to form the plot of *A Winter's Tale.* In origin it was historical. Something like the events narrated took place in the fourteenth century, when a Polish king or duke, suspecting his Bohemian wife, threw her into prison, where she bore him a son.[3] The queen was put to death and the boy sent away, but eventually restored to his penitent father. Greene remodelled the tale in the Greek romantic way and changed the scene to Bohemia and Sicily; Shakespeare turned these countries round about, giving the part of Pandosto of Bohemia to Leontes of Sicily, and that of Egistus of Sicily to Polixenes of Bohemia. He rechristened several other characters also, and gave important rôles to three new ones—

[1] See Volume I., chap. ix.: "Popular Tales."

[2] It is discussed by Dr Wolff in "Robert Greene and the Italian Renaissance" (*Englische Studien*, vol. 37, 1906-1907, pp. 348-350) and by Dr Jordan, p. 27 *et seq.*

[3] Sec. ed., by P. G. Thomas, *Shakespeare Library*, 1907, and Caro (*Eng. Stud.*, 1878-1888).

Antigonus, Paulina and Autolycus. Otherwise the plot is the same in its rough outlines, although the significance of the chief episodes is profoundly different.

After developing the first part of the story, in which Pandosto has grown violently jealous of Egistus, who returns to his kingdom to avoid a treacherous attack, and Pandosto thereupon throws his wife into prison, Greene begins to borrow from the Greek romancers. From Heliodorus he takes the incident of the casting away of the infant Fawnia (Perdita)—"as he thought, it came by fortune, so he would commit it to the charge of fortune." In the trial of the wrongly suspected mother Bellaria (Hermione), in the oracle declaring her guiltless and announcing that "the king shall live without an heir, if that which is lost be not found," and in the strange concatenation of events by which the princess is restored and the estranged monarchs brought together again by the union of their children, Greene shapes his little romance on the lines of the vast and complicated *Ethiopica*. But it is Longus who lent him the pastoral scenes occupying the middle of the piece. Like Chloe, the child is cast ashore on the coast of Sicily, and is brought up by a shepherd foster-father, who preserves the rich jewels round her neck, afterwards to be the tokens by which she is recognized and restored to her birthright. From *Daphnis and Chloe* was derived also the episode of Fawnia's life as a shepherdess and her wooing by rustic suitors. Then Dorastus (Florizel) comes into the story. He is the young prince of Sicily, son of Pandosto's former friend, Egistus. Rumour has apprised him of the loveliness of Fawnia, and he comes to see her for himself. He woos her ; but their only hope is to escape to another land, and they take a vessel and flee. They are driven ashore on the coast of Bohemia ; and now Greene follows Achilles Tatius, making Pandosto fall in love with the beautiful unknown, who is really his daughter, an unsavoury incident which Shakespeare rejected. Greene's details of the final disclosure are, however, taken over by the dramatist, but put together and amplified with others in a manner incomparably finer than this rude sketch. Greene's Bellaria was dead ; Shakespeare preserved his Hermione, to be the most touching figure in one of his greatest scenes. And, throughout his play, for Greene's facile handling of chance and coincidence, he substituted the natural operation of circumstance and human motive.[1]

Sidney's influence on Greene

Greene's characters, here as elsewhere, are merely puppets moved mechanically; but they utter the sentiments appropriate to the situation, and this gives them a certain charm. He is at his best in such a tender passage as Bellaria's lament when her ruthless husband commits their babe to the mercies of the sea:

"Alas, sweet unfortunate babe, scarce born, before envied by fortune, would the day of thy birth had been the term of thy life: then shouldest thou have made an end to care, and prevented thy father's rigour. Thy faults cannot yet deserve such hateful revenge, thy days are too short for so sharp a doom; but thy untimely death must pay thy mother's debts, and her guiltless crime must be thy ghastly curse. And shalt thou, sweet Babe, be committed to Fortune, when thou art already spited by Fortune? Shall the seas be thy harbour and the hard boat thy cradle? Shall thy tender mouth, instead of sweet kisses, be nipped with bitter storms? Shalt thou have the whistling winds for thy lullaby, and the salt sea foam instead of sweet milk? Alas, what destinies would assign such hard hap? What father would be so cruel? Or what gods will not revenge such rigour? Let me kiss thy lips, sweet infant, and wet thy tender cheeks with my tears, and put this chain about thy little neck, that if fortune save thee, it may help to succour thee. Thus, since thou must go to surge in the gastful seas, with a sorrowful kiss I bid thee farewell, and I pray the gods thou mayest fare well."[2]

There one can see the disciple of the prose-poet Sidney, and in much of the narrative portion Greene writes with a limpidity and grace not inferior to the best passages in the *Arcadia*. Greene is as fond as Sidney of rhetorical speeches and soliloquies; but in these he sticks to the euphuistic idiom, as in Fawnia's answer to Dorastus, when he appears before her clad in shepherd's weeds:

"Truth," quoth Fawnia, "but all that wear cowls are not monks: painted eagles are pictures, not eagles. Zeuxis' grapes were like grapes, yet shadows: rich clothing makes not princes, nor homely attire beggars: shepherds are not called shepherds because they wear hooks and bags, but that they are born poor and live to keep sheep;

[1] Greene's loans from Greek romance and Shakespeare's departures from Greene are fully tabulated by Wolff (*Greek Romances*, pp. 445-458).

[2] *Pandosto*, ed. P. G. Thomas, pp. 47-48.

so this attire hath not made Dorastus a shepherd, but to seem like a shepherd."

"Well, Fawnia," answered Dorastus, "were I a shepherd, I could not but like thee, and, being a prince, I am forced to love thee. Take heed, Fawnia: be not proud of beauty's painting, for it is a flower that fadeth in the blossom. Those, which disdain in youth, are despised in age. Beauty's shadows are tricked up with time's colours, which, being set to dry in the sun, are stained with the sun, scarce pleasing the sight ere they begin not to be worth the sight; not much unlike the herb Ephemeron, which flourisheth in the morning and is withered before the sun setting. If my desire were against law, thou mightest justly deny me my reason; but I love thee, Fawnia, not to misuse thee as a concubine, but to use thee as my wife. I can promise no more, and mean to perform no less." [1]

In his other pastoral, *Menaphon* [2] (1589), Greene made a public avowal of his debt to Lyly, and his later publishers officiously advertised the debt to Sidney. The first sub-title ran: "Camilla's alarum to slumbering Euphues, in his melancholy Cell at Silexedra"; later editions are entitled *Greene's Arcadia, or Menaphon*. The plot is a tissue of absurdities. Trying to compete with Sidney's fantastic exploit in the love entanglement of Zelmane, Philoclea, Basilius and Gynecia, disguised lover and lady, and lady's father and mother, all in a net of forbidden love, Greene evolves a still more monstrous situation.[3] The shipwrecked Sephestia, who believes her husband drowned, and has been rescued by the shepherd Menaphon, who woos her and is gently repulsed, loses her little son Pleusidippus, who is carried off by pirates. All the rusty machinery of Greek romance is set in motion again to bring about the central paradox—a long-lost wife courted by the husband who does not know her, by the father who many years ago turned her adrift, and by the son who was kidnapped and has grown to manhood in another land.[4] Compared with this, Thomas Hardy's *Well-Beloved* has a modest and reasonable plot. It is an interesting study to disentangle the

"*Menaphon*"

[1] *Pandosto*, ed. P. G. Thomas, p. 57.
[2] *Complete Works*, vi.
[3] Wolff, pp. 422-445.
[4] Greene may have got the first suggestion for his plot, the idea of princes and princesses living as shepherds and shepherdesses, not recognizing each other, and falling in love, from Warner's story of Argentile and Curan, in *Albion's England* (see J. Q. Adams' "Menaphon and the Thracian Wonder" in *Modern Philology*, iii., pp. 317-318), and Wolff, pp. 442-443).

threads of Sidneian rhetoric from the euphuistic skein in passages like the following :

> Well, to breakfast they went ; Lamedon and Samela fed hard, but Menaphon, like the Argive in the date gardens of Arabia, lived with the contemplation of his mistress's beauty. The salamander liveth not without the fire, the herring from the water, the mole from the earth, nor the cameleon from the air ; nor could Menaphon live from the sight of his Samela : whose breath was perfumed air, whose eyes were fire wherein he delighted to dally, whose heart the earthly paradise wherein he desired to ingraft the essence of his love and affection. Thus did the poor shepherd bathe in a kind of bliss, while his eyes, feeding on his mistress's face, surfeited with the excellency of her perfection.[1]

Here is a scene of high-pitched flyting, where Samela's long-lost son Pleusidippus sees the portrait of the mother whom he has never known :

> Pleusidippus, who all this while heard his tale with attentive patience, no sooner beheld the radiant glory of this resplendent face, but as a man already installed in eternity, he exclaimed thus abruptly : "O, Arcadia ! Arcadia ! storehouse of nymphs, and nursery of beauty !" At which words Olympia, starting up suddenly, as if she, a second Juno, had taken her Jove in bed with Alcmena, and overcasting the chamber with a frown, that was able to mantle the world with an eternal night, she made passage to her choler in these terms of contempt : "Beardless upstart, of I know not whence, have the favours of my bounty (not thy desert) entered thee so deeply in overweening presumption, that thou shouldst be the foremost in derogation of our dignity, and blaspheming of my beauty ? I tell thee, recreant, I scorn thy clownish Arcadia, with his inferior comparisons, as one that prizeth her perfection above any created constitution."
>
> Pleusidippus, upon this speech, stood plunged in a great perplexity, whether he should excuse himself mildly, or take her up roundly ; but the latter being more level to his humour than the former, he began thus to rouse up his fury : "Disdainful dame ! that upbraidest me with my birth as it were base, and my youth as it were boyish, know that although my parents and progeny are envied by obscurity, yet the sparks of renown that make my eagle-minded thoughts to mount, the heavenly fire imprisoned in the panicles of my crest, inciting me to more deeds of honour than stout Perseus effected

[1] *Green's Arcadia or Menaphon* (English Scholars' Library, 1814), p. 36.

with his falchion in the fields of Hesperia, ascertaineth my soul I was the son of no coward, but a gentleman: but sith my inequality of parentage is such an eyesore to thy envy, hold, take thy favours (and therewith he threw her her glove) and immortalize whom thou wilt with thy toys, for I will to Arcadia in spite of thee and thy affinity, there either to seek out mischance, or a new mistress." [1]

"Philomela: the Lady Fitzwater's Nightingale"

Even in one of his latest stories, *Philomela: the Lady Fitzwater's Nightingale* [2] (1592), which, though it purports to be a work written earlier, probably belongs to the time when it actually appeared, Greene keeps to the same composite strain.[3] Philippo, a Venetian nobleman, who had given his friend Lutesio leave and opportunity to test his wife Philomela as Posthumus gave leave to Iachimo in *Cymbeline*, ruminates in the following conceits:

Philippo, thou wert too fond to plot Lutesio a means of his love, granting him opportunity to woo, which is the sweetest friend to love. Men cannot dally with fire, nor sport with affection; for he that is a suitor in jest, may be a speeder in earnest. Have not such a thought in thy mind, Philippo, for as Lutesio is thy friend, so is he faithful; as Philomela is thy wife, so she is honest; and yet both may join issue, and prove dissemblous. Lovers have Argus' eyes, to be wary in their doings, and angels' tongues, to talk of holiness, when their hearts are most lascivious. Though my wife returned a taunting letter to him openly, yet she might send him sweet lines secretly; her satiable answer was but a cloak for the rain; for, ever since they have been more familiar and less asunder; nor she is never merry if Lutesio begin not the mirth: if Lutesio be not at table, her stomach is queasy: as when the halcyons hatch, the sea is calm, and the phœnix never spreads her wings but when the sunbeams shine on her nest; so Philomela is never frolic but when she is matched in the company of Lutesio. This courtesy grows of some private kindness, which if I can find out by just proof and circumstance, let me alone to revenge to the uttermost.[4]

"Greene's Mourning Garment"

Greene's Mourning Garment: given him by Repentance at the Funerals of Love (1590), which bears the motto, "*Sero sed serio*," and is his fullest version of the parable of the prodigal, has for its chief

[1] *Greene's Arcadia, or Menaphon*, pp. 68-69.

[2] *Complete Works*, xi.

[3] Dunlop calls this "the most beautiful . . . and best known of Greene's productions," and gives a very full epitome of the plot (*History of Fiction*, c. 14). It resembles now *Cymbeline* and now *Othello*, in its rudimentary way.

[4] *Philomela* (Archaica, Part I., 1814), p. 33.

exponent the headstrong Philador, younger son of a wealthy rabbi in Callipolis, a city on the rivers Gihon and Euphrates, which flow from Eden. Against the old man's will Philador goes off to see the world, and comes first to Thessaly, where he has a brief experience of pastoralism. But he travels on to the city of Saragunta, and despite the friendly warnings of his shepherd guide takes up his abode at "The Unicorn," the house of three beautiful sisters, who are courtesans. These sirens ere long strip him of money, and even of his clothes; and he is turned out, in time of famine, to eat husks with the swine. At length, like Acolastus in the play, he makes his way miserably home, confesses his folly in euphuistic language, and is entertained at the traditional banquet.

"Never too Late" and "Francesco's Fortunes"

Just such another as Philador is Francesco, in *Greene's Never too Late*, and the second part, *Francesco's Fortunes* [1] (1590); but the story of selfish dissipation takes other lines, a faithful and neglected wife being substituted for the prodigal's father, with other features betokening that Greene had his own sorry career before his eyes as he wrote. Francesco's story is related by a palmer who roams about endeavouring to draw men from devotion to Venus. He listens to the pleasant love-story of Francesco and Isabel. Then Francesco tells him how he went to Troynovant and fell a victim to the courtesan Infida. He goes to the bad for three years, loses his money, is thrust out by Infida, and falls into utter destitution. But he prospers again by joining a troupe of actors and writing plays —that is, by taking to Greene's own profession. Meanwhile his forsaken wife has been tried like Susannah, an episode for which a rehash of the early work, *The Myrrour of Modestie*, is made to do duty. Francesco hears of her ordeal and her uncomplaining fidelity and goes home a penitent.[2]

Auto-biographical pamphlets: the "Groats-Worth of Witte"

In *Greene's Groats-Worth of Witte, bought with a Million of Repentance* [3] (1592), he is undisguisedly telling his own story; towards the end he throws off the mask of allegory or parable, and speaks frankly in the first person. Gorinius had two sons, to the elder of whom, the scholar Roberto, who used to sneer at his

[1] *Complete Works*, viii.

[2] M. Jusserand pointed out that, for some of the incidents in *Francesco's Fortunes*, Greene was a borrower from Warner's tale of Opheltes, in *Syrinx*; see *The English Novel in the Time of Shakespeare* (new impression, 1899, p. 149, n.).

[3] Reprinted in Bodley Head Quartos, vi., 1923.

usurious mode of life, he bequeathed an old groat, leaving his large fortune to the more pliable Lucanio. After the old man's death Roberto plots with a friendly courtesan to pay his brother out. Between them they are to flay him and share the spoils. The plot succeeds, so far as the lady is concerned : Lucanio is relieved of his estate and reduced to beggary. But when Roberto demands his share of the proceeds she laughs in his face, and shows up his villainy to the brother. Roberto sinks to the lowest depths. Greene has hisown depravity in mind, and as was his wont overcharges the picture. But he was never more in earnest.

After such a review of lost opportunities and unredeemed baseness—none the less painful for being thrown into the indirect form of fiction—it is no wonder that poor Greene's feelings were too much for him, and that he broke into sobs of self-reproach :

Here (Gentlemen) break I off Roberto's speech ; whose life in most parts agreeing with mine, found one self punishment as I have done. Hereafter suppose me the said Roberto, and I will go on with that he promised : Greene will send you now his groat's-worth of wit, that never showed a mite's-worth in his life : and though no man now be by to do me good : yet ere I die I will by my repentance endeavour to do all men good.[1]

Then he holds forth in a regular sermon :

But now return I again to you three, knowing my misery is to you no news : and let me heartily entreat you to be warned by my harms. Delight not (as I have done) in irreligious oaths ; for, from the blasphemer's house, a curse shall not depart. Despise drunkenness, which wasteth the wit, and maketh men all equal unto beasts. Fly lust, as the deathsman of the soul, and defile not the Temple of the holy Ghost. Abhor those Epicures, whose loose life hath made religion loathsome to your ears : and when they soothe you with terms of Mastership, remember Robert Greene, whom they have often so flattered, perishes now for want of comfort. Remember, gentlemen, your lives are like so many lighted tapers, that are with care delivered to all of you to maintain : these with wind-puft wrath may be extinguisht, which drunkenness put out, which negligence let fall : for man's time is not of itself so short, but it is more shortened by sin. The fire of my life is now at the last snuff, and for want of wherewith

[1] *Greene's Groats-Worth of Witte* (Bodley Head Quartos, vi., 1923, p. 39).

to sustain it, there is no substance left for life to feed on. Trust not then (I beseech ye) to such weak stays: for they are as changeable in mind, as in many attires. Well, my hand is tired, and I am forst to leave where I would begin: for a whole book cannot contain their wrongs, which I am forst to knit up in some few lines of words.

Desirous that you should live, though himself be dying.

ROBERT GREENE.[1]

"The Repentance of Robert Greene"

The Repentance of Robert Greene [2] was yet to be written, but that is only a continuation of the same homily, and followed almost at once. Both tracts are written in a direct and forcible style that Greene had never attained in his wanton love-pamphlets: there is only an occasional lapse into euphuism in the *Groats-Worth of Witte*, not one in the *Repentance*. He speaks with the simple eloquence of strong feeling. He had misused his talents, never taken real pains with anything that he did; he had outraged the ties of kinship, brought himself and all who belonged to him to dependence on others, and was now sinking into an untimely and dishonoured grave. Yet in these autobiographical pieces and in the *Vision* he does himself a certain injustice. His "wanton love-pamphlets" had never done anyone a ha'p'orth of harm. Greene as a writer was always a lover of virtue, full of good counsel and shining instances, a pattern of puritanism and respectability, at a time when, in the making and selling of books, the two things were synonymous. As a man, he was at the mercy of idle, extravagant and debauched companions. But if the conscience of the man of letters pinched him, it ought to have been because he was capable of better things, but had been satisfied with the worse. Sidney had found time, in the midst of a thousand calls upon his energies, to write and rewrite the *Arcadia*, and make it as perfect as his genius could compass: Greene's masterpiece was the slight and slovenly *Pandosto*, which we read now because it had the honour of lending a plot to Shakespeare. He claimed a patriot's wreath for his services in exposing the cony-catching fraternity; but no one knew better than Greene how largely those pamphlets of his were ill-digested collections of facts stolen without acknowledgment from better-informed writers, eked out with sensational anecdotes such as an expert story-teller could easily provide. But of this

[1] *Greene's Groats-Worth of Witte* (Bodley Head Quartos, vi., 1923), pp. 46-47.
[2] *Ibid.*

group of his writings, in which the romancer addresses himself to the description of real life, more will be said hereafter.

Greene's puritanism

Greene has received applause from various critics as a propagator of Renaissance ideas and an apostle of the new culture.[1] At this, again, he would probably have been amused if he could have seen himself taken so seriously. Greene never dreamed that he had a mission of any sort, except in regard to the cony-catching pamphlets, and here it was not much more than a useful pretence. His job was to amuse the public for his livelihood, and to know beforehand what would please them best. But even those writers whose lives seem to evince a lack of it are prone to show in their books that they have a conscience after all; and a man will turn his best side to the reader, even when he will not exert himself to do the best work of which he is capable. Greene's fictions almost invariably inculcated a wholesome lesson; he was kind to those persons in them who behaved with probity, and severe on the evildoers. It was not, however, the lofty ideals of the Renaissance humanists that he stood for, so much as the restricted rule of life laid down by Protestant moralists. Like Lyly, like all his brethren in the craft, he usually began preaching when there was no more story to tell, and the doctrine he preached was the conventional puritanism of his day. He sounds the usual alarum against the wickedness of Italy, in *Greene's Never Too Late*, and elsewhere; but he is not very earnest about it, or indeed about any of the questions canvassed in his books, until the near prospect of death arouses him. Like Lyly, again, he takes the side of wisdom rather than that of wit, of the mediæval conception of submissive goodness rather than the Renaissance ideal of humane culture. His ethical vision is limited by the seven deadly sins, which are vaguely implied by his adjective "Machavilian."[2] A man of culture himself, at any rate an educated man who had done a good deal of miscellaneous reading though he was no great scholar, Greene rarely, if ever, sings the praises of learning. Roberto the scholar comes to a bad end.

It is usually said that Greene was unsuccessful with his men characters, but did better with his women. The truth is that he had

[1] *E.g.* S. L. Wolff: "Robert Greene and the Italian Renaissance" (*Eng. Stud.*, vol. 37, 1906-1907, pp. 321-374).

[2] *Ibid.*, p. 328.

Greene's character-drawing

scarcely any powers of characterization at all. He could tell a story, but his human figures are merely abstract counters. Creativeness was hardly to be expected of one so lacking in personality as Greene. It was not his personages but their lives that he was interested in. A certain charm that distinguishes his female characters confirms the generalization : for them he idealized, investing his chaste and long-suffering heroines with the poetry of his aspiration, and the rapacious harlots with another kind of poetry. But, even so, none of them has many marks to separate her from the others, except the circumstances in which she is placed. Bellaria and Sephestia, Mamillia and Publia, Isabel and Philomela are sets of twins, and all of them sisters ; Lais, Infida and Mistress Lamilia are only different names for the genus courtesan, though courtesan drawn by one well acquainted with her ways. He was good at one thing—a story ; even his plays are merely stories that never culminate in drama.

He was not, like Sidney, able to visualize a scene and give his incidents a background. This general absence of local colour is the only consideration that might persuade us to accept his statement that he once visited Italy and Spain ; he never manages to bring the foreign places in which he lays the action before our mental eye ; yet he is equally at fault when the events occur in England.[1]

His indebtedness to foreign writers

In the miscellaneous stories that have now been reviewed Greene is evidently carrying to a further stage the work of his predecessors, the translators ; he is putting the romance and the *novella* into a somewhat makeshift English dress, and is hardly any more original than men like Whetstone and Rich, who slipped a story or two of their own into a bundle of translations. Apart from the puritanism, any native element in his fiction is as rare as a character who is recognizably English. But, while Sidney studied the art of Heliodorus until he was able to write Greek romance in English, Greene was content to take what he wanted from Heliodorus or Sidney without much insight into their method. His actual borrowings from the Greek romancers and the Italian *novellieri* have, to a large extent, been earmarked by Dr S. L. Wolff.[2] He did succeed in writing a few *novelle* in English when he had become an experienced

[1] *Cp.* Wolff, pp. 370 and 402.

[2] *The Greek Romances in Elizabethan Fiction*, Part II., c. 3.

hand at lifting plots and motives from Boccaccio, Giraldi Cinthio, Bandello and others, and copying their procedure. He borrowed most from Boccaccio among the moderns, from Achilles Tatius among the ancients. A French translation of *Clitophon and Leucippe* had appeared in 1568—Greene was hardly scholar enough to read it in Greek—and he found here the varied and exciting incident, with little dependence on motive, the sentimental attitude to life, and the showy rhetoric, that appealed to him before anything. Perhaps it was Achilles Tatius that was responsible for Greene's subjection to the idea of chance or fortune as the arbiter of human affairs ; perhaps they both fell back upon this easy way of contriving events to fall out as they desired from sheer inability to work out the causal nexus in character and motive.

CHAPTER VII

EUPHUISM AND ARCADIANISM—LODGE AND OTHERS

Thomas Lodge

THOMAS LODGE was slightly Greene's senior, being born in 1557 or thereabouts, and he lived twice as long, dying about 1625. His output was as varied, though—if his translations are omitted—not so extensive as Greene's, with whom he was on friendly terms, collaborating with him in a play, *A Looking Glasse for London and England*, and perhaps giving him the hint, in his *Alarum against Usurers*, for the profitable series of revelations in the cony-catching pamphlets. Lodge was the son of a wealthy Londoner, who became Lord Mayor and was knighted. He went to Oxford, and after taking his Bachelor's degree started reading law. His legal knowledge, and no doubt his own mishaps at the hands of moneylenders and lawyers, came in useful when he wrote the *Alarum*; but he did not proceed to the Bar; the muses claimed him, and he was disinherited by his unsympathizing father.

Like Sidney, Lodge had been provoked by Gosson's pharisaical *Schoole of Abuse* to take up the cudgels "in defence of Poetry, Musick, and Stage Plays"; this tract, however, failed to secure publication. His next work was *An Alarum against Usurers* (1584), professedly a public-spirited exposure of the exactions of money-lenders; it shows some feeling signs of personal acquaintance with the evils denounced, though the career of the young spend-thrift need not be read as mere autobiography. This is one of the earliest of a very numerous class of Elizabethan writings that, on more or less trustworthy grounds, unmask the practices of various enemies of the public—thieves, sharpers, swindlers, fraudulent tradesmen, and others of the same kidney. Like Greene, Lodge was naturally inclined to illustrate his argument with a story; but he gives his imaginary instance of a young man's ruin in an impersonal way that is not very effective. We have the young

"An Alarum against Usurers"

gentleman and the knavish broker, who plays the part of cony-catcher with a usurious bond. Then comes in Mistres Minxe the harlot, Scrape-Penie the usurer's tool, "a stale for young novices, and a limb of Satan himself." The rake's progress is rapid, and the young dupe ends as the moneylender's decoy.

"Forbonius and Prisceria"

"Annexed" to this tract, as the title-page has it, was a very different item, *The delectable historie of Forbonius and Prisceria* (1584), his first piece of avowed fiction. The style is euphuistic; the narrative overweighted with soliloquies and addresses, and with letters of the familiar stamp, all lamenting the father's opposition to the young people's love-match, and swearing fidelity and firmness of purpose. Lodge shares Sidney's admiration for Heliodorus. His Prisceria is the granddaughter of Theagenes and Chariclea. But there are no Heliodorian complications. The plot is simple and amateurish. The lady's father, viceroy of the province adjoining the city of Memphis, frowns on the suit of Forbonius, and to get rid of him carries his daughter off to Farnusium, a manor of his. Forbonius thereupon attires himself in shepherd's clothes, and enters the service of a farmer near his mistress's abode. The path of the lovers is now as smooth as could be wished. Prisceria being in a state of dejection, the poetical shepherd Arvalio is called in to cheer her: this rustic swain is of course the faithful Forbonius. He sings her a delectable eclogue, which is a love-letter in disguise. The blissful episode is cut short by the arrival of the irate father. But the reader is not kept long in pain. With a change of front that is not adequately explained, the father gives way at all points, and on the morrow the lovers post back to Memphis to be united by the high priest of the Sun. Lodge dedicated the whole volume to Sidney.

Lodge's adventures in the New World

His next book was a series of poems, *Scillaes Metamorphosis* (1589); but in the meantime he had been differently employed. Lodge was one of those Elizabethan authors who liked a bout of adventure in reality as well as on paper. He went on two buccaneering voyages against the Spaniards and Portuguese; the first was an expedition to the Canaries and Azores, with Captain Clarke (1587-1588); the other, under Thomas Cavendish (1591-1593), a more daring enterprise which almost ended in complete disaster, took him to Brazil and the Straits of Magellan, till, after storms and mutiny, the adventurers returned sadly reduced in numbers. Lodge's share of the booty consisted of two romances. *Rosalynde* (1590) he describes as "Fetcht from the Canaries," and he pretends that the second, *A Margarite of America* (1596), was a translation, done whilst storm-bound in the Straits of Magellan, of a Spanish work that he found in the Jesuits' library at Santos, a town in Brazil which the squadron had seized.

"Rosalynde"

Rosalynde: Euphues golden legacie; found after his death in his Cell at Silexedra; Bequeathed to Philautus sonnes noursed up with their father in England, bears its provenance on its face. Lodge repeats the Lylian antitheses, zoological similes and parallel cadences. But the story is a pastoral. Based on the old English tale of Gamelyn, it is the story from which Shakespeare took the plot of *As You Like It*. He added the melancholy Jaques, and the inimitable Touchstone and Audrey, to Lodge's bevy of characters; but the novelist was responsible for that enchanting wild-wood air which makes the forest of Arden as famed poetically as the forest of Broceliande, and that he caught the fancy of the public is attested by a large number of editions. The harangue entitled "Sir John of Bordeaux' legacy he gave to his sons" is unadulterated euphuism:

Climb not, my sons: aspiring pride is a vapour that ascendeth high, but soon turneth to a smoke; they which stare at the stars stumble upon the stones; and such as gaze at the sun (unless they be eagle-eyed) fall blind. Soar not with the hobbie, lest you fall with the lark, nor attempt not with Phaeton, lest you drown with Icarus. Fortune when she wills you to fly, tempers your plumes with wax; and therefore either sit still and make no wing, or else beware the sun, and hold Daedalus' axiom authentical (medium tenuere tutissimum). Low shrubs have deep roots, and poor cottages great patience. Fortune looks ever upward, and envy aspireth to nestle with dignity. Take heed, my sons, the mean is sweetest melody, where strings high stretched either soon crack or quickly grow out of tune. . . . The outward show makes not the inward man, nor are the dimples in the face the calendars of truth. When the liquorice leaf looketh most dry, then it is most wet! when the shores of Lepanthus are most quiet, then they forepoint a storm. The baatan leaf the more fair it looks, the more infectious it is, and in the sweetest words is oft hid most treachery. Therefore, my sons, choose a friend as the Hyperborei do the metals, sever them from the ore with fire, and let them not bide the stamp before they be current: so try and then trust.

But Lodge at his best improved on Lyly; the following is a pretty example:

Rosalynde returning home from the triumph, after she waxed solitary, Love presented her with the idea of Rosader's perfection, and taking her at discovert, struck her so deep, as she felt herself grow passing passionate; she began to call to mind the comeliness of his person, the honour of his parents, and the virtues that, excelling both, made him so gracious in the eye of every one. Sucking in thus the honey of love, by imprinting in her thoughts his rare qualities, she began to surfeit with the contemplation of his virtuous conditions, but when she called to remembrance her present estate, and the hardness of her fortunes, desire began to shrink, and fancy to vail bonnet, that between a chaos of confused thoughts, she began to debate with herself in this manner:

Rosalynde's Passion

Unfortunate Rosalynde, whose misfortunes are more than thy years, and whose passions are greater than thy patience. The blossoms of thy youth are mixed with the frosts of envy, and the hope of thy ensuing fruits perish in the bud. Thy father is by Torismond banished from the crown, and thou the unhappy daughter of a king detained captive, living as disquieted in thy thoughts as thy father discontented in his exile. Ah, Rosalynde, what cares wait upon a crown! what griefs are incident to dignity! what sorrows haunt royal palaces! The greatest seas have the sorest storms, the highest birth subject to the most bale, and of all trees the cedars soonest shake with the wind; small currents are ever calm, low valleys not scorched in any lightnings, nor base men tied to any baleful prejudice. Fortune flies, and if she touch poverty, it is with her heel, rather disdaining their want with a frown than envying their wealth with disparagement. Oh, Rosalynde! hadst thou been born low, thou hadst not fallen so high, and yet being great of blood, thine honour is more if thou brookest misfortune with patience. Suppose I contrary fortune with content, yet Fates unwilling to have me anyways happy, have forced love to set my thoughts on fire with fancy. Love, Rosalynde! becometh it women in distress to think on love? Tush, desire hath no respect of persons, Cupid is blind and shooteth at random, as soon hitting a rag as a robe, and piercing as soon the bosom of a captive as the breast of a libertine. Thou speakest it, poor Rosalynde, by experience, for being every way distressed, surcharged with cares, and overgrown with sorrows, yet amidst the heap of all these mishaps, Love hath lodged in thy heart the perfection of young Rosader: a man every way absolute as well for his inward life, as for his outward lineaments, able to content the eye with beauty and the ear with the report of his virtue. But consider, Rosalynde, his fortunes and thy present estate; thou art poor and without patrimony, and yet the daughter of a prince; he a younger brother, and void of such possessions as either might maintain thy dignities or revenge thy father's injuries. And hast thou not learned this of other ladies, that lovers cannot live by looks; that women's ears are sooner content with a pound of *give me*, than a drachm of *hear me*; that gold is sweeter than eloquence: that love is a fire, and wealth is the fuel: that Venus's coffer should ever be full? Then Rosalynde, seeing Rosader is poor, think him less beautiful because he is in want, and account his virtues but qualities of course, for that he is not endued with wealth. Doth not Horace tell thee what method is to be used in love:

Quærenda pecunia primum, post nummos virtus.[1]

Another euphuistic tract was brought out for him by Greene whilst Lodge was away with Cavendish and Davis on the American voyage. *Euphues Shadow, the Battaile of the Sences; wherein youthfull folly is set downe in his right figure, and vaine fancies are prooued to produce many offences* (1592), is, however, of slighter interest even than two pieces of book-making in which he has left us a clumsy sort of historical romance. *The Life of Robert second Duke of Normandy, surnamed for his monstrous birth and behauiour, Robin the Diuell; wherein is contained his dissolute life in his youth, his deuout reconcilement and vertues in his age: interlaced with many straunge and miraculous aduentures* (1591), is Lodge's amplified version of a legendary biography that was already going about as a chap-book.[2] The other is a still slenderer example of pseudo-history, entitled *The Life and Death of William Longbeard, the most famous and witty English traitor, borne in the Citty of London*[3]*: Accompanied with manye other pleasant and prettie*

Lodge's historical tales

[1] *Rosalynde.*

[2] *Robert the deuyll* was twice printed by Wynkyn de Worde.

[3] Professor F. W. Chandler recognizes an English *pícaro*, "a supple rogue," in the hirsute William, a crafty and self-seeking demagogue, who was shown up and came to a bad end (*Lit. of Roguery*, i. 142). For the sources of some of the pretty histories see Miss Scott, *Elizabethan Translations*, pp. 62-63.

histories (1593). Like Greene's *Ciceronis Amor*, they are curiosities in the history of prose fiction, but less interesting than Nash and Deloney's use of material clumsily appropriated from the chroniclers or drawn from local tradition. Whilst Lodge was away in the western hemisphere his tragedy of Roman history, *The Wounds of Civill War*, and the religious play, *A Looking Glasse for London and England*, in which Greene was his collaborator, were both printed (1594). On his return he brought out a medley of poems, largely satirical, *A Fig for Momus* (1595), which was followed the next year by his best romance, *A Margarite of America* (1596). This stands apart from most of its class in being a long story of love, war and intrigue, evidently modelled on the heroical parts of the *Arcadia*, but with a tragic instead of a happy conclusion.

"*A Margarite of America*"

The narrative opens with a martial scene. The armies of Artosogon, Emperor of Cusco, and of Protomachus, King of Mosco, are drawn up in battle array, and about to fight for the possession of Mantinea, when an aged man intervenes, and proposes that the monarchs should make peace by joining the hands of their two children, Arsadachus, son to Artosogon, and Margarita, daughter of the king of Mosco. A treaty is thereupon concluded; and from this point the story runs on in a succession of spectacular scenes, tournaments and pageants, and slaughters grandiosely staged, in which Lodge indulges his pictorial bent to the full. He describes the chamber of the princess in flowery and resplendent images that recall the *Hypnerotomachia*, or Sidney in his most gorgeous word-painting. In general, his style is a mixture of euphuistic antithesis with the more flexible and poetical diction of the *Arcadia*, the episodes of action punctuated with lyrical interludes, in the regular pastoral manner.

But Arsadachus is a second Catiline. So irredeemably villainous is he that Lodge goes so far as to call him "Machiavellian." Counterfeiting passion for Margarita, he tries to debauch her lady-in-waiting, Philenia, the betrothed of the knightly Minucius, and a pattern of the truest love. Repulsed with indignation by Philenia, he treacherously waylays and assassinates Minucius, Philenia falling dead in her lover's defence. This pathetic episode is evidently an attempt to rival the tragic loves of Argalus and

Parthenia. The dastardly crime is revealed to Philenia's father, Arsinous, by a page who escaped the fray. Arsadachus is guilty of further outrages and treasons; but Arsinous finds it difficult to bring him to book, although the emperor begins to suspect his son. When, however, he intrigues with Diana, daughter of Argias, one of the emperor's dukes, and it comes out that he has secretly married her, the monarch is furious. He has Argias torn to pieces by wild horses, and, in another episode copied from the *Arcadia*, lays siege to the castle where Diana takes refuge. And now the lawlessness of the young prince breaks all bounds. He dethrones his father, and proceeds to torture him. Rumours of his misdeeds have reached the princess Margarita. She sends him a magic potion, which if Arsadachus is true to her will increase his affection, if disloyal, will drive him mad. He goes mad with a vengeance. Raging and storming, he dashes out the brains of his infant son, and wades in carnage, last of all running Margarita through the body as a sacrifice to his lost Diana. In bare outline, the story sounds cruder than it actually is; it is a long way inferior to the *Arcadia*, but of all Elizabethan efforts in the same style it certainly comes closest to Sidney.

Lodge, who had turned Roman Catholic, took up the study of medicine in middle age, and obtained the degree of Doctor of Physic at Avignon, practising in England chiefly in the families of his own religion. He wrote *A Treatise of the Plague* (1603); but his chief literary labours in his later years were devoted to translating the works of Josephus and of Seneca the philosopher.

Other euphuists—Munday, Melbancke, Warner

Anthony Munday, the most industrious of Elizabethan translators, wrote one euphuistic novel of his own, *Zelauto, the Fountaine of Fame: Erected in an Orcharde of Amorous Aduentures: Containing a Delicate Disputation, gallantly discoursed betweene two noble Gentlemen of Italye: Given for a friendly entertainment to Euphues, at his late arrival into England* (1580). Into the same category fall Brian Melbancke's *Philotimus: the Warre betwixt Nature and Fortune* (1583), and William Warner's *Pan his Syrinx, or Pipe, Compact of seven Reedes* (1584). This last is a framework story comprising the following tales: "Arbaces," "Thetis," "Belopares," "Pheone," "Deipyrus," "Aphrodite," "Opheltes," with a return to "Arbaces," *pars calami primi.*

"*Pan his Syrinx*"

In the frame-tale, Sorares and his company of Assyrian troops are driven by tempest on a desolate isle, where they come across Arbaces and another castaway Mede. The party devote their leisure time to speeches and discussions, on ambition and avarice, the levity and vanity of women, the allurements and the incommodities of seafaring, and on ingratitude, fortitude, and similar themes. Meanwhile, Atys and his brother sail in quest of their father, Sorares, but are detained in the castle of a Scythian noble. "Thetis" is the tale of this nobleman's temptation by Thetis, a treacherous seductrix, and his escape. "Pheone" is a story of love at cross-purposes told by the pilot. "Deipyrus" concludes with an incident that revives the young princes' hopes that their father is still alive; but "Aphrodite," an oratorical duel on the praise and dispraise of women, leads to their being cast into prison. At length, with some further incidents and seasonable discourses, Sorares is discovered by his sons. Warner follows Lyly closely in the continual debates upon women, whose whimsical fashions in dress and deportment, as well as their subtleties in the undoing of men, are uncharitably described. The general features of his plot indicate that he was under the spell of Greek romance. Underdowne's translation of Heliodorus had appeared in 1569.[1]

John Dickenson

Both Lyly and Greene were the influences that, as the mere titles show, led the poet, John Dickenson, to write his *Arisbas, Euphues amidst his slumbers: or Cupid's Journey to Hell* (1594), and *Greene in Conceipt: New raised from his graue to write the Tragique historie of faire Valeria of London* (1598). In the one, Dickenson presents "a Myrror of Constancie, a Touch-stone of tried affection, begun in chaste desires, ended in choise delights: and emblasoning Beauties glorie, adorned by Natures bountie; with the Triumph of True Loue, in the foyle of false Fortune." In the tale of Valeria he glances at the seamy side of London life, and tries to portray a courtesan in the admonitory manner of Greene, of whom the frontispiece of the book is a woodcut, showing him draped in his shroud.

Henry Chettle, who acted as Greene's literary executor, editing the *Groats-Worth of Witte*, and summoned Nash, in his own *Kind-Harts Dreame* (1592), to refute the base insinuations of Gabriel

[1] Wolff, p. 433, n.

Chettle's "Piers Plainnes"

Harvey against their dead friend, was probably the author of a curious little book, *Piers Plainnes seaven yeres Prentiship* (1595), which opens as a pastoral novelette and then turns into a picaresque tale with an unmistakable likeness to *Lazarillo de Tormes*.[1] A party of Thessalian shepherds are discovered talking together and reciting tales in the vale of Tempe. One of them, Piers himself—the name was stolen from Nashe, who dubbed himself Pierce Pennilesse—relates his experiences under a succession of masters, seven in all, the same number as Lazarillo's. The seventh is one of the present company, Corydon the plow-swain. He describes the hectoring and cowardly soldier, the intriguing courtier, the fraudulent broker who tries to swindle the usurer with whom Piers next takes service; and then plunges into more romantic events, the story of Æliana, virgin-queen of Crete, who was in peril from a usurper and from the incestuous passion of her uncle, regent during her minority. She is delivered from her troubles by the heroic young prince Æmilius, who after various ups and downs of fortune weds her, and is crowned king of Crete. This is the first English story in which direct imitation of Spanish picaresque fiction is evident. Touches like the account of the starvation fare provided at the house of the miserly Ulpian—a humorous topic recurring in almost every Spanish story of the kind—leave no shadow of doubt as to Chettle's sources. But the tales are deftly intertwined with the dialogue and the incidents of a shepherd's day, and there are some pleasant lyrics in between; though the mixture seems to have been too heterogeneous even for the easy-going tastes of that day, and Chettle never had the book reprinted nor went on with a half-promised continuation.

Lady Mary Wroath's "Urania"

The most direct imitation of the *Arcadia* was a performance by a niece of Sidney's, the Lady Mary Wroath, daughter of the Earl of Leicester. She called it, *The Countess of Mountgomeries Urania* (1621), and blazoned her kinship to Sir Philip and his sister, the Countess of Pembroke, at the head of a pictorial title-page. Carried away by ingenuous enthusiasm for her brilliant relative, the Lady Mary, who at all events had personality enough—or noble lineage—to impress Ben Jonson and receive the dedication of his *Alchemist*, copies and outdoes Sidney's utmost extravagances, both in the story and in the mode of telling it. For Arcadia she substitutes the

[1] *Piers Plainnes* is epitomized by Chandler (vol. i., pp. 200-202).

Morea, with excursions to Constantinople, Rhodes, Delos, Negropont, Pamphilia, Mytilene. Shepherd princes and shepherdesses of royal blood go through the conventional adventures, make high-flown speeches and exalted love, compose a vast number of indifferent elegies and eclogues, and attain the rewards ordained for their constancy and valour, with the discomfiture of a host of enemies.

Emanuel Forde

Another of Sidney's followers, Emanuel Forde, is counted by M. Jusserand among the disciples of Lyly and Greene.[1] Forde may well have been incited by Greene's success with the public to enter the same line of business. But, like Sidney, he chose to follow the romantic manner of the Amadis cycle, and that with a remarkable absence of originality: any closer resemblance to Greene is hard to detect. Nor was Forde a euphuist. Such graces were quite beyond the scope of his pen. "Expect not the high style of a refined wit," he says in his preface to *Parismus*, "but the plain description of valiant knights, and the constant truth of loyal friends." Forde's modest estimate of his literary ability is correct: he writes a plain, dull, straightforward style, which anyone could read, and he was by far the most popular of all the Elizabethan and Jacobean romancers, mainly because he was incapable of anything superior.

"Parismus and Parismenos"

Anthony Munday's translations of *Palmerin d'Oliva*, *Amadis of Gaule*, *Palmendos*, and *Primaleon* [2] were coming out in large instalments when Forde began his dogged career in 1598 with *Parismus, the Renoumed Prince of Bohemia: his most famous, delectable and pleasant Historie; containing his Noble Battailes fought against the Persians, his love to Laurana, the Kings Daughter of Thessaly; and his straunge Aduentures in the Desolate Island.* It is a debased and entirely mechanical effort in Amadisian and Arcadian romance, without any pastoralism. Parismus prosecutes his suit in knight-errant fashion, with the usual disguises, feats of arms, and contests with hostile enchanters. He wins fame as the Black Knight. Then he turns up, disguised as a page, on the Desolate Island, the princess of which, when he has overthrown her champions, defends herself in the last resort by casting him into a magic sleep. Laurana is

[1] Jusserand, p. 193. See also *Cambridge History of English Literature*, vol. iii., p. 359.

[2] See Volume I., p. 254. *Palmerin d'Oliva* was the model for *Parismus*.

carried off by the tyrant Andrasmart to the Island of Rocks. A sequel went on with "the adventurous travels and noble chivalry of Parismenos, the Knight of Fame, with his love to the beautiful and fair Angelica, the Lady of the Golden Tower." Parismenos is the son of Parismus, and his rival in prowess ; and more battles, sieges, jousts, encounters with Brandamore and other giants, disguises, mysteries and recognitions are provided. All the tricks of the trade—beauteous ladies seen in dreams, strange prophecies, and stranger fulfilments—which have come down from ancient romance and been used over and over again in the later cycles, are mechanically employed ; romance had become a matter of routine. Forde made a baser appeal to his readers with his fondness for risky situations, like that where Pollipus, in bed with Violetta who is disguised as a page, tells her the pathetic story of his love. She does not reveal herself as the object of his passion till later, so the convenances are saved.

"Ornatus and Artesia" and "Montelyon, Knight of the Oracle"

Parismus went on being published, at full length or in different abridgments, from the end of the sixteenth century to the first three decades of the eighteenth, at frequent intervals ; two similar productions of his were only a trifle less in demand. These were *The Most Pleasant Historie of Ornatus and Artesia ; wherein is contained the vnjust Raigne of Thæon King of Phrygia, who with his sonne Lenon (intending Ornatus death) right Heir to the Crowne, was afterwardes slaine by his own Seruants, and Ornatus after many extreame miseries, Crowned King* (1607), and *The Famous Historie of Montelyon, Knight of the Oracle, and Sonne to the Renowned Persicles King of Assyria* (1633). The case of Emanuel Forde shows how easy it was for a novelist without a spark of genius to satisfy, by mere industry, and continue to satisfy, the cravings of a certain large section of the reading public. Sidney ran him close in sustained popularity, no doubt, with a more fastidious body of devotees ; otherwise none of the early novelists or romancers had anything like such a hold on generations of readers. To those who are interested in the vagaries of the herd instinct in matters of literary taste, Forde's enormous vogue furnishes material for a generalization which is not yet out of date. It is a curious incident in the literary history of the English, but has little to do with the history of English literature, unless in an indirect way, since it might be argued that the demand for rubbish is a deterrent to those who would write better. Otherwise, its only traceable effects seem to be to have given rise to some ridicule and parody, and to have contributed to the romantic craze satirized later on by Mrs Lennox in *The Female Quixote*.

CHAPTER VIII

THE BEGINNINGS OF REALISTIC FICTION

Fiction and other kinds of narrative literature

ESPECIALLY at times that are afterwards seen to have been transitional, there is always much give and take between fiction and those various kinds of narrative and portraiture that are not fiction except by default. Bacon had in mind the deep affinity between the art that is tied down to verifiable fact and the art that is not so tied down when he spoke of poesy as "feigned history." Ages before Macaulay, historians tried to make their presentation of events as interesting as a novel. They studied, or at any rate practised, the methods of the story-teller in relating what was in the main matter of fact, and when facts failed them did not hesitate to add those touches of character and dialogue which give life to a scene. On the other hand, the composer of fiction, in order to win the reader's trust, continually assumed the guise of biographer, historian, or direct reporter. Both parties learned from each other. On either side there were continual loans and repayments with interest.

Their reciprocal influence

This reciprocal contribution of matter and method went on steadily with the most honest motives, so many of the aims on both sides being identical. But when the maker of fiction does not want his work to be recognized as fiction, or when the biographer or historian tries to dissemble gaps in his information, their exchange of means and apparatus is not so legitimate. Many of the examples of prose fiction to be studied from now onwards to the time of Defoe were not put forward avowedly as fiction, but purported to be true accounts of actual occurrences. To counterbalance which, many memoirs and similar works of the same period have a much larger proportion of imaginary stuff in their composition than of authentic record.[1] What we find over and over again is, that which

[1] Lives of notorious persons were continually put together from gossip and hearsay with the smallest basis of genuine fact. A case in point is the

always emerges in the infancy of prose fiction, a furtive transition from the honest to the dishonest, from plain fact or frank invention to a cunning intermixture of truth and falsehood, with intent to deceive. And this violation of the rules presently results in some decisive advance in craftsmanship or art. It is in sailing under false colours that fiction opens fresh routes and seizes new territory.

Genuine and fictitious exposures of social evils

The smugglers and pirates followed in the track of explorers whose motives were straightforward and aboveboard. Distressed by the state of the country, a man wrote an account of the outcasts and criminals infesting London and the Home Counties. Another called attention to the misdoings of moneylenders and swindlers, the tricks of greedy tradesmen, the chicanery of lawyers. Their books dealt frankly with scandals that touched every private individual on the raw. They were illustrated with anecdotes as spicy as those of the jest-books and which gave point to what was no laughing matter. More mercenary writers, seeing the welcome given to these exposures and their rapid sale, were quickly in the field with further anatomies of abuses, revelations and caveats, in which they made up for their lack of first-hand knowledge by covert thefts from their better-informed predecessors, with incidents which they easily worked up from common report, and with downright fiction. In the fervid Puritan and the earnest advocate of social reform it was neither surprising nor very blameworthy if they erred on the side of vividness and were sometimes carried away by the impulse to be sensational and alarmist. But when the professional writer began making capital out of the scare he went a great deal further, outdoing Jeremiah and Jonah with his lamentations and denunciations, depicting London as the city of destruction prefigured in holy writ, and stopping at nothing that

Life and Memoirs of Mrs Behn (1696), probably by Charles Gildon, which is a mixture of some fact, some deductions from statements in her novels, and a large amount of ingenious padding. It has been examined by Dr Ernest Bernbaum ("Mrs Behn's Biography a Fiction," *Modern Language Association of America*, v. 28, 1913). He says: "The more worthless the *Life and Memoirs* as a biographical document, the greater its value for the history of fiction. . . . The probabilities are that later research will reveal a whole school of such fiction masquerading as fact." Mr Montagu Summers is more conservative in his attitude to the *Life and Memoirs* (*Works of Aphra Behn*, 1925, I. introduction).

would excite the public and lead them to buy his tracts rather than those of his rivals.[1]

Realism and the preference for the ugly aspects of life

This insistence on the depravity of the world was a new thing in the literature written for and read by the crowd concerning themselves and their neighbours. Vices and follies had been caricatured before, in the horseplay that was the most popular element in the mystery plays, and in the tales that preceded the jest-books as well as in the jest-books themselves. But the object had been to provide suitable fare for appetites that loved nothing better than a boisterous joke, especially when there was no mistaking at whose expense it was made. Popular literature, hitherto, so far as

[1] Take, for instance, this from Nashe in his best apocalyptic manner: "If we would hunt after signs and tokens, we should ominate from our hardness of heart and want of charity amongst brethren, that God's justice is hard entering. No certainer conjecture is there of the ruin of any kingdom than their revolting from God. Certain conjectures have we had that we are revolted from God and that our ruin is not far off. In divers places of our land it hath rained blood, the ground hath been removed, and horrible deformed births conceived. Did the Romans take it for an ill sign when their Capitol was strooken with lightning, how much more ought London to take it for an ill sign when her chief steeple is strooken with lightning? They with thunder from any enterprise were disanimated, we nothing are amated. The blazing star, the earthquake, the dearth and famine some few years since, may nothing affright us. Let us look for the sword next to remembrance and warn us. As there is a time of peace, so is there a time of war. No prosperity lasteth always. The Lord by a solemn oath bound himself to the Jews; yet when they were oblivious of him, he was oblivious of the covenant he made with their forefathers, and left their city desolate unto them. Shall he not then (we starting from him, to whom by no bond he is tied) leave our house desolate unto us? Shall we receive of God (a long time) all good, and shall we not look in the end to receive of him some ill? O ye disobedient children, return, and the Lord shall heal your infirmities. Lie down in your confusion, and cover your faces with shame. From your youth to this day have you sinned, and not obeyed the voice of the Lord your God. Now, in the age of your obstinacy and ungrateful abandonments, repent and be converted. With one united intercessionment thus reconcile yourselves unto Him" ("Christs Teares over Jerusalem," *Works*, ii. 172-173). This was written at the time of the plague of 1592-1593; Dekker wrote in a like tone of the plague in 1603, the year of Elizabeth's funeral, of which he descants also in unmeasured terms, as in these phrases: "Her hearse (as it was borne) seemed to be an island swimming in water, for round about it there rained showers of tears, about her deathbed none: for her departure was so sudden and so strange, that men knew not how to weep, because they had never been taught to shed tears of that making. . . . Oh what an earthquake is the alteration of a State! Look from the chamber of presence to the farmer's cottage, and you shall find nothing but distraction: the whole kingdom seems a wilderness, and the people in it are transformed to wild men." As he comes to his chief topic, the plague, he cries out: "A stiff and freezing horror sucks up the rivers of my blood: my hair stands on end with the panting of my brains: mine eyeballs are ready to start out, being beaten with the billow of my tears: out of my weeping pen does the ink mournfully and more bitterly than gall

it dealt with everyday life, had been broadly satirical, or at any rate humorous. But we now begin to discern, through the efforts of story-tellers to appease it, a craving to hear the facts of life, to see things as they are, which usually means distinctly worse than they are. The comic tends to disappear; humour and satire become merely sardonic. Deloney is the only delineator of ordinary, unromantic people who keeps up the old spirit of fun. Greene and Dekker's pamphlets on cony-catching were written ostensibly to put readers on their guard against evildoers; but they were no doubt read with gusto for the sake of their grim sketches of the seamy side. Realism, indeed, was continually identified with portraiture of the ugly and unclean, and the tradition maintained by Defoe has lasted down to modern times.

The literature of vagabondage

The actual starting-point of this literature of rascality was John Awdeley's *Fraternitye of Vacabondes* (1561), which was followed and supplemented by Harman's *Caveat for Commen Cursetors* (1567), this in turn being shamelessly pilfered by Dekker

drop on the pale-faced paper, even when I do but think how the bowels of my sick country have been torn." He conjures up the most ghastly images to heighten the descriptions that follow:—"What an unmatchable torment were it for a man to be barred up every night in a vast, silent charnel-house, hung, to make it more hideous, with lamps dimly and slowly burning, in hollow and glimmering corners; where all the pavement should, instead of green rushes, be strewed with blasted rosemary, withered hyacinths, fatal cypress and yew, thickly mingled with heaps of dead men's bones; the bare ribs of a father that begat him lying there, here the chapless, hollow skull of a mother that bore him; round about him a thousand corses, some standing bolt upright in their knotted winding-sheets, others half mouldered in rotten coffins, that should suddenly yawn wide open, filling his nostrils with noisome stench, and his eyes with the sight of nothing but crawling worms? And to keep such a poor wretch waking, he should hear no noise but of toads croaking, screech-owls howling, mandrakes shrieking: were not this an infernal prison? Would not the strongest-hearted man, beset with such a ghastly horror, look wild, and run mad, and die? And even such a formidable shape did the diseased city appear in; for he that durst, in the dead hour of gloomy midnight, have been so valiant as to have walked through the still and melancholy streets, what think you should have been his music? Surely the loud groans of raving sick men, the struggling pangs of souls departing, in every house grief striking up an alarum, servants crying out for masters, wives for husbands, parents for children, children for their mothers: here he should have met some frantically running to knock up sextons; there others fearfully sweating with coffins to steal forth dead bodies, lest the fatal handwriting of death should seal up their doors. And to make this dismal concert more full, round about him bells heavily tolling in one place, and ringing out in another. The dreadfulness of such an hour is unutterable: let us go further" (*The Wonderfull Yeare*, reprint of 1924, 38-39). When in this attitude, and most of them assumed it one time or another, the Tudor pamphleteers were as gloomy and pessimistic as any of the churchyard poets of the eighteenth century.

and others, who revived the subject for their own purposes at a later date. Awdeley was not the first English writer to depict the canting tribe; this had been done with less accuracy but more force and humour by the author of *The Hye Way to the Spyttel Hous* (*c.* 1531), printed and probably written by Robert Copland. In rude but trenchant verse a graphic picture is drawn of the rabble of vagrants, beggars, cripples, malingerers, coseners, unfortunates and impostors haunting the gate of St Bartholomew's Hospital. It is in the familiar vein of German satires on folly, vice and roguery, though it is obvious that the writer had seen all this himself. Awdeley's motive was different. He proposed to give an unvarnished, matter-of-fact account of the English vagabond tribe and their orders, after the model of the German *Liber Vagatorum* (*c.* 1512-1514), of which there had been many editions, one in 1528, with a preface by Martin Luther. Awdeley was a printer in Little Britain, London, and hints in the doggerel verses prefixed to the tract that he got his information from a member of the vagabond brotherhood who turned king's evidence.[1] It is a little book with a very long title: *The Fraternitye of Vacabondes, As wel of ruflyng Vacabondes, as of beggerly, of women as of men, of Gyrles as of Boyes, with their proper names and qualities. With a description of the crafty company of Cousoners and Shifters. Wherunto also is adjoyned the xxv Orders of Knaves, otherwyse called a Quartern of Knaves. Confirmed for ever by Cocke Lorell.* There follow two quatrains, in which the tinker-captain of the famous English ship of fools, *Cocke Lorelles Bote*, assures an Upright Man that some of his own crew will be found in the vagrant brotherhood. Awdeley had his eye on the present day; but he was not forgetful of the skits and satires—some of them coming down from the Middle Ages: in which the lowest orders had cut a picturesque figure.

Awdeley's "Fraternitye of Vacabondes"

The first part of his tract is a descriptive catalogue of the different kinds and grades in the fraternity—Abraham men, rufflers, prygmen,

[1] The earliest extant edition of the tract is dated 1565; but there is an entry in the Stationers' Register of a "ballett" under date 1560-1561, which no doubt refers to the same work, the prefatory verses being the reason for its inadvertent description as a ballad. That Awdeley preceded Harman and could not have plagiarized from Harman is clearly shown by Furnivall (*The Rogues and Vagabonds of Shakespeare's Youth*, ed. E. Viles and F. J. Furnivall, 1907, where both Awdeley and Harman are reprinted at length).

The hierarchy of rogues

swygmen, palliards, doxies, etc. The highest rank is that of the Upright Man, who is "of such authority, that meeting with any of his profession, he may cal them to accompt, and commaund a share or snap unto him selfe, of al that they have gained by their trade in one moneth. And if he doe them wrong, they have no remedy agaynst hym, no though he beate them, as he useth commonly to do. He may also commaund any of their women, which they cal Doxies, to serve his turne. He hath ye chiefe place at any market walke, and other assembles, and is not of any to be controled." In the next section are set forth at length the tricks peculiar to three descriptions of rogue: the Curtesy Man, who disguises his calling under the garb and behaviour of respectability; the Cheatour or Fingerer, who decoys young gallants to strip them at cards; and the Ring Faller, a rascal who drops worthless trinkets about and then extorts money from the finders by claiming to go halves. A third part is a list of tricks and tricksters, with names and descriptions that have a humorous tang, as in these:

9. NICHOL HARTLES

Nichol Hartles is he, that when he should do ought for his Maister hys hart faileth him. This is a Trewand knave that faineth himselfe sicke when he should woorke.

18. CORY FAVELL

Cory Favell is he, that wyl lye in his bed, and cory the beds bordes in which he lyeth in steede of his horse. This slouthfull knave wyll buskill and scratch when he is called in the morning, for any hast.

Harman's "Caveat"

Thomas Harman was a gentleman of moderate fortune who lived at Crayford, near Dartford Heath, for twenty years keeping a house "where unto poverty dayely hath and doth repayre." He was a Justice of the Peace for Kent, in Mary's reign, but not apparently at the time he was writing his book. The depredations and immorality of the rascal rabblement drove him at last to make a thorough inquiry into their practices, and expose them to the authorities and the public, "to the end that they might be stopt, and sin and wickedness might not so much abound." Harman's book, *A Caveat or Warening for Commen Cursetors vulgarely called Vagabones* (1567), is a great advance on Awdeley's scheme. He gives a full account of each type of rogue, with information about the localities they chiefly haunt, and, best of all, anecdotes of their doings, for most of which he can avouch his own experience. Whether Harman perceived the humour of many of these recitals may be doubted ; but a good story is often none the worse when the humour is unconscious.

"A Ruffeler," says Awdeley, "goeth with a weapon to seek service, saying he hath been a servitor in the wars, and beggeth for his relief. But his chiefest trade is to rob poor wayfaring men and market women." Harman paints a lurid portrait of this type of rogue, placing him first, "as the worthiest of this unruly rabblement." He illustrates with an anecdote :

I had of late years an old man to my tenant, who customably a great time went twice in the week to London, either with fruit or with peascods, when time served thereto. And as he was coming homeward on Blackheath, at the end thereof next to Shooters Hill, he overtook two rufflers, the one mannerly waiting on the other, as one had been the master, and the other the man or servant, carrying his master's cloak. This old man was very glad that he might have their company over the hill, because that day he had made a good market ; for he had seven shillings in his purse, and an old angel, which this poor man had thought had not been in his purse, for he willed his wife over night to take out the same angel, and lay it up until his coming home again. And he verily thought that his wife had so done, which indeed forgot to do it. Thus after salutations had, this master ruffler entered into communication with this simple old man, who, riding softly beside them, commoned of many matters. Thus feeding this old man with pleasant talk, until they were on the top of the hill, where these rufflers might well behold the coast about them clear, quickly steps unto this poor man, and taketh hold of his horse bridle, and leadeth him into the wood, and demandeth of him what and how much money he hath in his purse. "Now, by my troth," quoth this old man, "you are a merry gentleman. I know you mean not to take away any thing from me, but rather to give me some if I should ask it of you." By and by, this servant thief casteth the cloak that he carried on his arm about this poor man's face, that he should not mark or view them, with sharp words to deliver quickly that he had, and to confess truly what was in his purse. This poor man, then all abashed, yielded, and confessed that he had but just seven shillings in his purse ; and the truth is he knew of no more.

This old angel was fallen out of a little purse into the bottom of a great purse. Now, this seven shillings in white money they quickly found, thinking in deed that there had been no more; yet farther groping and searching, found this old angel. And with great admiration this gentleman thief began to bless him, saying, "Good lord, what a world is this! how may" (quoth he) "a man believe or trust in the same? See you not" (quoth he) "this old knave told me that he had but seven shillings, and here is more by an angel: what an old knave and a false knave have we here!" quoth this ruffler; "our lord have mercy upon us, will this world never be better?"—and therewith went their way. And left the old man in the wood, doing him no more harm. But sorrowfully sighing, this old man, returning home, declared his misadventure, with all the words and circumstances above showed. Whereat, for the time was great laughing, and this poor man for his losses among his loving neighbours well considered in the end.[1]

In another branch of the industry the hookers or anglers "be perilous and most wicked knaves"; they carry rods with a hole at the end, wherein after dark they insert a hook, and so pluck down linen and other stuff.

I was credibly informed that a hooker came to a farmer's house in the dead of the night, and putting back a draw window of a low chamber, the bed standing hard by the said window, in which lay three persons (a man and two big boys), this hooker with his staff plucked off their garments which lay upon them to keep them warm, with the coverlet and sheet, and left them lying asleep naked saving their shirts, and had away all clean, and never could understand where it became. I verily suppose that when they were well waked with cold, they surely thought that Robin Goodfellow (according to the old saying) had been with them that night.[2]

Harman tells a pleasant story of a glimmering mort—that is, a woman who begs charity on the plea of having been burnt out of house and home. The unthrifty son of an innkeeper, having nothing else to give, bestowed a silver whistle belonging to his widowed mother on a wanton lass of this occupation; the whistle was missed, the young man owned up to an ostler who was sent to cross-question him, and the ostler went off in pursuit. When he comes up with the

[1] Harman's *Caveat*, ed. Viles and Furnivall, pp. 30-31.
[2] *Ibid.*, p. 36.

damsel, he finds her in company with a sturdy rogue, whom she appeals to as her husband. All the ostler gets for demanding back the whistle is a dry thrashing from the man and a crack on the head with a big stone from the woman. They also relieve him of his purse, and he crawls home to bed, where his mistress comes to inquire what is the matter.

"What is the cause ?" quoth this ostler ; "your whistle, your whistle"—speaking the same piteously three or four times. "Why, fool," quoth his mistress, "take no care for that, for I do not greatly weigh it ; it was worth but three shillings four pence." "I would it had been burnt four years agone." "I pray thee why so," quoth his mistress ; "I think thou art mad." "Nay, not yet," quoth this ostler, "but I have been madly handled" ; and he recounts how, for the sake of the wretched whistle, he had been mauled and robbed of all he had, and was now like to be mocked and laughed to scorn by all who heard of his mishap. "Now, out upon you knaves both," quoth his mistress, and laughs out the matter ; for she well saw it would not otherwise prevail.

The humour is of the brutal, elementary kind that consists in laughing at other people's misfortunes ; and the subsequent story of a walking mort, and the retribution she contrives to inflict on an amorous farmer, might also have been told with a richer sense of the comic. She makes an appointment to meet the scapegrace husbandman in the barn after supper, and meanwhile informs his wife, who arranges with her gossips to lie in ambush behind the hay till her faithless spouse is in no condition to defend himself. The plot is thoroughly successful, and the farmer gets a fearful drubbing. He is discovered later on, bound and helpless, by one of the farm hands, and swears revenge ; but thinks it better after all "not, as the proverb saith, to awake the sleeping dog." The lesson does him good, and he becomes an exemplary husband—the moral of the story being well rubbed in.

CHAPTER IX

THE CONY-CATCHING PAMPHLETS

Greene's cony-catching pamphlets

WHEN Greene started his campaign against the cony-catchers of the metropolis he had a mine of information at hand in Harman's *Caveat*, of which he made good use. The clear account of the different kinds of rogue and the part each played in a complicated swindle was a guide in his own descriptions of rogueries with which he probably had but little direct acquaintance ; but he abstained from wholesale borrowing. In 1608, however, when Harman's book was twice as old and he probably hoped had been quite forgotten, Dekker pillaged from it, in his *Bel-man of London*, without even troubling to cover up his tracks. Dekker also lifted a large part of his material from Greene, and from a work usually ascribed to Samuel Rowlands, *Greenes Ghost Haunting Conie-catchers.* The succession is complete from Awdeley and Harman to the latest of the wits who prosecuted the discovery of roguery as a literary business. But Greene was not so chary of borrowing from a work considerably older than Awdeley. From this early tract, *A Manifest detection of the most vyle and detestable use of dice play and other practices like the same* (1552),[1] Greene, according to Dr Jordan, learned all that he knew about the ways in which the unsuspicious were fleeced by card-sharpers.[2] Lodge's *Alarum against Usurers* also preceded Greene's pamphlets, and must have taught him something ; though it must be remembered that Lodge was not altogether unindebted to the same predecessors as Greene.[3]

"*A Notable Discouery of Coosnage*"

Greene opened fire in December 1591 with *A Notable Discouery of Coosnage, Now daily practised by sundry lewd persons, called Connie-catchers, and Crosse-biters.* The same day, 13th December, was licensed *The Second and last part of Conny-catching. With new*

[1] Probably by Gilbert Walker.
[2] Jordan, 89-91.
[3] *Ibid.*, 92-93.

additions containing many merry tales of all lawes worth the reading, because they are worthy to be remembered, which was published almost, if not quite, simultaneously, as the title-page bears the same date, 1591. By 7th February 1592 was registered *The Thirde and last Part of Conny-catching. With the new devised knauish Art of Foole-taking*, which was brought out soon after by another publisher. The dates are important. The second part must have been well in hand, if not actually finished, when the first part went to press ; yet this second part alleges that his enemies, the cony-catchers, have already been badly hit by his exposures, and refers to people who have taken warning at his revelations, and others who had not read the first book in time to escape being duped.[1] These disingenuous tactics naturally incline one to the belief that Greene was much more intent on a profitable sale for his writings than on the patriotic object indicated in the new motto adopted in his cony-catching series, *Nascimur pro patria.* Other suspicious circumstances come to light as the campaign goes on.

The first part of "Conny-catching"

The first part denounces two principal tricks by which the unwary, especially countrymen, are swindled in London : the art of cony-catching or cheating at cards, and the art of cross-biting. Greene describes the former as similar to the old barnard's law, a method expounded in the *Manifest Detection of Dyce Play* ; but adds : "Yet is the Art of Cunny-catching so farre beyond it in subtiltie, as the devill is more honest than the holiest Angell." Four performers were required in the practice of barnard's law : the taker up, the verser, the barnard, and the rutter. The first is the decoy ; the second, "a man of worship," with whom they go to a tavern ; there the barnard stumbles in, an unwary-looking, half-drunken old farmer, with whom they start gaming ; and when the victim has lost all his money the rutter plays his part, which is to start a row, under cover of which the barnard steals off with the plunder. Greene really has nothing to add to the explanation of the process borrowed from the older book, though he talks glibly about having consorted with rogues, " as a spie to have an insight into their knaveries, that seeing their traines I might eschew their snares." He rings the changes on some of the technical terms, which were apt to alter with the usual shifts of cant lingo ; yet he fails to

[1] See Jordan, 85-87.

convince us that he always knows the meaning of the terms he uses. The other trick explained in the first part, cross-biting, is one that has had vogue in very ancient and in very modern times. A harlot takes a man home, and the supposed husband bursts in, extorting money with threats of the law. Not having filled the required number of pages with instances of these two forms of cheating, Greene goes on to describe how London colliers take in their customers by a system of short weight and inferior quality.

This initial pamphlet is mainly descriptive. The way the conies are entrapped is related graphically enough ; and there are two stories of card-sharping, two illustrating the coal-vendors' cheats, and a lame anecdote of a man who had the best of it in a tussle with cross-biters. But as Greene proceeds he gives freer rein to his talent for stories. There are nine in the second part, which sets forth the method of the black art or lock-picking ; the courbing law, or how the hookers steal linen out of windows ; Vincent's law, a bowling cheat ; the prigging law, or horse-stealing ; and so on. The third part is a set of ten stories, exemplifying the modes of deceit that have been expounded. It opens adroitly with an account of a supper at which the conversation turned on the villainies that had been recently laid bare—by Robert Greene. Thus the tales that ensue fall into a sort of framework, like that of his earlier romantic stories. One of the best, staged in St Paul's Church, is about a notable knave that scorned the name of cony-catcher, and for his mastery of the art would be termed fool-taker. Whilst a female confederate holds a man of the law in conversation, the fool-taker comes up behind, and like a frolicsome acquaintance puts his hands over the gentleman's eyes, asking him to guess who it is. When the lawyer had guessed wrong several times he takes away his hands, pretends to have made a mistake, for which he gracefully apologizes, and walks away. The confederate has, of course, removed the lawyer's well-lined purse. In another excellent tale a gentleman from the country, strolling in St Paul's, sporting a gold chain, is accosted by a pretended acquaintance, who has found out his name by a stratagem much employed by these gangs. He warns the countryman of the snares of London, and counsels him to put the chain in a safer place. The gentleman wraps it in his handkerchief and hides it in his sleeve. When they are going out, the cony-catcher

The second and third parts of "Conny-Catching"

drops a key, and, whilst he is stooping, is set upon by one of his accomplices, who pretends a quarrel.

> The gentleman at his standing up, seeing it was he that gave him so good counsel, and pretended himself his very friend, but never imagining this train was made for him, stepped in his defence, when the other following tripped up his heels, so that he and his counsellor were down together, and two more upon them, striking with their daggers very eagerly, marry indeed the gentleman had most of the blows, and both his handkerchief with the chain, and also his purse with three and fifty shillings in it, were taken out of his pocket in this struggling, even by the man that himself defended. . . . But they vowing that they would presently go for their weapons, and so to the field, told the gentleman he laboured but in vain (in trying to pacify them) for fight they must and would, and so going down by Paul's Chain, left the gentleman made a cony going up towards Fleet Street, sorry for his new counsellor and friend, and wishing him good luck in the fight; which indeed was nothing but wine pots, for joy of their late-gotten booty.[1]

In *The Second Part of Conny-catching* Greene dropped various remarks about the damage he had inflicted on the cosening tribe, and their bloodthirsty threats to "make a massacre of his bones" and cut off his right hand "for penning down their abominable practices." He goes so far as to hint that they have got hold of a "scholar," whose name he does not know, "to make an invective against me." Sure enough, in April, there appeared *The Defense of Conny-catching, or a Confutation of those two injurious Pamphlets published by R. G. against the practitioner's of many nimble-witted and mysticall Sciences*, by Cuthbert Conny-catcher. Ostensibly this is an attempt to retaliate on Greene—who is accused of being himself a cony-catcher—for having sold his play, *Orlando Furioso*, to the Queen's Players for twenty nobles, and when they were in the country palmed it off on the Lord Admiral's men for a larger sum. Incidentally, Cuthbert Conny-catcher supplies Greene with a valuable testimonial by remarking that when he came out of Newgate he found his trade completely paralysed through the warnings spread about by his enemy's pamphlets. But the gist of his remonstrance is to upbraid Greene with wasting his indignation on such small fry when far more grievous offenders—rogue lawyers,

"The Defense of Conny-catching"

[1] *Third Part of Conny-Catching* (Bodley Head Quartos, iii.), 45-46.

to wit, and usurers, deceitful tradesmen, fortune-hunters and the like—go undetected. Cuthbert follows his adversary's lead in interweaving stories to substantiate his invective,[1] and lets fly at Greene with much noisy but not very damaging abuse.

Greene, in truth, was not a stiver the worse, and did not take the trouble to answer Cuthbert, or even to clear himself of the allegation that he had sold a play twice over, for which no evidence has been discovered beyond Cuthbert Conny-catcher's statement. Most likely it is pure make-believe. The controversy was unquestionably good for business. The output of tracts against the cony-catchers went on more prosperously than ever, each one promising further revelations to follow. Thus the suspicion can hardly be avoided that Cuthbert Conny-catcher must have been Greene himself, or else some friend he had suborned to do him a good turn whilst pretending to do him a bad one. The "scholar" predicted so opportunely in Greene's second pamphlet—which, be it remembered, was penned almost at the same time as the first,[2] and at any rate long before the hue and cry could have made itself heard—can we believe for a moment that he belonged to the other side? The passage is too much in the style of Greene's habitual puffs preliminary. Formidable authorities have taken the transaction at its face-value, and tried to exonerate Greene from any fraudulent complicity[3]; but the plain man cannot help suspecting such a slippery person. Perhaps the decisive argument that Cuthbert Conny-catcher was not really a cony-catcher nor really Greene's enemy is that he failed to plant the dagger where it would really have done Greene's business—failed, that is, to demonstrate, as he

[1] One of the best, "A Pleasant Tale of an Usurer," has a heroine, the wife of a Cockermouth gentlemen who has got into embarrassed circumstances and falls into the clutches of a usurer. This worthy rival to the cony-catchers persuades his client to make over his estate by deed of gift, and then pretends it was a square deal. But the wife turns the tables on the cozener. She gets him into the house, and, by a stratagem, pillories him in a window, threatening to cut off his ears. The usurer has no alternative but to make restitution (Greene's *Works*, xi.).

[2] *The Notable Discovery* was printed by John Wolfe for T.N. (1591); the *Second Part*, by John Wolfe for William Wright (1591); Thomas Scarlet printed the *Third Part* for Cuthbert Burbie (1592).

[3] Grosart, for instance, is convinced that the *Defense* is a genuine attack on Greene (Greene's *Works*, xi. 40). Professor H. C. Hart agrees with the opinion that it was a sham attack, but will not admit that Greene wrote it (*Notes and Queries*, 10th series, v. 84, 3rd February 1906). For a summary of the discussion see Jordan, 96-105.

surely would have done, that the intimate knowledge of the rascally crew which he boasted was all a literary pretence.

The fact that Greene had got up the subject from sources open to everyone did not, however, escape the observation of all his contemporaries. That same year, 1592, some anonymous person seized the opportunity of the general interest in the subject to resurrect the original text-book, Harman's *Caveat*, and bring it out under the significant title, *The Groundworke of Conny-catching.* An enormous sub-title was added and a new introduction with two new stories—otherwise Harman was reproduced verbatim. This must have fetched more blood than all Cuthbert Conny-catcher's execrations would have drawn from Greene.

"The Groundworke of Conny-catching"

His next addition to the series is the most workmanlike of the lot; it holds together more consistently, and as a piece of fiction tells itself more naturally than any of the other cony-catching tales. This is *A Disputation, Betweene a Hee Conny-catcher, and a Shee Conny-catcher, whether a Theefe or a Whoore, is most hurtfull in Cousonage, to the Common-wealth. Discovering the secret villanies of alluring Strumpets. With the Conuersion of an English Courtizen, reformed this present yeare, 1592.* Nan and Lawrence debate in a friendly way on the relative powers of mischief possessed by the abandoned of either sex, each telling stories that come in for the most part with considerable aptness. Nan admittedly has the best of it. Over and above the arts that any evil-minded person may acquire, she can exert the compelling power of sex, and is ruthless in applying it to those marked down for her prey.

"A Disputation, etc."

Oh Lawrence enter into your own thoughts, and think what the fair words of a wanton will do, what the smiles of a strumpet will drive a man to act, into what jeopardie a man will thrust himself for her that he loves, although for his sweet villainy, he be brought to loathsome leprosy, tush Lawrence they say the pox came from Naples, some from Spain, some from France, but wheresoever it first grew, it is so surely now rooted in England, that by S. it may better be called A Morbus Anglicus than Gallicus, and I hope you will grant, all these French favours grew from whores, besides in my high loving or rather creeping, I mean where men and women do rob together, there always the woman is most bloody, for she always urgeth unto death, and though the men would only satisfy themselves with the party's coin, yet she endeth her theft in blood, murthering parties so deeply as she is malicious. . . . For mine own part, I hope you do not imagine but I have had some friends besides poor George my husband, alas, he knows it, and is content like an honest simple suffragan, to be corrival with a number of other good companions, and I have made many a good man, I mean a man that hath a household, for the love of me to go home and beat his poor wife, when God wot I mock him for the money he spent, and he had nothing for his pence, but the waste beleavings of others' beastly labours. Lawrence, Lawrence, if concubines could inveigle Solomon, if Delilah could betray Samson, then wonder not if we, more nice in our wickedness than a thousand such Delilahs, can seduce poor young novices to their utter destructions.[1]

Lawrence admits himself beaten when Nan has finished her recital :

I confess it Nan, for thou hast told me such wondrous villainies as I thought never could have been in women, I mean of your profession, why you are crocodiles when you weep, basilisks when you smile, serpents when you devise, and the devil's chiefest brokers to bring the world to destruction. And so Nan let's sit down to our meat and be merry.

In the supplementary story a courtesan is shown the error of her ways by a godly young man who, when she has repented, marries her.[2] There is a fine poetical touch in the scene where she takes him from chamber to chamber, because there is too much light, and at length brings him to a back loft, " so dark at noonday it was impossible for any man to see his own hands."

How now sir, quoth I, is not this dark enough? He sitting him down on the bedside fetched a deep sigh, and said, indifferent, so so, but there is a glimpse of light in at the tiles, somebody may by fortune see us. In faith no, quoth I, none but God. God, says he, why can God see us here? Good sir, quoth I, why I hope you are not so simple, but God's eyes are so clear and penetrating that they can pierce through walls of brass, and that were we enclosed never so secretly, yet we are manifestly seen to him.

And alas, quoth he, sweet love, if God see us shall we not be more ashamed to do such a filthy act before him than before men?

[1] *Disputation* (Bodley Head Quartos), pp. 36-38.
[2] Inset in this is the story borrowed from Gascoigne, see p. 29.

Some of Greene's old euphuistic trappings cling to his style in this late tract; or was he using up old material? The English courtesan describes her days of giddiness in such terms as these:

> But now I find, in sparing the rod, they hated the child, that over-kind fathers, make unruly daughters. Had they bent the wand while it had been green, it would have been pliant, but I, ill grown in my years, am almost remediless. The hawk that is most perfect for the flight and will, seldom proveth haggard, and children that are virtuously nurtured in youth, will be honestly natured in age: fie upon such as say, young saints, old devils: it is no doubt a devilish and damnable saying, for what is not bent in the cradle, will hardly be bowed in the saddle. . . .
>
> And as the Agnus Castus leaf when it looks most dry, is then most full of moisture, so women's wantonness is not qualified by their wariness, nor doth their chariness for a month warrant their chastity for ever.[1]

Like Defoe at a later date, but of course with a better excuse than Defoe, Greene insists on the actual truth of his story. The life of his courtesan, he affirms in the preface, is not a fiction; and she herself, like Moll Flanders, tells us that she conceals her name and parentage out of consideration for others, and lest envy might taint her for wantonness. Defoe would also, no doubt, have inserted the same telling kind of allusions to the fury and threats his veracious deposition excited, and the same timely advertisement of further disclosures soon to be on sale. "Nan," he says, "hath sworn to wear a long Hamborough knife to stab me, and all the crew have protested my death, and to prove they meant good earnest, they beleaguered me about in the St John's Head, within Ludgate, being at supper." One of his company, he declares, was sore hurt. But the cony-catching business is at a standstill, his enemies are wasting away, and before long he will deal them a final blow with his *Black Book*, divulging particulars of four laws not yet described, and a bead-roll of all the foists, nips, lifts, and priggers in and about London. Greene did not live to publish his *Black Book*, but he did bring out *The Blacke Bookes Messenger*, which is probably the tract to which Cuthbert Conny-catcher refers when he writes, in the *Defense*, that it is reported "you are

[1] *Disputation*, pp. 43-44, 56.

in hand with a book called *The Repentance of a Conny-catcher*—another indication that Greene wrote the *Defense*.

"A Quippe for an Upstart Courtier"

Meanwhile Greene published a tract entitled *A Quippe for an Upstart Courtier*, which is but slightly connected with the war against the cony-catchers, yet shows again how much at this period his mind was absorbed by social disorders and moral obliquity. Incidentally, Greene retorts in the course of this pamphlet upon the Harveys, who had libelled his character. The *Quippe* is described in the sub-title as "A Quaint Dispute between Velvet Breeches and Cloth Breeches," the question being whether the courtier or the tradesman is better entitled to the realm of Britain. Plan and theme were suggested by the poem of a certain F.T., called *The Debate between Pride and Lowliness*, which Greene skilfully remodelled and made more realistic in his best prose. In the pithy dialogue of the rival claimants, and in the process of challenging the jury of citizens, Greene manages to review, in an amusing way, some sixty different grades and occupations, hitting off types in the pointed manner of the character-writers. He is entirely on the populist side, and gives Cloth Breeches an easy victory over the genteel fop.

"The Blacke Bookes Messenger"

In the next number of the cony-catching series, *The Blacke Bookes Messenger, laying open the Life and Death of Ned Browne* (1592), there is a resemblance, which must not be pressed too far, to such sardonic glorifications of villainy as Fielding's *Jonathan Wild* and Thackeray's *Barry Lyndon*. Greene, however, was not a master of irony; he was not even clear-headed enough to keep to the same point of view to the end. Ned recounts five episodes in his career, from boyish disobedience to crime: "I lived wantonly, and therefore let me end merrily, and tell you two or three of my mad pranks and so bid you farewell." The pranks are mostly variants of snares and swindles already described. A new one is Ned's dodge for bilking a priest, to whom he sells his own good horse, taking the priest's nag in exchange together with twenty nobles. Ned ties a hair over a vein on his horse's fetlock, and when the beast which he has sold goes lame offers to show the new owner how to ride him. Before mounting, he cuts the hair unperceived, and then gallops off, with the animal, the money, and the horse's furniture belonging to the priest. Finding England too hot to hold him he migrates to the Low Countries, and is arrested for robbing a church, sentenced to death, and, in default of a gallows, is about to be hanged at a window. With the halter round his neck he tells his tale, announcing that he will not repent even at the point of death. But with sad inconsistency Greene makes him preach an edifying sermon before he springs out of the window and dies. Thus a promising tale ends in feeble rodomontade.

Greene's contribution to realistic fiction

In his cony-catching series, Greene started the exploitation of shady life for literary purposes. It may be said that the jest-books had been doing this already. This is true to a certain extent. But the jest-books were merely what they were intended to be—collections of broad anecdotes of hoaxes and rascality, the point of which was the fun of the thing. Some of Greene's anecdotes were comic enough ; but the declared object was to show up craft and villainy, and the majority were nearer akin to the police news than to the jest-book. Greene puts on the knowing airs of a special commissioner sent out by a modern newspaper to investigate a case. But his evidence would not have received a moment's attention in a police court, and was a mere imposition on the public. He worked up, and profited by, a scare, and so far as he exposed anything it was an exposure of scandals already exposed by men who knew what they were talking about. From the literary point of view, however, we are concerned solely with his success in painting a realistic picture of low life, or at least in doing some promising sketches. It is, of course, no business of the realistic painter of life to provide any evidence save that of verisimilitude. If Greene had been simply a story-teller the falsity of his attestations would have been neither here nor there ; the sole objection would have been to their clumsiness. His real service was to have penned some graphic scenes from a side of life that he knew only in part from immediate observation, and to have initiated a kind of story-telling which, through the rogue-stories and criminal biographies, led to epoch-making developments in the hands of Defoe.[1]

[1] As it is frequently asserted that the jest-books—especially those recounting the feats of such a celebrity as Skelton or Scoggin—were tending to develop into something like the picaresque fiction soon to be imported from Spain, or into a realistic portrayal of low life, it may be worth while to glance at one of these, *The Jests of George Peele*, which has as much as any of the unity pertaining to a book about one hero. The title of the best version emphatically suggests something of the nature of continuous narrative: it

Greene's imitators —Chettle

Greene's mantle did not fall peaceably on the shoulders of any one successor, but was snatched at by a number of eager scribes. He had a sort of literary executor in Henry Chettle, who revised and published his *Groats-Worth of Witte*, and took up the cudgels against the Harveys and other of Greene's detractors in *Kind-Harts Dreame, conteining five Apparitions, with their Invectives against abuses raigning. Delivered by severall Ghosts unto him to be publisht, after Piers Penilesse Post had refused the carriage* (1592). Pierce Pennilesse—as already explained in reference to Chettle's later tract, the picaresque *Piers Plainnes*[1]—is Nashe, to whom Greene's spirit appeals for revenge upon his foes. He also assures Nashe that his intent in the pamphlets had been merely "to reprove vice, and lay open such villainies as had been very necessary to be made known, whereof my *Blacke Booke*, if ever it see light [which it never did] can sufficiently witness." The strolling dentist, Kind-Hart, falls asleep after incautious potations in an ancient tap-house not far from Finsbury, and dreams that he is accosted by five personages—old Anthony Now-now, a well-known fiddler; the famous Tarlton; William Cuckoe, juggler, recently deceased; Dr Burcot, a notorious quack, and the late Robert Greene. With them was the devil who played knight of

runs thus: *Merrie Conceited Jests, of George Peele gentleman, sometimes student of Oxford. Wherein is shewed the course of his life, how he lived: a man very well knowne in the City of London, and elsewhere* (1607). The claim that the course of Peele's life is shown does not hold water; the jests, which are of the cony-catching order and not very amusing, are perfunctorily connected into a sort of narrative. There are about a dozen of these. One is how Peele, who had done a certain barber out of a lute, and other persons out of a horse and mare, all of which had been sold, tricks the barber again and decamps. The hackneyed device of leaving the gull to pay the score, and other jests that consist of swindling someone or relieving him of his portable belongings, would be boring to such as have not outgrown the kinds of comedy that have no point except some harmless individual's misfortune. The most elaborate jest, if not the most entertaining, is that in which Peele passes himself off as a physician, attends several patients, and of course pockets the fees. There is something like it in *Guzman d'Alfarache*, and it was served up again even so recently as in *Harry Lorrequer*. The best feature of the little book is the terse and natural dialogue, which might have done duty in a light comedy of the period. The hero is to be identified with the playwright, and is described as "an excellent poet," having acquaintance "of most of the players in England." *Scoggin's Jests*, which were very popular in the sixteenth century, are more amusing, but not more original, being largely derived from tales preserved in older collections; and are even less connected into any sort of unity. Much the same may be said of the *Merie Tales newly imprinted and made by Master Skelton Poet Laureat*, of similar date. See Chandler, i., pp. 59-70.

[1] See p. 122.

the post in carrying *Pierce Penilesse his Svpplication to the Divell.*[1] The five worthies deliver themselves of "friendly admonitions" on the chief pests of the time, and in the course of their denunciations add a few more to the standing catalogue of tricks and rogueries. The tract is a kind of gloss upon Greene, and is best known for its reply to those who had taxed him with slandering Shakespeare.

Other followers

Greene was hardly cold in his grave when some anonymous writer came out with a tract entitled *Greenes Newes both from Heaven and Hell* (1593),[2] which takes the same side as Cuthbert Conny-catcher in the *Defense*, St Peter reviling Greene for not having called more venerable and more mischievous knaves to account, those who walk the streets in long gowns and velvet coats, and sometimes ride in coaches. In the other place, he is greeted by the cony-catchers with threats and invectives, and Lucifer himself refuses the hapless spirit admittance. Dickenson's *Greene in Conceipt*, telling the tale of the fair Valeria, has already been mentioned.[3] Rowlands and Dekker were the best-known among those who followed in Greene's footsteps, sometimes pilfering from him without acknowledgment, whilst anonymous tracts such as *Questions concerning Coniehood and the Nature of the Conie*, or *Nihil Mumchaunce, his Discoverie of the Art of Cheating in false Dyce play, and other unlawful games* (1597), were actually attributed to Greene.[4]

Rowlands

Samuel Rowlands—boldly plagiarizing when he was short of matter, whilst reprehending Nashe for doing the same thing[5]—brought out *Greenes Ghost haunting Conie-catchers* (1602) and *Martin Mark-All, Beadle of Bridewell, his Defence and Answere to the Bel-man of London* (1610). The former was a collection of stories of a journalistic stamp, evidently written to order for the booksellers, and cribbed from Greene and others. Among the fifteen stories there is hardly one with the slightest claim to novelty, unless it be that the reader's friendliness is now claimed

[1] Recently published by Nashe; see p. 156.
[2] Attributed to Barnaby Rich in *Camb. Hist. of Eng. Lit.*, iv. 528.
[3] See p. 121.
[4] Chandler, i. 104-105.
[5] Dekker seems to have meant Rowlands by his reference to the Belman's brother in *Lanthorne and Candlelight*, see p. 215.

for the rogues. Yet in the other work Rowlands had the assurance to call Dekker over the coals for his thefts from Harman's *Caveat*, with serene disregard for his own larcenies. He tactfully ignores Dekker's raids upon two more recent authors—Greene and himself—that would have provoked a dangerous retort. The work is neither a single story nor a collection of cony-catching stories, but a fabulous chronicle of English vagabondage and roguery from Jack Cade to Cocke Lorell—that is, from the time of Henry VI. to the twenty-sixth year of Henry VIII., "gathered out of the Chronicle of Crackeropes," with an account of the gipsies and their language. Rowlands inserts a map of the land of roguery, drawn in a fanciful style, to illustrate the allegorical introduction to the chronicle. He may also be the author of another tract, furnished with anecdotes of the usual type, *The Art of Jugling or Legerdemaine* (1612), unmasking the wiles of conjurers and gamesters.[1]

Nicholas Breton's stories—"Mavillia"

Nicholas Breton, the poet (*c.*1545-*c.*1626), Gascoigne's stepson, who dabbled in all the fashionable modes of verse and prose, apprenticed himself for a while to Greene, and in his first story, *The Miseries of Mavillia ; the most unfortunate Ladie that ever lived* (1596), attempted something betwixt and between Greene's romantic tales and the later portrayals of low life. He came down badly between the two stools. Mavillia tells her plaintive story in five chapters, entitled after her five miseries. Turned adrift as a child of four or five, through the sack of the town where she lived and the slaughter of her parents, she seems doomed to misfortune. The young page to whom she is given in charge by a friendly officer is wounded to death in killing a savage boar ; and though a shepherd takes her home his vixen of a wife makes her a drudge, and defrauds her of her money. Then she is accused of stealing, and is about to be convicted, when the real culprits—there are three of them implicated in varying degrees—one after another confess the crime and beg for her acquittal. Breton seizes the occasion for a display of sentimental heroics. Mavillia is released, and being now in the flower of her youth and beauty is wooed by an aged lecher, whom she sketches with the merciless pen of a Smollett :

[1] Chandler thinks so (see Chandler, 104).

But the fool will be kissing, and the stubble of his old shaven beard new come up so pricks me and tickles my lips, that I am ready to scratch them after every kiss : but yet his nose is so great that he hath much ado to kiss kindly ; besides he hath a stinking breath and a hollow eye. Further, I fear by his complexion, he hath been a traveller into some low countries, where he hath been infected with some unwholesome air : I guess it the more by his speaking in the nose, and never a good tooth in his head. He is as deaf as a door ; I must tell him a tale in his ear, that all the town must be privy to, or else he cannot hear me. He hath the gout in one of his legs, and blind of one of his eyes : he hath almost no hair on his head, and he hath lost one of his ears : he goes crup-shouldered, and sits down by leisure : he is continually coughing, and betwixt every three words spitting : he never plays at tables or cards without a pair of spectacles. Oh, what sport I have to deal him the knave of clubs : his play is not great, thirteen games for three farthings, and yet wrangle too, and in the end look upon both sides whether it be a penny or no : yet will he have his purse full of gold to make a brave show withal : a brooch in his hat with a good deal of gold in it, and a seal ring on his finger with an ounce of gold at least. Marry, sir, who would not be glad of such a bargain ? Faith, not I. Oh, this filthy fellow now must I meet, and have a little talk withal, and a kiss as good, saving your reverence. But patience, we must now to the matter.[1]

The character-writer is already beginning to get his hand in ; but the story-teller makes a childish conclusion. Mavillia avoids this "old gander," and marries a man more to her liking. But the aged wooer comes with two knaves and with swords drawn and sets upon Mavillia and her husband, reviling her for a jilt and threatening revenge. He offers her the choice of two things : to lose her husband or her nose. She implores that he will put her to death rather.

Well then (quoth he), come hither, let me have a kiss for all the love I have borne thee, and so I will bid thee farewell. I with tears in mine eyes, leaping in heart for joy of this good promise, ran to him, and taking him about the neck to kiss him, the cankered old villain (with the ill-favoured teeth that he had) bit off my nose, and so with his two villains like himself away he goes.[2]

[1] *Works* of N. Breton, ed. A. Grosart, ii. : *The Miseries of Mavillia*, pp. 48-49.
[2] *Ibid.*, p. 51.

This is the last of the miseries of Mavillia !

"Two Princes" and "A Mad World my Masters"

Breton's next story was an Italianate romance, *The Strange Fortunes of two excellent Princes : in their lives and loves, to their equall Ladies in all the titles of true honour* (1600), in which the euphuistic and the arcadian ingredients are again compounded in the manner of Greene and Lodge. Fantiro and Penillo are the only sons of two enemy dukes, and they have each a beauteous sister. The time-honoured result of this promising situation is brought about after a medley of time-honoured adventures. Breton comes a little nearer to real life in two of his dialogues. *A Mad World my Masters, Mistake me not* (1603), is a didactic piece ; two travellers, Dorindo and Lorenzo, the Taker and the Mistaker, discuss their experiences of life. Lorenzo is always making mistakes. The first thing he was mistaken in was himself : "For, with only a little observation, I was persuaded that there was no matter of worth, but I had it by heart ; and for trifles, I would not be troubled with them." He goes to sea, but when bad weather sets in finds he was entirely mistaken about the merry life of a mariner. It is no better, however, on land. Where he expects hospitality he meets with churlishness, and where honesty, fraud. "In courting," he says, "I found more cost than comfort ; in war, more danger than ease ; in learning, more study than profit ; in traffic, more gain than conscience ; in service, more pain than honour ; in marriage, more care than quiet ; and in love, more pleasure than virtue : so that in all my courses being mistaken, that I found a cross to my comfort in every of them, I fairly left the courtier to his courtesies, the soldier to his marches, the scholar to his studies, the merchant to his traffic, the married man to his purgatory, and the lover to his vanity : and home returned to my poor cottage that my parents left me." Dorindo is a self-confident young man, with a touch of the rogue, who takes things as he finds them. He also has ill haps as well as good to relate, and sums up his experiences :

To be short, if I should tell you all the courses that I have taken, and how I have been taken in every of them, I should make you think all your mistaking a trifle in comparison of many a miserable taking that I have been in.

The wise part, he concludes, is to take things as they come and think oneself lucky if the reality turns out as good as or better than appearances.

Take a courtier for a fine man, a lawyer for a wise man, a soldier for a valiant, a divine for a learned man, a merchant for a rich man, a clown for a painful man, and a beggar for a poor man : but for an honest man, take him as you find him, in what estate so ever he be. If he be in a great one, give him honour : if in a mean one give him praise. Now if you find wealth, valour, wisdom, learning, labour, and honesty, all in one man : note him for a rare man, and take him for the best man. But, because in many it falleth out, that wealth causeth pride ; wit, cunning ; learning, policy ; valour, discord ; pains, grief ; and poverty, misery ; take good notice of every man you have to deal withal, and have to do with as few as you can. And for an end, if a good occasion may be taken, slip it not ; if a good gift may be taken, refuse it not ; and if you have taken a good course leave it not."

"Grimello's Fortunes"

Grimello's Fortunes. With his Entertainment in his Travaile (1604), is another didactic dialogue, between a young fellow out of a place and Signior Ganuzido, who wants a man. They overtake each other by the wayside, and the gentleman questions Grimello about his character, which appears to be without blemish, and then about his life, which hardly comes up to the same standard. Grimello has been a failure in a variety of occupations ; and he more than hints that it is because he has been too good for this wicked world. Satisfied, however, with the wholesome sentiments he has expressed, Ganuzido promises to make him his steward and ranger of his forest and now and then to wait upon his wife ; and next, as they have still three miles to go, asks him to beguile the way with some of his experiences. Grimello at once comes out with several stories. The first is how an amorous coxcomb was hoaxed by a page dressed up as a young woman—he half admits that he sustained the part himself. The gull sends letters and presents, and at last is emboldened by the other pages, who are in the plot, to give the supposed lady a banquet. Next morning he is to attend her on her way out of town ; but his wine is drugged, he oversleeps himself, and when he awakes it is to find the young wags wearing the favours he had sent to his charmer. Better than this is the caricature of a certain commander of a garrison, who was such a poltroon that when there was a false alarm of the enemy

. . . he, in a cold sweat, what with fear and the weight of his armour, called presently for his captains, gave every one their charge what to do : which done, providing as well as he might for one : barricaded all his gates without, and all his doors within : and in the midst of a low room, within a wall of twenty yards thick of stone, barricaded himself within a great wall of earth, which was made for a furnace to cast metal in for ordnance. There over head and ears in fear sits he with his two pages, the door fast locked to him, till anon, the people being come in with their merry show, went a messenger from the captain of the watch, to entreat his lordship to be partaker of the pastime, and to entreat the people with some kindness. The messenger being come to the door and let in, before he could deliver his message : Well, quoth he, imaging the enemies before the walls, What is the parley that he offereth thee ? Parley, my lord, quoth the messenger, it is a pastime : there is no enemy, all friends : your poor neighbours are come to make you merry with a morrice dance and a May game. Yea, quoth he, is it none other ? and with looking in his purse, and giving him just nothing, It is well : stay awhile, boy, give me my sword and my target, that my neighbours shall see how ready I was to meet the enemy upon the least alarum. And with these words, causing the trumpet to sound a merry note for joy of the deliverance of his fear, out he comes among them, and like an ass, as ever man was, shows himself. After a little gratulation, leaving them in their sports, got him again into his lodging, and there calling for his breakfast, put off his armour, and went to bed again : where let him lie till I raise him.[1]

Breton's dialogues and letters

Grimello's other stories are of the cony-catching or the jest-book kind. Breton may have got the idea of the page and his escapades from Nashe's *Unfortunate Traveller*, which had appeared ten years before. He is less sprightly and more solemn and sententious in the rest of his dialogues—a form into which he put what another writer would have made into an essay. Such are *Wits Trenchmour, in a Conference betwixt a Scholler and an Angler* (1597), *The Wil of Wit, Wits Will, or Wils Wit, chuse you whether* (1599), and *An Olde Mans Lesson, and a Young Mans Love* (1605). He also brought out two

[1] *Works*, ed. A. B. Grosart, ii : *Grimello's Fortunes*, pp. 11-12.

collections of letters and answers by imaginary correspondents, which are more curious than amusing, under the title of *A Poste with a Packet of Mad Letters* (1603-1637). Breton is numbered among the early character-writers, and under that head will be referred to again.

CHAPTER X

THOMAS NASHE

Thomas Nashe

BRETON's long life has carried us forward to a point from which we must hark back to the more important figure of Thomas Nashe, who was only seven years junior to Greene. Both Nashe and Greene died in the early thirties, and in other respects were not dissimilar. Nashe (1567-1600), born at Lowestoft, son of a clergyman, was nearly seven years at St John's College, Cambridge (1582-1589), and then came to London, where he wrote more works than ever got into print, but presumably relied for support less upon literary earnings than upon various patrons for whom he no doubt performed secretarial or other services. Nobody can be described as one of the university wits with more appropriateness. Wit was his aim in writing, such erudition as he loved to display, miscellaneous rather than genuine, being subsidiary to that accomplishment—wit not so much in the modern sense as in that of general intellectual alertness and sprightly address. More than Greene, or any other of the fellowship, he took himself very seriously as a champion of learning, and a lynx-eyed critic of innovations and eccentricities, whether in literary or in social manners. But it was not the new learning that Nashe defended. He was proud of belonging to an ancient university. He was orthodox and conservative by breeding and education, showing this at the outset, when he satirized the modern woman of his day, in *The Anatomie of Absurditie*, and vented a tirade on mishandlers of the English language, in the epistle prefixed to Greene's *Menaphon*, and also at the end, when he composed his loyal masque, *Summers Last Will and Testament*, published in the year of his death. Excitable and insubordinate in temper, he was often in bad odour with authority ; at heart he was uniformly on the side of all that was established and respectable, and of all that was English.

More versatile even than Greene, Nashe made himself a writer of

His versatility

all work, trying his hand at nearly every style of writing that the age affected—anatomies of abuses, denunciations, burlesque, story, play, the controversial tract, the personal lampoon. He gave some a new turn, in some he compounded old ingredients in singular ways. Nashe was possessed of little originality, or anything that could be called genius, but he had plenty of talent, and such a passion for writing that he could inspire himself with enthusiasm for any object to which he turned his pen. His driving force was a robust and defiant self-confidence ; kept up by that, his animal spirits and energy never flagged. He was arrogant, combative, pugilistic, always spoiling for a fight, yet good-tempered, even when he was showering scurrilities on the foe.

His devotion to matters of fact

These characteristics of the man are as evident in the one work of his which is fiction all through as in the remainder. But Nashe's share in the development of realistic fiction is not confined to *The Unfortunate Traveller*. He was always railing at the foppery of romance. His thoroughly English common sense, while it fettered in no way his zest for playful flights of extravagance, kept him close to fact in every allusion to contemporary life. In his satirical and in his controversial works, he had to carry conviction into the minds of a more critical class than the readers addressed by Robert Greene ; even when he exaggerated he had to hit the nail on the head—and hit it he did, not only harder but also with a much truer aim than the others who tried.

"The Anatomie of Absurditie"

The Anatomie of Absurditie and the preface to *Menaphon* were the work of the young Cambridge student. The former, written not later than 1588,[1] is a rambling series of animadversions on women, Puritans, astrologers, ballad-mongers, and other foolish people, followed by a eulogy of poetry and learning, and on the best way to acquire the latter. It is in an attack on literary follies and babble book-mongers that Nashe lets fly at those who would revive "that forgotten legendary licence of lying, to imitate afresh the fantastical dreams of those exiled abbey-lubbers, from whose idle pens proceeded those worn-out impressions of the famed nowhere acts of Arthur of the Round Table, Arthur of Little Britain, Sir Tristram, Huon of Bordeaux, the Squire of Low Degree, the Four Sons of Aymon, with infinite others." Here Nashe sounds the

[1] McKerrow, iv. 1.

challenge which he was to maintain to the end of his short career : bearing in mind that this was his attitude throughout, we shall understand what he was after when he came to write fiction himself.

The star of *Euphues* was not yet below the horizon when Nashe was writing the *Anatomie* ; echoes of Lyly are heard both in the style and in the exhortations to study.

There be three things which are wont to slack young students' endeavour, Negligence, want of Wisdom, and Fortune. Negligence, whenas we either altogether pretermit, or more lightly pass over, the thing we ought seriously to ponder. Want of wisdom, when we observe no method in reading. Fortune is in the event of chance, either naturally happening, or whenas by poverty or some infirmity, or natural dullness, we are withdrawn from our studies, and alienated from our intended enterprise, by the imagination of the rareness of learned men : but as touching these three, for the first, that is to say, negligent sloth, he is to be warned : for the second, he is to be instructed : for the third, he is to be helped. Let his reading be temperate, whereunto wisdom, not weariness, must prescribe an end, for as immoderate fast, excessive abstinence, and inordinate watchings, are argued of intemperance, perishing with their immoderate use, so that these things never after can be performed as they ought in any measure ; so the intemperate study of reading incurreth reprehension, and that which is laudable in his kind is blameworthy by the abuse. . . . We read many things, lest by letting them pass, we should seem to despise them ; some things we read, lest we should seem to be ignorant in them ; other things we read, not that we may embrace them, but eschew them. Our learning ought to be our lives' amendment, and the fruits of our private study ought to appear in our public behaviour.[1]

Still closer to the style of *Euphues* is this passage from his sarcastic observations on the folly of love—a congenial topic to both writers :

Well worthy are the Essenians to be extolled for their wisdom, who abhor the company of women and detest the possession of gold and silver, and they to be deemed as soothing flatterers, who spend so much paper about a proposition of praise, set apart from any appearance of probability. Peradventure they think, that as the poets invent that Atlas upholds the heavens with his shoulders, because by an excellent imagination he found out the course of the stars, even so they by compiling of pamphlets in their mistress' praises, to be

[1] *Works*, ed. McKerrow, i. 42-43.

called the restorers of womankind. But idle heads are usually occupied about such trifling texts, wanton wits are cumbered with those wonted fittes, such busy brains sow where they reap small gains. When wit gives way to will and reason to affection, then folly with full sail launcheth forth most desperately into the deep.[1]

The preface to "Menaphon"

The letter written as a preface to *Menaphon* (1589) is less euphuistic ; Nashe was already intent on forming a style entirely his own, and traces are plainly observable of the exuberant, slashing, robustious rhetoric which in a year or two was to flow so readily from his pen. In this short piece Nashe lays down the law, with the confidence of a new-fledged graduate, on literary affectations, especially in the employment of un-English terms, and winds up with a panegyric of Cambridge's share in the revival of learning. In both these works there is more about literature than about life ; the life that Nashe does treat of is that of the student and lover of wisdom. It is noteworthy that he cannot away with pamphleteers and exposers of abuses, a class into which he himself could not help gravitating without much lapse of time.

Nashe's controversial tracts

With Nashe's part in the great Martin Marprelate controversy there is no need to deal here. What his precise share was is very difficult to determine[2] ; at any rate it gained him the name of a formidable duellist. Nor is this the place to dwell on his still more momentous campaign against Gabriel Harvey and his brothers, excellent as much of the fighting was from the literary point of view, and a first-rate opportunity for the exercise of his powers of wit and raillery.[3] More relevant to the present theme is the general satire on the inhabitants of London, *Pierce Penilesse his Supplication to the Divell* (1592), which seems to have been the most popular work of our "Young Juvenal," as Greene entitled him in the *Groats-Worth of Witte*. Here, after a characteristic lament for the poor esteem in which wit and learning were now held, and for the many evils that the Church had failed to remedy, Nashe proposes to send a supplication to the Devil, and looks round for a knight of the post to deliver it. The whole petition is then rehearsed. It is in the name of Pierce Penilesse, the impecunious man of letters, and

"Pierce Penilesse his Supplication to the Divell"

[1] *Works*, ed. McKerrow, i. 19.
[2] It is fully discussed by Dr McKerrow, v. 34-65.
[3] *Ibid.*, 65-110.

entreats his infernal majesty to hand over to him the superfluous wealth of the rich, enforcing the request with a long catalogue of the sins infesting the world : avarice, niggardliness, pride, envy, murder, wrath, gluttony, drunkenness, sloth, lechery, and — the Harveys. These " ridiculous asses " are not named, but serve to show how he could rail were he called upon to do so. The iniquities denounced are obviously the seven deadly sins of the Middle Ages brought up to date. Nashe's satire falls heavier, be it noted, on Dutchmen, Spaniards, Frenchmen and Italians than on his own countrymen. His knight of the post brings back news from hell, and supplies matter for an account of its polity and inhabitants.

Manifestly, the *Supplication* is an example of that species of writing which Nashe had previously decried, and not a bad example either. He displays as wide and racy an experience of all sorts and conditions as any of his forerunners, and far more caustic powers of ridicule, in spite of his too often preferring crude invective to the finer weapons of satire. He paints realistic vignettes of foolishness, vice and extravagance which, with allowance for satirical animus and for the intentional coarseness, would take an advantageous place on the walls of that gallery of characters which was now beginning to be hung. Regard this portrait :

In another corner, Mistress Minx, a merchant's wife, that will eat no cherries, forsooth, but when they are at twenty shillings a pound ; that looks as simperingly as if she were besmeared, and jets it as gingerly as if she were dancing the Canaries : she is so finical in her speech, as though she spake nothing but what she had first sewed over before in her samplers, and the puling accent of her voice is like a feigned treble, or one's voice that interprets to the puppets. What should I tell how squeamish she is in her diet, what toil she puts her poor servants unto, to make her looking-glasses in the pavement ? how she will not go into the fields, to cower on the green grass, but she must have a coach for her convoy ; and spends half a day in pranking herself if she be invited to any strange place ? Is not this the excess of pride, signior Satan ? Go to, you are unwise, if you make her not a chief saint in your calendar.

A slighter piece, probably one of " two or three trivial volumes " spoken of by Nashe in the preface to *Christes Teares*, was *The*

" Christes Teares "

[1] *Works*, i. 173.

Terrors of the Night; or A Discourse of Apparitions (1593), in which the crass superstitions rampant in that day are ridiculed in a random discourse on a sick man's dreams. There are specimens of charactery in Nashe's famous jeremiad, *Christes Teares over Jerusalem, whereunto is annexed a comparative admonition of London* (1593).[1] Written probably at the time of the plague that afflicted London (1592-1593), this owes its tone of judgment and retribution to that grievous experience. Nashe first gives a terror-striking account of the siege and destruction of Jerusalem,[2] by which the Jews were punished for their sins. Then, turning to his own time and country, he says:

Whatsoever of Jerusalem I have written was but to lend her a looking-glass. Now I enter into my true tears, my tears for London, wherein I crave pardon though I deal more searchingly than common soul-surgeons accustom; for in this book wholly have I bequeathed my pen and my spirit to the prosternating and enfurrowing the frontiers of sin. So let it be acceptable to God and his Church what I write, as no man in this treatise I will particularly touch, none I will semovedly allude to, but only attaint vice in general."[3]

Then comes his parallel picture of the demoralization, depravity and crimes of London, which cry out for a like castigation. The sons and daughters of Pride—Ambition, Avarice, Vainglory, Atheism, Discontent, Contention, Disdain, Glorious Attire, Delicacy, Gluttony, Lust, Sloth—and all their familiars, riot unchecked. Nashe can only pray that the vengeance of Heaven may be pretermitted.

He probably wrote *The Unfortunate Traveller* before *Christes Teares*,[4] but a review of this, eminently his chief contribution to fiction, may as well be left until some later writings have been considered. Nashe had a hand, to what extent is uncertain, in a comedy, not now extant, *The Isle of Dogs*, which got him into trouble with the Privy Council. Described as a lewd play, "containing very seditious and slanderous matter," it drew down an order for the apprehension of some of the players, and for a search to be made in Nashe's lodgings for incriminating papers (1597). He does not

[1] See below, p. 223.

[2] H. V. Routh notices that "the terrors of the siege recalled the downfall of Antwerp, still fresh in men's minds" (*Camb. Hist. of Eng. Lit.*, iv. 324).

[3] *Works*, ii. 80.

[4] McKerrow, *ibid.*, v. 124.

appear to have been arrested, but he states that he took flight from the tempests that were raised, and found a refuge at Great Yarmouth in his native East Anglia. There he was hospitably entertained, and probably wrote his *Lenten Stuffe* (1599) as a thank-offering to the town.

"Lenten Stuffe"

Nashes Lenten Stuffe . . . with a new Play never played before, of the praise of the Red Herring, is a jovial, robustious piece, in the rollicking, fantastic style which Nashe had fashioned for himself, as if to outrival all his competitors. It reads sometimes as a sort of caricature of euphuism; often its sallies of audacious fancy make one think of Rabelais, whom, however, Nashe had probably never read.[1] He had long ago expressed his aversion for "new fangles," "candle-stuff," "tapsterly terms," and the language of "inkhorn men" and "trivial translators." He cultivated a style of his own as sedulously as any Carlyle or Stevenson; and, though indebted to many predecessors and rivals, he was influenced more by wilful opposition and a resolve to be different at all costs than by imitation, even unconscious, except of one avowed model, the audacious Aretino. With his wonted skill at collecting scraps of information from diverse sources, learned and unlearned, and serving them up in a well-spiced dish, Nashe produces an historical and descriptive account of Great Yarmouth, and then launches out into a bombastic eulogy of the red herring. A comic version of the tale of Hero and Leander, who were changed into the immortal shapes of the Red Herring and the Ling, is followed by the story of how the herring was made king of the fishes. Myths, legends and fables about fishes, especially the herring, are culled from ancient literature and folk-lore, and jostle facts extracted from Camden or gleaned from local authorities. He adapts all admirably to his purpose; and the whole piece must have been read with delight, and by others than mere natives of Yarmouth. The narrative skill shown in his humorous perversions of history and legend is finer than that of any episode in *The Unfortunate Traveller*; his hand was growing in dexterity. It would be impossible to better his tale of Hero and Leander, whose after fate is thus related:

The dint of destiny could not be repealed in the reviving of Hero and Leander, but their heavenly-hoods in their synod thus decreed,

[1] McKerrow, *ibid.*, v. 129-131.

that, for they were either of them sea-borderers and drowned in the sea, still to the sea they must belong, and be divided in habitation after death, as they were in their life-time. Leander, for that in a cold, dark, testy night he had his passport to Charon, they terminated to the unquiet cold coast of Iceland, where half the year is nothing but murk night, and to that fish translated him which of us is termed Ling. Hero, for that she was pagled and tympanized, and sustained two losses under one, they footballed their heads together, and protested to make the stem of her loins of all fishes the flaunting Fabian or Palmerin of England, which is Cadwallader Herring, and, as their meetings were but seldom, and not so oft as welcome, so but seldom should they meet in the heel of the week at the best men's tables, upon Fridays and Saturdays, the holy time of Lent exempted, and then they might be at meat and meal for seven weeks together.[1]

"The Unfortunate Traveller, or Jack Wilton"

Euphues, the *Arcadia*, and *The Unfortunate Traveller, or the life of Jack Wilton* (1594), are the three most notable works of Elizabethan prose fiction before Deloney. Deloney was to make the most substantial contribution to realism; failing him, Nashe would have had that credit. In everything he wrote, Nashe announced himself an anti-romantic, an anti-sentimentalist, a hard-headed, superior person. Exaggeration and hyperbole came natural to one with his force of mind; but, except when he was undisguisedly fabling, the reference was always to fact; he exaggerated to make the truth more biting. He could spin a preposterous yarn with the best—as in *Lenten Stuffe*—but when he applied himself to a more extended and more serious task—as in *Jack Wilton*—it was the man's very nature to stick to realities. Not that he troubled himself about literal accuracy. His literary conscience was not over-sensitive. What Nashe appears to have intended in *The Unfortunate Traveller* was to show that real life, as men saw it or read about it in the current narratives of travellers and historians, was as rich in savour and as wildly exciting as the lawless inventions of the romancers. They had told tales of heroes, lovers and adventurers in other times and places, times and places usually remote, or of shadowy personages of no determinable time or place at all. Nashe came definitely down to earth by putting his story in the mouth of a scapegrace page, and linking it to events that everyone could give a date to, from the siege of Tournay at the beginning to the

[1] *Works*, iii. 199-200.

Field of the Cloth of Gold at the end. The autobiographical form was itself a guarantee that the writer was going to deal out something like fact, if not literal fact itself. Fact, of course, gives better opportunities for downright lying, if need be, than romance can possibly give, as no one knew better than Thomas Nashe. He was a predecessor of Defoe, though Defoe probably knew nothing about him.

Outline of the story

The scene opens in the camp before Tournay and Thérouanne, besieged by Henry VIII., in 1513, where Jack introduces himself as "a certain kind of appendix or page, belonging or appertaining in or unto the confines of the English court," with more creditors than money; one of many good fellows who are "quickly blown to nothing with bearing a light heart in a light purse." Jack, in short, is remarkably like a *pícaro* of Spanish extraction. But there is an essential difference. The Spanish rogue lives by his wits. Jack Wilton lives to enjoy himself. "Amongst this chaff was I winnowing my wits to live merrily." He is not a rogue, though he plays the scallywag, and later on makes his story lurid with scenes of hair-raising scoundrelism into which he is plunged by the course of events. Roguery and practical joking are two different things, thorough-paced villainy is a third. Nashe may have heard of *Lazarillo de Tormes*, translated by David Rowland in 1576; he may at least have known that it was written as an autobiography. There is no evidence, however, in his novel or elsewhere, that he had ever read it, or had any appreciation of the distinctive method and design of picaresque fiction.[1] There are no comic changes of masters, and the one master is not lampooned, but is the partaker in many of the adventures.

[1] Perhaps the only thing that suggests it is a curious touch in Nashe's hyperbolical painting of character. Thus he describes the stinginess of the Pope's Jew-physician in terms that remind one of Aleman and Quevedo—*e.g.* "Nor did he it so much for clarifying physic, as to save charges. Miserable is that mouse that lives in a physician's house; Tantalus lives not so hunger-starved in hell, as she doth there. Not the very crumbs that fall from his table, but Zachary sweeps together, and of them moulds up a manna. Of the ashy parings of his bread, he would make conserve of chippings. Out of bones after the meat was eaten off, he would alchemize an oil, that he sold for a shilling a dram. . . . His rheumatic eyes when he went in the wind, or rose early in a morning, dropped as cool alum water as you would request. He was Dame Niggardise' sole heir and executor." His virulent, pictorial method of setting a personage before us, again, is the method afterwards employed with Hogarthian effect by Smollett, who was a disciple of Le Sage.

Jack at once describes his first exploit. There is in the camp a huge tavern-keeper, who sells cider and cheese to the soldiers, a tun-bellied man, "his great velvet breeches larded with the droppings of this dainty liquor," a man who condescends with the air of a baron of long descent to act as victualler to the army, but is frightened to death when Jack pretends that he is suspected of dealings with the enemy. Many critics are quite sure that this blustering coward of the lordly person was the direct progenitor of Falstaff; however that may be, he is undoubtedly a character, and one of the first of the genus to appear in English fiction. Jack hoaxes him to the top of his bent. There is one infallible method, says Jack, by which he can prove his loyalty and make everyone his friend—it is to sell his cider free of charge. So he does, to the uproarious delight of the camp. But Jack's trick comes to light, and he is whipped by order of the king. It was well worth it, he thought; and soon he is engaged in another plot. This time he avenges himself on a captain who has cheated him at dice-play, by inducing him to go over to the enemy in the guise of a deserter and win fame and reward by bringing back information. The captain's real character is easily seen through by the French, who give him a taste of the wheel, and then whip him back to the English lines for a cully. In these and other comic knaveries Jack plays the part of a Tarlton, Scoggin, or Peele—that is, of one of those jest-book heroes whose performances make up a continuous story.

Loose handling of history

His adventures now take a new turn. He comes back to England on the capture of the two towns, is there during the sweating sickness, and then goes over sea again, in time to witness the battle of Marignano, describing horrible scenes of carnage with immense gusto; after which he finds his way to Münster, where he is a spectator of the rising of the Anabaptists and its bloodthirsty suppression. The interval of nineteen years between Marignano (1515) and the Münster insurrection is calmly ignored. All the facts are borrowed, of course, from the historians; here the source is Sleidan's *Commentaries*, later on there is actual mention of Lanquet's *Chronicle*,[1] which is drawn upon wholesale. But the historical account is followed far from accurately, whether from carelessness or design.

[1] Thomas Lanquet's *Epitome of Chronicles* (*c.* 1549 or *c.* 1565).

Nashe puts his own opinions in Jack's mouth without scruple, often ruining consistency by intruding his comments into the narrative. He has no sympathy to spare for John of Leyden or his followers; to Nashe they were merely Puritans of a more outlandish and outrageous kind:

> Hear what it is to be Anabaptists, to be puritans, to be villains; you may be counted illuminate botchers for a while, but your end will be, Good people, pray for us.

Now there is a change in the story again. Back in England once more, Jack falls in at Middleborough with Henry Howard, Earl of Surrey, and is taken into his service. Surrey confides to him, in poetical language, his passion for the stately Geraldine—a fable that may have originated with Nashe. Entirely fictitious also is the relation that ensues of Surrey and Jack Wilton's adventurous travels on the Continent. Nashe himself had never been far from his native land,[1] and made up these imaginary experiences, by the method followed later on by Defoe, from written or oral accounts of travel, and also to an extent that must not be overlooked from the current translations of *novelle*.

Jack and the Earl of Surrey

The strangely matched couple visit Rotterdam and Wittenberg. They come across Sir Thomas More and Erasmus, witness a scholastical entertainment in honour of the Duke of Saxony, and a performance of *Acolastus*. They hear Luther and Carolostadius dispute, and are introduced to the learned Cornelius Agrippa, reputed the greatest conjurer in Europe. He shows them in a magic mirror the lively image of Geraldine, weeping for the absence of her lover. After a visit to the emperor's court they go on to Italy. Before leaving Germany they agreed to exchange names and conditions, Jack being now for a while known as the Earl of Surrey. The reasons given for this manœuvre are not very plausible: Surrey desired "to take more liberty of behaviour"—that is, to have full fling as an adventurer. But the true reason, more probably, was that Nashe wanted to reproduce the romantic situation beloved of old-fashioned story-tellers in a new setting. The disguise nearly costs them dear. At Venice they are brought to the house of a courtesan, Tabitha the

[1] McKerrow, v. 12-15.

Temptress, who, taking Surrey to be the servant, plots with him to kill and rob his supposed master.[1]

Of course Surrey tells Jack what is in the wind, and they arrange to discomfit the would-be murderess. Jack has his eye on her coffers, and exacts an enormous bribe not to bring her to justice. But the crafty quean passes off a quantity of counterfeit coin on her accusers, and our adventurous pair find themselves in durance. Jack bursts into a violent invective against the rascal who has led them into these straits :

> Detestable, detestable, that the flesh and the devil should deal by their factors. I'll stand to it, there is not a pander but hath vowed paganism. The devil himself is not such a devil as he, so be he perform his function aright. He must have the back of an ass, the snout of an elephant, the wit of a fox, and the teeth of a wolf ; he must fawn like a spaniel, crouch like a Jew, leer like a sheep-biter. If he be half a puritan, and have scripture continually in his mouth, he speeds the better.

Abuse and avoid euphuism as he might, Nashe cannot get away from the influence of Lyly.

The pair are released through the good offices of no less a person than Pietro Aretino—an episode that gives opportunity for a high-flown eulogy of that writer, whom Nashe admired and would fain imitate in his style. Whilst in prison, Jack picks up with Diamante, the ill-used wife of a magnifico, who has put her there on a false charge of unfaithfulness. The husband dies, and Jack makes off with Diamante and her ducats to ruffle it in Florence as the earl. Surrey is left in the lurch, but when they meet again Jack has a flattering excuse ready and they make it up ; but they resume their proper relationship, and Jack is again Surrey's servant.

Burlesque of chivalric romance

Romance is further travestied at Florence. Surrey visits the house where his Geraldine was born, and breaks into magnificats, eclipsing the sun and moon with comparisons, to the amusement of his page. Then, to signalize the event, he holds a tourney challenging all comers to dispute the beauty of his mistress. The narrative

[1] A curious instance of Nashe's ignorance of the country he was writing about occurs here. Tabitha's house, we are told, "stood upon vaults, which in two hundred years together were never searched" ; in these vaults she proposes to fling the body when the crime is completed. Commentators have tried in vain to explain away the absurdity of a house in Venice built upon vaults.

of the jousting outdoes the heroics of the *Arcadia* ludicrously; in the description how the knights were caparisoned the extravagances of both Sidney and the author of the *Hypnerotomachia* are burlesqued. Surrey's armour

was all intermixed with lilies and roses, and the bases thereof bordered with nettles and weeds, signifying stings, crosses, and overgrowing encumbrances in his love; his helmet round proportioned like a gardener's water-pot, from which seemed to issue forth small thrids of water, like cittern strings, that not only did moisten the lilies and roses, but did fructify as well the nettles and weeds, and made them overgrow their liege lord's. Whereby he did import thus much, that the tears that issued from his brain, as those artificial distillations issued from the well-counterfeit water-pot on his head, watered and gave life as well to his mistress' disdain (resembled to nettles and weeds) as increase of glory to her care-causing beauty (comprehended under the lilies and roses). The symbol thereto annexed was this, ex lachrimis lachrimæ.

Surrey being recalled to England, Jack and Diamante continue their journey to Rome, and are there during a famous plague. Nashe again seizes the opportunity to dilate on horrors, working up his description from Lanquet:

To smell of a nosegay that was poisoned, and turn your nose to a house that had the plague, it was all one. The clouds, like a number of cormorants that keep their corn till it stink and is musty, kept in their stinking exhalations, till they had almost stifled all Rome's inhabitants. Physicians' greediness of gold made them greedy of their destiny. They would come to visit those with whose infirmity their art had no affinity; and even as a man with a fee should be hired hang himself, so would they quietly go home and die presently after they had been with their patients. All day and all night long car-men did nothing but go up and down the streets with their carts and cry, "Have you any dead bodies to bury?" and had many times out of one house their whole loading: one grave was the sepulchre of seven score, one bed was the altar whereon whole families were offered.

Exaggerated descriptions of Italian life

Jack and his mistress become involved in events of the most melodramatic kind. Nashe accepted unquestioningly the view commonly held by his countrymen that Italy, in respect to morals, was a hell upon earth, a view corroborated by their reading of the *novelle*; and from his reading in the *novelle* he had no difficulty in improvising the villainous characters, motives and crimes required to paint what he probably thought an honest picture. In the general collapse of order during the plague all sorts of atrocities are perpetrated ; so Jack Wilton alleges. With the gusto of a modern exponent of "unshrinking realism," with the healthy appetite for horrors of a Kyd or Marlowe, he describes the doings of two hideous cut-throats, Esdras of Granada and Bartol, a desperate Italian, who break into plague-stricken houses, and steal all they can find of value, ravishing and murdering without remorse. Diamante is carried off, and Jack is seized as one of the criminals. He is saved at the foot of the gallows by a banished English nobleman, who lectures him on the folly of travelling abroad when England has so much that is better to offer. The sermon is in Nashe's best vein, and sufficiently shows what was the motive of the Italian episodes :

The first traveller was Cain, and he was called a vagabond runagate on the face of the earth. Travel like the travail wherein smiths put wild horses when they shoe them, is good for nothing but to tame and bring men under. God had no greater curse to lay upon the Israelites, than by leading them out of their own country to live as slaves in a strange land. That which was their curse, we Englishmen count our chief blessedness ; he is nobody who hath not travelled : we had rather live as slaves in another land, crouch and cap, and be servile to every jealous Italian's and proud Spaniard's humour, where we may neither speak, look, nor do anything but what pleaseth them, than live as freemen and lords in our own country.

He that is a traveller must have the back of an ass to bear all, a tongue like the tail of a dog to flatter all, the mouth of a hog to eat what is set before him, the ear of a merchant to hear all and say nothing : and if this be not the highest step of thraldom, there is no liberty or freedom.

From this satire on the tourist craze he proceeds to the peculiar objectionableness of Italy :

If thou dost but lend half a look to a Roman's or Italian's wife, thy porridge shall be prepared for thee, and cost thee nothing but thy life. Chance some of them break a bitter jest on thee, and thou retortest it severely, or seemest discontented : go to thy chamber, and provide a great banquet, for thou shalt sure to be visited with guests in a mask the next night, when in kindness and courtship thy throat shall be cut, and the doers return undiscovered. Nothing so long of memory as a dog; these Italians are old dogs, and will carry an injury a whole age in memory: I have heard of a box on the ear that hath been revenged thirty year after. The Neapolitan carrieth the bloodiest mind, and is the most secret fleering murderer: whereupon it is grown to a common proverb, I'll give him the Neapolitan shrug, when one intends to play the villain and makes no boast of it.

Meanwhile, Diamante has been playing him false, and Jack, stumbling into a cellar, finds her kissing an apprentice. All three are arrested on the allegation of a rascally Jew that they were engaged in robbing him, and Jack is handed over to the Jew to be his bondman. The Jew sells him to a physician for anatomical purposes. Jack's sensations on learning his fate are described with sardonic facetiousness:

O, the cold sweating cares which I conceived after I knew I should be cut up like a French summer doublet. Methought already the blood began to gush out at my nose: if a flea on the arm had but bit me, I deemed the instrument had pricked me. Well, well, I may scoff at a shrewd turn, but there's no such ready way to make a man a true Christian, as to persuade himself he is taken up for an anatomy. I'll depose I prayed then more than I did in seven year before. Not a drop of sweat trickled down my breast and my sides, but I dreamt it was a smooth-edged razor tenderly slicing down my breast and my sides. If any knocked at door, I supposed it was the beadle of Surgeon's Hall come for me. In the night I dreamed of nothing but phlebotomy, bloody fluxes, incarnatives, running ulcers.

He escapes dissection. The Pope's mistress happens to see Jack, and manages to get hold of him for the sake of his handsome person. The Jew sends her Diamante as a present, with secret instructions to poison her. The plot is revealed and the Jew put to horrible tortures, which are recounted in full. But while the lady Juliana is gone to salute the Pope on St Peter's Day, Jack and Diamante make off with her money and jewels, and escape to Bologna. There they witness the execution of another desperado, one Cutwolfe, Bartol's brother. Cutwolfe relates with cold-blooded glee how he had put Esdras to death for murdering his confederate, Bartol. In the hope of mercy he made him renounce God and devote his soul to hell, with terrible imprecations; then shot him dead, trusting to have destroyed both soul and body. The lesson is not lost upon Jack. He marries his light-o'-love, performs many alms-deeds, and hurries out of Italy, arriving at the English camp at the Field of the Cloth of Gold, that is, in 1520, fourteen years before the Münster rising—Jack ignores chronology right to the end.

Nashe's attitude in "Jack Wilton"—a counter-blast to other story-tellers

Nashe in his dedication calls *The Unfortunate Traveller* "this phantastical Treatise," and promises "some reasonable conveyance of history, and a variety of mirth." We have seen how well he fulfils this programme. It would be going too far to describe this as the first of the anti-romances; rather is it an effort to present the romance of actuality. Nashe beat his antagonists by shifting the ground. But there was hardly one of the varieties of fiction then before the public which Nashe omitted from his miscellany. His "cosening page" is not merely a jest-book hero, but also versed in the arts of cony-catching. He says: "I have done a thousand better jests if they had been booked in order as they were begotten," and he glories in being counted among the "fool-catchers." Greene's tales of foreign adventure, and the medley of history and fiction produced by Sidney, Greene, Lodge, and the other romancers, are left far in the rear. Nashe painted a more vivid though not a more accurate picture of Italy than his rivals had painted of darkest London, and vied in sensational interest with the *novella* whilst recounting the successive haps and hazards of a grand tour. He parodied Sidney's feats of chivalric prowess and his love-lorn elegies, yet thrilled his readers by unearthing a magic mirror in a real town of Germany, and evoking the seraphic image of Surrey's Geraldine. Scott was to draw inspiration from that incident, and Coleridge from the lady's name; the poets invented a whole love-romance for her and Surrey. The one thing Nashe did not do was to imitate the Spanish rogue-story.[1]

Nashe, however, was only a pioneer. His story is as forced and as unlikely as the romances that it parodies. But he was undoubtedly

[1] Most critics will have it that Nashe was trying to emulate *Lazarillo de Tormes*, and that his is the first English example of picaresque fiction. Professor F. M. Warren is one of the most positive, and finds a singularly close resemblance in *Jack Walton*—as he persistently calls the book—to Aleman's *Guzman de Alfarache*, published five years later. He thinks that Nashe and Aleman, both having Lazarillo before them, may have been indebted further to picaresque stories that have disappeared (*History of the Novel before the Seventeenth Century*, pp. 339-342). There is not the slightest need to postulate any such thing.

successful in the competitive task that he undertook. No man could tell a tale more vigorously. Though no better than the rest of his group at character-drawing, a thing little understood or expected in prose fiction as yet ; nevertheless his pusillanimous cider-seller is more than a good rough daub in the low-comedy style. His merit was to have substantiated the claims of real life as material for a rousing story, and to have mingled the comic with the grim and terrifying in a new and remarkable way.

CHAPTER XI

DELONEY AND OTHERS

Thomas Deloney's place in the history of fiction

ALTHOUGH two of his three works of fiction were reprinted during the nineteenth century,[1] the novelist Deloney was strangely overlooked by chroniclers of literature, and his right to a foremost place in the history of Elizabethan fiction passed unrecognized until, in 1908, a critical edition of his whole works was published by F. O. Mann. His name does not occur in the fullest account hitherto written of the Elizabethan novel. Even from his contemporaries he never had his due. That he was widely read among people of his own rank in life there can be no question ; his stories were continually reprinted for more than a century after his death. But Greene, Nashe, Harvey, and others of like pretensions speak of him only in disparagement as a vulgar ballad-monger, and Strype condemns him as a disreputable fellow who had stirred up discontent among the lower orders by a scurrilous ballad on the scarcity of corn, and was in hiding to escape arrest.[2]

His life and work

Thomas Deloney (? 1543-1600) was not born in the upper middle class, nor was he educated at a university. It might well be said that he belonged to no class at all, for as a ballad-maker voicing popular grievances he was a nuisance to the magistrates, and was liable, not merely to be lumped with the unfortunates and ne'er-do-wells described by Awdeley and Harman, but to be summarily apprehended as a vagrant, branded and put in the pillory.[3] Such were the laws brought about by stagnation of trade, unemployment, high cost of living, and the consequent destitution and disorder. Deloney obtained his education, and his acquirements were far from contemptible, in the school of adversity ; and, like Bunyan, Burns,

[1] *Thomas of Reading* (W. J. Thoms's *Early English Prose Romances*, 1858) and *The Pleasant History of John Winchcomb*, ed. J. W. Halliwell (1859).

[2] *Works of Deloney*, ed. F. O. Mann : introduction, viii.-ix.

[3] Chevalley, A., *Thomas Deloney : le roman des métiers au temps de Shakespeare* (Paris, 1926).

and other writers nearer our own time, he profited by these circumstances when he became an author. Greene and Dekker could hardly be accepted as infallible witnesses on the social conditions about which they were so fluent. Deloney wrote from intimate acquaintance; he knew the people whom he portrayed, he had shared their lot, and was, in fact, writing for them to read. Hence his transparent truth and raciness, and the charm of unsophisticated ease and simplicity.

About the man few facts are extant. He is supposed to have been a native of Norwich, but the date of his birth can only be conjectured. His name suggests a French origin, and his family may have come over with the Flemish and Walloon refugees who settled in Norfolk in the fourteenth century, or with the Huguenots who arrived in the sixteenth.[1] Both these immigrations helped to strengthen the position of Norfolk as a centre of the textile industry. Deloney was a silk-weaver; this craft was largely in the hands of foreign operatives. Strype mentions a book of his written for the silk-weavers, containing "foolish and disorderly matter"; but whether this was another story-book is unknown, as the work has vanished. From his wide and accurate knowledge of towns and villages and of the roads of England it may be gathered that he led an unsettled life down to the period, about 1596, when he is found living in Cripplegate, earning a precarious livelihood by his ballads, and then by his prose tales of the clothing and shoemaking industries. He had succeeded Elderton as the laureate of the working classes.

Deloney a pamphleteer on behalf of the great clothiers, etc.

1596 was the year of the great dearth, which came as a terrible aggravation of the ills from which his fellow-workmen were suffering, through a complicated series of checks and disturbances in the textile trade. It was desirable that public attention should be called to the effects of the legal restraints which were hampering the industry, as Deloney does, in *Jack of Newbery*, in a cautious and roundabout way.[2] It was also eminently desirable that the nation

[1] *Op. cit.*,, pp. 33-37, on Deloney's probabe French ancestry; and *passim* on the effect of the influx of foreigners on the weaving industry.

[2] The economic questions underlying Deloney's three works of fiction are admirably set forth by M. Abel Chevalley, in his *Thomas Deloney: le roman des métiers au temps de Shakespeare* (Paris, 1926). The Tudor period was a critical time in the evolution of industry. The mediæval guild system was obsolescent, and the guilds themselves, bolstered up by royal charters, were degenerating into close corporations that strove by every device to keep down

and the Government should realize that the manufactures based upon wool were the staple industries of the country, and the main source of its wealth, as coal was to be in the future. The latter object Deloney could pursue without fear of censure. It may be that he was actually employed by the manufacturing houses whose praises he sings to write his novels of industrial life, and that he was suitably rewarded for his services. Perhaps, without any promise of reward, he voluntarily took up the task which he had at heart.[1] The dedication of his first story "to all famous Cloth-workers of England" merely states that if his offering be kindly accepted he will think his pains well recompensed, and that "finding your gentleness answering my hope" he will proceed with the history of Thomas of Reading and other distinguished clothiers. But the possibility that he was not unmoved by the expectation of reward gains in likelihood the more his accounts of commercial enterprise are studied in connexion with

or extinguish competitors. Manufactures were tending to move from the towns into the country. In the provincial towns and villages large businesses were growing up, like Jack of Newbury's or Thomas of Reading's. These represented the transition from the guild to the domestic system of manufacture. It was a stage in the gradual progress towards modern capitalism, and it performed most of the functions of modern capitalist enterprise; yet it preserved the community of interest and the social equality between master and worker that had characterized the guild. The workers were not yet mere hands; the master was a friend and associate, not a mere employer. In the metropolis the change had hardly begun. A London tradesman with his journeymen and prentices still formed a self-contained establishment not far removed from that of the mediæval guildsman. The welfare of the City merchant depended on the loyalty and good will of those who worked for him, or rather with him. The organization of his business was simple, and hinged upon none of those complex external conditions which were controlling factors in the other case. But the great clothier in the West or the North had to see to the production of wool, to weaving, dyeing, fulling, and other operations in the manufacture of cloth, and to the vital business of marketing; and commercial success depended on his carrying on these varied activities undisturbed. He stood for the principle of *laissez-faire*, the conservative guilds for protective regulation and monopoly; and the Government was on the side of the guilds, not perceiving the inevitability of the change that was occurring, not realizing the great access of wealth it was bringing in its train. Hence much hostile legislation aimed at the cloth trade. Such a measure as the Weavers Act of 1555 was a bulwark in defence of the guilds. Other restrictions were due to the exigencies of foreign policy. Strikes, unemployment and vagabondage were the results of these blows at a thriving industry; other causes aggravated the state of unrest, which was at its worst in 1596, the year of the great scarcity of corn, and the year before Deloney's *Jack of Newbery* appeared.

[1] The question is discussed by Chevalley (pp. 239-245), who concludes from the absence of any mention of remuneration in his preface to the first part of *The Gentle Craft* that Deloney was at any rate not actually commissioned to write up the clothing business.

the economic history of the period, and if it be a fact it would not be to his discredit. He makes no overt bid for patronage, in any extant passage of his works ; it was hardly necessary to do so. In the inscription of the second part of his *Gentle Craft*, however, to the master and wardens of the worshipful company of Cordwainers, his reference to the " gentle look " they had lent to the previous volume can hardly mean anything else than a monetary acknowledgment of his services, and a trust in favours to come. However this may be, Deloney's three books show no injurious signs of having been written to order. He retained the confidence of his fellow-artisans, and died in poverty the last year of the century.

"Jack of Newbery"

The Pleasant Historie of John Winchcomb, in his younger yeares called Jack of Newbery, the famous and worthy Clothier of England (1597), is no doubt an imaginative account of a real person, though the history it contains is merely traditional. Jack lived at Newbury under Henry VII. and his son, and is known to have died in 1519. Deloney, who must at some period have dwelt at Newbury, as his familiarity with the place and its traditions shows, composes a sort of popular biography, describing the rise of a successful tradesman ; who starts life as a mechanic, marries his master's widow, and becomes the head of a thriving business, entertains royalty, and is offered knighthood by the king, but prefers to remain in his russet suit, the friend and equal of the men and women who labour under him. His huge establishment at Newbury is stated to be one of many in different parts of the kingdom, all providing employment and a comfortable living for a multitude of workers, and adding abundantly to the country's wealth. Within one room there were two hundred looms, each tended by a man and a boy ; in a place hard by a hundred women were carding wool, and two hundred maidens spinning in another ; sevenscore children were picking wool, fifty men shearing, and fourscore rolling cloth, besides dyers, fullers, and those at work in the brewery, bakehouse and kitchen, to furnish good cheer for this vast household. It is a typical example of the system that was superseding the city guilds of the Middle Ages—a prosperous and contented community, the master not yet a mere employer of hands, but rather the head of a family for whose welfare he felt himself responsible, and every member of which was his social equal and knew that their interests were identical. The episode of Government interference under Henry VIII., Jack's tactful protest, and Wolsey's discomfiture, are Deloney's indirect way of pleading against similar interferences that were ruining the trade at the time of writing. What could be more effective than his detailed picture in impressing upon his readers the value of such a busy hive to the nation, and the widespread loss any stoppage would entail? John Winchcomb's career, with this significant episode, is the main theme; but the story is filled out with other features, some much the worse for wear, some entirely new.

The older are borrowings from the jest-books and the collections of popular tales, and occasionally, though not so often as in *The Gentle Craft,* from the romances. The new were Deloney's homely picturing of a sphere of life that the romancers would never have humbled themselves to allude to, and the humorous handling of idiosyncrasy. Jack himself, though not half so good as some later figures, is an interesting person clearly drawn. Rather a stolid and sheepish fellow at first, he seems to be too dull to perceive what his mistress is after. But he knows very well on which side his bread is buttered. Jack, indeed, is a prototype of Samuel Smiles's industrious young men, who combine moral and economic self-interest, acquire both wealth and a virtuous character, and enjoy the very best of both worlds.[1] Further, he is a bit of a humorist, and, as Deloney's purpose demanded, has vision and courage enough to take the lead in facing and conciliating the king and parrying the malicious thrusts of the cardinal. Though transformed from poor prentice to wealthy magnate, he is consistently drawn from beginning to end.

Deloney's natural dialogue

His mistress has cast an amorous eye on Jack, but the discreet journeyman does not respond until she takes the irrevocable step. Meanwhile, she is courted by the tailor, the tanner and the parson. Here is a snatch of the best dialogue that had been seen as yet in an English prose tale:

Quoth she, "For want of the Sexton, here is the Priest if you need him."

"Marry," quoth the Tanner, "in good time, for by this means we need not go far to be married."

[1] The mercenary, utilitarian spirit of Deloney's typical characters, combined with the spirit of independence and honest self-respect, appears again in Defoe's tradesmen, not to mention Pepys. It is a thoroughly English trait.

"Sir," quoth the Parson, "I shall do my best in convenient place."

"Wherein?" quoth the Tanner.

"To wed her myself," quoth the Parson.

"Nay soft," said the Widow, "one swallow makes not a summer, nor one meeting a marriage: as I lighted on you unlooked for, so came I hither unprovided for the purpose."

There is a touch of the *Mery Tales and Quicke Answeres* here, but less than in several passages of coarser repartee. Deloney is probably the first English writer to spice his conversations with dialect, and probably also the first to make play with the malaprop. After his marriage to the widow and her demise, Jack seeks another partner, and sees the makings of a good housewife in a comely maid who is the daughter of a poor man dwelling at Aylesbury in Buckinghamshire. The old peasant is amazed when he beholds Jack's warehouses, full of wool and broadcloth and kerseys:

"Sir," quoth the old man, "I wis che zee you be bominable rich, and cham content you shall have my daughter, and God's blessing and mine light on you both."

"But father," quoth Jack of Newbery, "what will you bestow with her?"

"Marry, hear you!" quoth the old man, "I' vaith cham but a poor man, but I thong God, cham of good exclamation among my neighbours, and they will as zoon take my vice for anything as a richer man's. Thick I will bestow, you shall have with a good will, because che hear very good condemnation of you in every place; therefore chil give you twenty nobles and a weaning calf; and when I die and my wife, you shall have the revelation of all my goods."

When Jack heard his offer, he was straight content, making more reckoning of the woman's modesty than her father's money.

The wedding endured ten days, "to the great relief of the poor that dwelt all about." Jack receives the daughter's portion from the old man and his wife, thanking them for their good will and courtesy, and in requital making them handsome presents of money for their expenses and of broadcloth for their apparel.

"O my good zon," quoth the old woman, "Christ's benizon be with thee evermore; for to tell thee true, we had zold all our kine to make money for my daughter's marriage, and this zeven year we should not have been able to buy more. Notwithstanding, we should have zold all that ever we had, before my poor wench should have lost her marriage."

"Ay," quoth the old man, "chud have zold my coat from my back, and my bed from under me, before my girl should have gone without you."

The healthy sentiment, so naturally expressed, makes one think of the corresponding situation in *Pamela* ; the contrast between Deloney's sturdy independence and Richardson's obsequiousness is not more remarkable than the natural way in which he puts in his strokes of tenderness and pathos. Deloney was obviously a man, like all his protagonists, with his heart in the right place, which is no small virtue in a novelist, and with as much sense as sensibility, which is a greater.

Mockery of euphuism

Deloney makes mock of euphuism ; though, unfortunately, when he has to mount the high horse of romance, in *The Gentle Craft* and elsewhere, he drops into a feeble echo of it himself. Here, however, we see him poking fun at all such affectations. Jack's first wife is the speaker, after a tussle of wills in which she has come off best.

"Husbands," quoth she, "think that women are like starlings, that will burst their gall before they will yield to the fowler ; or like the fish Scolopendra, that cannot be touched without danger. Notwithstanding, as the hard steel doth yield to the hammer's stroke, being used to his kind, so will women to their husbands, where they are not too much crossed. And seeing ye have sworn to give me my will, I vow likewise that my wilfulness shall not offend you. I tell you, husband, the noble nature of woman is such, that for their loving friends they will not stick (like the pelican) to pierce their own hearts to do them good. And therefore forgiving each other all injuries past, having also tried one another's patience, let us quench these burning coals of contention, with the sweet juice of a faithful kiss, and shaking hands, bequeath all our anger to the eating up of this caudle."

Elsewhere it is often doubtful whether Deloney writes as a euphuist because an episode calls for magniloquence, or is smiling at the convention. At all events, there is a pretty quaintness about such a passage as the wooing of Crispine and Ursula, in *The Gentle Craft*, that is far from unpleasing.

The speech just quoted of Mistress Winchcomb's gives the moral of an incident borrowed, like a good many others, from the older story-books. When the widow and Jack are married, she takes to gadding about, and coming home late one night is locked out by her husband. Presently, when she has been knocking a long while, Jack looks out of the window and tells her to ask the constable for a bed.

Debts to older story-books

"I hope," quoth she, "you will not shut me out of doors like a dog, or let me lie in the streets like a strumpet."

"Whether like a dog or drab," quoth he, "all is one to me, knowing no reason, but that as you have stayed out all day for your delight, so you may lie forth all night for my pleasure. Both birds and beasts at the night's approach repair to their rest, and observe a convenient time to return to their habitation. Look upon the poor spider, the frog, the fly and every other silly worm, and you shall see all these observe time to return to their home: and if you, being a woman, will not do the like, content yourself to bear the brunt of your own folly: and so farewell."

Of course he relents when she has had her lesson. But she is not going to take her lesson meekly. As Jack lets her in, his wife pretends that she has dropped her wedding-ring, and entreats him to look for it. Whilst he is searching outside the door, she whips in and locks him out. Then the dialogue is repeated with the positions reversed. Jack begs her to let him in. She at the window gives him back his own sermon:

"How now, Jack, am I even with you? What, John, my man, were you so lusty to lock your dame out of doors? Sirra, remember you bade me go to the constable to get lodging, now you have leisure to try if his wife will prefer you to a bed. You, sir saucy, that made me stand in the cold, till my feet did freeze, and my teeth chatter, while you stood preaching of birds and beasts, telling me a tale of spiders, flies, and frogs: go try now if any of them will be so friendly to let thee have lodging."

It is an excellent adaptation of the story from Petrus Alphonsus in the *Alphabet of Tales*[1]; a closer version is that of Tofano and his wife, in the *Decameron*.[2] Other incidents of the *fabliau* kind are much more brutal—for instance, the one in which Jack's servants pay out a would-be seducer by putting him to bed with a drugged pig.

Jack grows so rich and powerful that he is able to provide two

[1] Volume I. pp. 271-273.

[2] VII., iv.

Protest against Government interference with trade

hundred and fifty men at his own cost to serve in the Flodden campaign. Henry VIII., on a progress into Berkshire, pays him a visit, and is royally entertained. Here, and in the chapter narrating how the clothiers of England joined together to petition the king against the hindrances to traffic into other countries, Deloney indirectly submits his case for a more liberal policy under Henry's daughter, Elizabeth. Jack of Newbury puts the economic situation in the form of an apologue enacted in pantomime. At the approach of the king, Jack's men are seen drawn up, with swords and bucklers, in front of an ant-hill, and when the king sends for him he refuses to budge. The king good-humouredly rides up and receives Jack's interpretation of the show. It is a covert protest at the policy of Wolsey, instigator of the war with the emperor which had ruined the cloth-merchants' Continental trade. Jack is Prince of the Ants, whose industrious commonwealth is disturbed by the Mole, the Grasshopper, the Caterpillar, but chiefly the Butterfly, who would take away the eggs. The Butterfly is Wolsey, who hides his resentment, and after further passages at arms over the petition of the merchants concedes their request; "so that within short space clothing was again very good, and poor men as well set on work as before."[1]

Before his second book on the clothing trade, Deloney was induced to take up the subject of the cordwainers. In this case he had no such battle to fight as in the other two books. His new patrons wanted it to be understood that their apprentices and journeymen were the happiest people in London, and Deloney was just the man to give them a first-class advertisement.

"The Gentle Craft"

The Gentle Craft. A most merry and pleasant Historie, not altogether vnprofitable, nor any way hurtfull: very fit to passe away the tediousnes of the long winters euenings (1598), came out in two parts, probably in 1597 and 1598; a third, promised in the preface to the second part, cannot be traced and may never have been written. *The Gentle Craft* celebrates the history and achievements of the shoemakers, beginning with the legendary stories of St Hugh and St Winifred, and of Crispin and Crispian, patron saints of the craft, and coming down to contemporary times. Deloney follows the same plan as had succeeded so well in *John Winchcomb.* The tales

[1] Chevalley, 83-87.

of old time are borrowed from *The Golden Legend* ; Grafton and Holinshed's chronicles supplied some historical details, more came from local tradition. Farcical anecdotes as old as the *fabliaux* are served up in a new shape, reminiscences of ballad-histories and of the debased popular versions of the romances are worked into the motley fabric ; even Shakespeare's *Romeo and Juliet* may have suggested the turn given to the love-story of Crispin, the runaway prince disguised as a shoemaker, and the emperor's daughter Ursula.[1] But it is Deloney's thorough knowledge of Westminster and the City, the streets, shops, taverns, and the manners and customs of the tradesmen and their apprentices, and the womenfolk, from the stately city dame to the alehouse wench, that gives life and colour to his patchwork of stories.

The career of Simon Eyre

Having conscientiously rehearsed the consecrated legends of the craft, Deloney dismisses St Hugh, Crispin, Crispian and Ursula, and brings the first of his modern heroes on the scene. This is the half-legendary Sir Simon Eyre, who, beginning life as a cobbler's apprentice, rose by dint of good luck and sagacity to be Lord Mayor of London, and is said to have founded Leadenhall (1419). Having had the pluck to buy the rich cargo of a foreign vessel that had been driven ashore, and making a large sum out of the speculation, Eyre sets up as a merchant, and grows very wealthy. He becomes sheriff, and in due course Lord Mayor, and the progress of him and his wife to the highest civic honours is described with abundant humour. There is an amusing underplot interwoven, how a Frenchman falls in love with one of Mistress Eyre's maids, and is circumvented by the apprentice, Haunce the Dutchman. Dekker appropriated both plot and underplot in his jovial comedy, *The Shoemaker's Holiday*, introducing more romantic business.[2] Haunce becomes the nephew of the Earl of Lincoln, who labours in the workshop as Hans, the apprentice from Holland, for the love of Rose, daughter of Lord Mayor Oateley, whom his father forbids him to marry.

Dekker's rumbustious Simon Eyre, with his "Prince am I none, yet am I princely born," is a much more expansive figure than Deloney's shrewd tradesman ; and his Dame Margery, with the

[1] F. O. Mann, notes to *The Gentle Craft*, 523.

[2] On the story of Crispin and Crispian in Part I. Rowley based his play, *A Shoomaker a Gentleman*, acted in 1609.

airs and graces she puts on after her promotion, is a different creature altogether. "Of a truth," says the lady in *The Gentle Craft*, after she and her husband had been entertained at the Lord Mayor's table, and plain Simon Eyre had been accosted as Master Eyre,

> although I sat closely by my lady's side, I could eat nothing for very joy, to hear and see that we were so much made of. And never give me credit husband, if I did not hear the officers whisper as they stood behind me, and all demanded one of another, what you were, and what I was. "Oh," quoth one, "do you see this man? Mark him well, and mark his wife well, that simple woman that sits next my lady: what are they?" "What are they?" quoth another; "marry this is the rich shoemaker that bought all the goods in the rich argosy: I tell you there was never such a shoemaker seen in London since the city was builded." "Now by my faith," quoth the third, "I have heard much of him to-day among the merchants in the street, going between the two Chains." Credit me, husband, of mine honesty this was their communication. Nay, and do you not remember, when the rich citizen drank to you, which craved pardon because he knew not your name, what my Lord Mayor said? "Sir," quoth he, "his name is Master Eyre," did you mark that? and presently thereupon he added these words: "This is the gentleman that bought," and so forth.

Richard Casteler

Part II. of *The Gentle Craft* gives the romance of another merchant prince, Richard Casteler, and follows this up with the exploits of a sturdy citizen, Master Peachey, and the adventures of divers other votaries of St Hugh, such as the happy-go-lucky apprentice, Tom Drum, which connect the several chapters in a random sequence. The most striking personage in the early chapters is certainly Long Meg of Westminster, already the heroine of a chap-book, *The Life and Pranks of Long Meg of Westminster* (1582), a young woman of great strength and stature who was credited with as many coarse practical jokes as was the average hero of the jest-books. Deloney makes her out to be a more personable sort of Madge Wildfire, with a touch of the Celestina in her cheerful fatalism. She and another maiden, Gillian of the George, who seems to be his own creation, nourish a secret fondness for his paragon of a shoemaker, Richard Casteler. This worthy had been celebrated already as the Cock of Westminster, and is mentioned by Holinshed and Grafton.[1] He turns a cold shoulder to the two young women

Long Meg of Westminster

[1] Mann, 531.

who pester him, having given his heart elsewhere. Riming Robin, a merry young journeyman who for his singing was held in high repute among the shoemakers, gives each of the lovesick maidens a private hint that Richard will be found in the evening in Tuttle Fields, the spot now commemorated by the name of Tothill Street, Westminster. Thither both severally repair, pretending to be looking for herbs, whilst Robin derides them for their infatuation.

When Meg saw that Gillian would not away, at last she came unto her, asking what she made there.

"Nay, what do you here?" quoth she; "for my own part I was sent for to seek heartsease, but I can find nothing but sorrel."

"Alack, good soul!" quoth Meg, "and I came to gather thrift, but can light on nothing but thistles, and therefore I will get my ways home as fast as I can."

"In doing so you shall do well," quoth Gillian, "but I mean to get some heartsease ere I go away."

"Nay Gillian," quoth she, "I am sure I shall find thrift as soon as you shall find heartsease, but I promise you I am out of hope to find any to-day."

"I pray you, get you gone then," quoth she.

"What would you so fain be rid of my company?" quoth Meg; "for that word I mean not to be gone yet. I' faith, Gill, I smell a rat."

"Then," quoth she, "you have as good a nose as our grey cat; but what rat do you smell, tell me? I doubt, I doubt if there be any rat in the field, you would fain catch him in your trap, if you knew how. But, i' faith, Meg, you shall be deceived, as cunning as you are."

"Then, belike," quoth Meg, "you would not have the rat taste no cheese but your own."

"All is one for that," said Gillian, "but wheresoever he run I would have him creep into no corner of yours."

"Your words are mystical," quoth Meg, "but if thou art a good wench, let us go home together."

"Not so," said Gillian, "as I came not with you, so I mean not to go with you."

"No?" quoth Meg, "before God I swear I will stay as long as thou for thy life."

"In troth," quoth she, "I will make you stay till midnight then."

"Yea?" quoth Meg, "now, as sure as I live I will try that." And in this humour sometimes they sat them down, and sometimes they stalked round about the field, till it was dark night, and so late, that at last the watch met with them, who, contrary to Gillian's mind, took pains to bring them both home together: at what time they gave one another such privy flouts that the watchmen took no little delight to hear it.

When Robin brought the maids two willow garlands in token that Richard is another's,

Meg, being merrily inclined, shook off sorrow in this sort, and gently taking the willow garland, said: "Wherefore is grief good? Can it recall folly past? No. Can it help a matter remediless? No. Can it restore losses or draw us out of danger? No. What then? Can grief make unkind men courteous? No. Can it bring long life? No, for it doth rather hasten our death. What then can it do. Can it call our friends out of their graves? No. . . . Then wherefore should I grieve? except I went to kill myself. Nay, seeing it is so, hang sorrow, I will never care for them that care not for me, and therefore a fig for the Cock of Westminster!"

This is obviously a flight inspired by Falstaff's soliloquy on honour.[1] Deloney, however, could rival Shakespeare in the dialogue of low comedy on his own account, as Professor F. W. Chandler has pointed out.[2]

Master Peachey

Exit Casteler and enter lusty Peachey, in the probably fictitious rôle of a shoemaker of Fleet Street, "who kept all the year forty tall men on work, besides prentices," and went to the court on St George's day with all his men about him, to attend upon his lord, the Duke of Suffolk. Two young bloods, Stuteley and Strangwidge, gallant sea-captains attired all in crimson velvet, are incensed at this presumption, and swear to take him down a notch. They seek out

[1] *1 Hen. IV.*, v. 1, 127 *et seq.*

[2] Chandler, F. W., *The Literature of Roguery*, i. 72. The passage instanced is from *Jack of Newbery*, where the maids revenge themselves on Dame Tittle-Tattle Gossip Pintpot, by making her drunk so that "she thought the world ran round." "Your master!" quoth she, "I knew your master a boy, when he was called Jack of Newbury, ay Jack, I knew him called plain Jack; and your mistress, now she is rich, and I am poor, but it's no matter, I knew her a draggle-tail girl, mark ye." "But now," quoth they, "she takes upon her lustily, and hath quite forgot what she was." "Tush! what will you have of a green thing?" quoth she. "Here I drink to you, so long as she goes where she list a-gossiping. And it's no matter, little said is soon amended. But hear you, my masters, though Mistress Winchcomb go in her hood, I am as good as she; I care not who tell it her. I spend not my husband's money in cherries and codlings, go to, go to, I know what I say well enough; I thank God I am not drunk. Mistress Winchcomb, mistress! No, Nan Winchcomb, I will call her name, plain Nan."

his shop in Fleet Street, and demand the master. The foreman comes forward and inquires what is their will.

"Why, knave," quoth they, "what carest thou, let us speak with thy master."

"Gentlemen," quoth he, "if you lack any such commodity as we make, you shall find me sufficient to serve you, for to that end hath my master set me in the shop."

"Why, Jack-sauce," quoth Stuteley, "you whoreson peasant, know you to whom you speak?"

The fellow being very choleric, and somewhat displeased at these disdainful speeches, made him this round answer: "Ask you to whom I speak?" quoth he.

"Aye, goodman Flat-cap," said Strangwidge, "we ask to whom you speak."

"Sir," quoth he, "I speak to a velvet fool, a silken slave that knows not how to govern his tongue."

With that Stuteley swore like a madman and presently drew out a dudgeon-haft dagger that he had by his side, and began to lay at the fellow; which one of his fellows seeing flung a last at his head and felled him to the ground. Strangwidge thereupon drew his sword, but by that time the fellow had took down his sword and buckler, which hung in the shop hard at hand, and therewith so well defended himself that Strangwidge could do him no hurt, and by that time Stuteley recovering crawled up again.

Prentices and journeymen

Master Peachey now appears, to inquire about the hurly-burly, and seeing whence the provocation had come espouses his journeymen's quarrels. Stuteley dares him to meet himself and his fellow with forty of his men. Peachey accepts the challenge, and, appearing on the field with one follower, gives the bullies a sound drubbing. Wherever they go the swashbucklers find themselves running up against Peachey's men, two at a time, and always getting the worst of it; so that at length they beg the Duke of Suffolk's intervention, and a peace is patched up, entirely to the credit of the redoubtable shoemaker. Deloney's democratic spirit is revealed, not only in these episodes of conflict between the courtier and the citizen, but also in his hearty enjoyment of such jolly, raffish characters as Riming Robin and Tom Drum. Tom, English counterpart to the Spanish *picaro*, but English to the backbone, is an original, who, sitting one day in his master's shop at Petworth, and seeing how sweetly the sun shines and how trimly the trees are decked with leaves, picks up staff and pack and betakes him to the road. He falls in by the wayside with Harry Neville, a young gentleman who has run away from home ; and proving to him by many instances that a shoemaker is as fine a fellow as any scion of gentility, carries him off to find a job under Master Peachey. Tom's tales are as astounding and as apocryphal as those of Sir John Mandeville, which they were perhaps intended to parody ; with them he beguiles the long trudge to London, and keeps everyone agog when he gets there. But his boastfulness is his undoing. Harry Neville presently enlists himself among the many aspirants to the hand of a wealthy widow of Fleet Street, with whom, Tom brags, he is such a favourite that she can refuse him nothing. He offers to take Harry to her house and recommend him to her good graces ; but when the pair knock at her door they receive such a snub that it becomes a proverb, when a man gets a shrewish welcome it is Tom Drum's entertainment. Tom runs away to hide his shame, and enlists with the Scots army in the Musselburgh campaign. He turns up again later, discoursing all his adventures in the wars,

> and according to his old cogging humour, attributed other men's deeds to himself, " for," quoth he, " it was I that killed the first Scot in the battle, yet I was content to give the honour thereof to Sir Michael Musgrave, notwithstanding," quoth he, " all men knows that this hand of mine killed Tom Trotter, that terrible traitor, which in despite of us kept the castle so long, and at last as he cowardly forsook it, and secretly sought to fly, with this blade of mine I broached him like a roasting pig."

Harry, after Tom's exit, continues his addresses to Mistress Farmer, and cuts out his formidable rival, Dr Burket (the Dr Burcot of *Kind-Harts Dreame* and popular renown) ; but both are eventually discomfited by a prentice dwelling in the widow's house, who leads her to the altar. The sentimental comedy of the masterful dame and the lovesick prentice, whose devotion she tries by making him do scullion's work, is a very quaint affair.

The final episode in *The Gentle Craft* is a variation on one of Deloney's pet themes, the bankrupt merchant rebuffed by those who had courted him in his days of prodigality. The shoemaker hero is an oddity known as the Green King, " a man very humorous, of small stature, but very courageous," who kept thirty or forty servants, and when he went walking always carried a two-handed sword on his shoulder. His substance wasted by these riotous expenses but his pride undiminished, the Green King goes abroad to repair his fortunes. His wife, however, has better luck than he, and by the time he returns she has put their business on its legs again. At this revival of prosperity she again receives polite attentions from her faithless friends; but she turns on them and gives them a piece of her mind:

The Green King and his wife

"Ay, neighbour," quoth she, "I know your kindness and may speak thereof by experience: well may I compare you to him that would never bid any man to dinner, but at two of the clock in the afternoon, when he was assured they had filled their bellies before, and that they would not touch his meat, except for manners' sake; wherefore for my part I will give you thanks, when I take benefit of your proffer."

"Why, neighbour, we speak for good will," quoth they.

"'Tis true," quoth she, "and so say they that call for a fresh quart to bestow on a drunken man, when they know it would do him as much good in his boots as in his belly."

"Well, neighbour," quoth they, "God be thanked that you have no need to use friends."

"Mary, Amen," quoth she, "for if I had, I think I should find few here."

One of the Green King's cronies is the celebrated ballad-singer, old Anthony Now-now (another of those who play a part in *Kind-Harts Dreame*). Deloney seems to have invented the incident of Tom Drum and the widow to furnish an explanation of the saying about Tom Drum's entertainment. So he here brings forward Anthony to give the origin of his nickname.

> When is the best time to drink with a friend?
> When is it meetest my money to spend?
> O Anthony, now, now, now.

So sings the old fiddler, as he and the Green King sit drinking in the tavern. Even in these small touches we see how closely Deloney tied himself to tradition.

Deloney's comedy is of a lowly type, not disdainful of high jinks and horseplay. The master who comes home unexpectedly and interrupts the maid's little party is accidentally paid out by sitting down on the scalding posset, in the unlucky place where they have hidden

Deloney's humour

it. Two other maids who were going to wash down their venison with a bottle of the best Rhenish in London are astonished to find that somebody has drunk the wine and refilled the bottle with water.

"We'll drink it out of the bottle," said Joan.

"Not so," quoth Florence, "I do love to see what I drink, and therefore I'll borrow a glass at the next house."

And while she goes for a glass, said Joan to herself, "I'll have a taste of it before she returns again"; and then setting her hand unto the bottle and the bottle to her mouth, she drank a good draught, and finding it to be something thin in the going down, she said to Bess that sat by, "Credit me now, but for the name of wine, I have drunk as good water."

"It is Rhenish wine," quoth Bess, "and that is never strong."

"It may be made of rain well enough," quoth Joan.

At which words Florence entered with a glass, and pouring it into the glass, she extolled the colour, saying, "See what a brave colour it hath; it is as clear, I do assure you, as rock water"; and therewithal drinking it off she said, "It drinks very dead: of a troth," quoth she, "this is but bad wine, it is even as dead as a door-nail." And so, filling the glass again, she gave it unto Bess.

She tasting thereof said, "Passion of me! this is plain water."

"Water?" said Joan, "is it water? Let me taste of it once again: by my maidenhead, it is water indeed," quoth she.

Of *fabliau* extraction is probably the story of the blind priest who cannot say mass without having the book in front of him and his spectacles on his nose. Bandello's tale of the priest who refuses to bury a dead man until the poverty-stricken widow pays his fee, the tale already found in Smyth's *Tragicall Hystories*,[1] is retold, and the summary act of the Duke of Milan in having him flung into the grave is ascribed to Sir John Rainsford, who finds a refuge from the arm of the law in Peachey's shop, and afterwards wins the royal pardon by his gallantry in a skirmish with the French. Leland had attributed the crime to a man named Neville.[2] Many of the names in Deloney's pages can be traced to local tradition or to ballad literature, though the name and the character, or the name and the story, are often curiously changed round about.

"Thomas of Reading"

Deloney's last novel, *Thomas of Reading or The sixe worthie yeomen of the West*, which deserves the name of novel better than either of the others, is made of the same kind of material, but is

[1] See p. 34.

[2] Mann, 534.

notably superior in construction. Thomas Cole, the rich clothier of Reading, is probably the offspring of tradition, and, as Fuller contended, at least as fictitious as King Arthur and Guy of Warwick.[1] The other five yeomen, Gray of Gloucester, Sutton of Salisbury, Fitzallen of Worcester, Tom Dove of Exeter, and Simon of Southampton, together with their northern brethren, Cuthbert of Kendal, Hodgkins of Halifax, and Martin Byrom of Manchester, are not more historical than the alliterative aptness of their names would lead one to expect. Deloney places them in the reign of Henry I., when no such merchant princes existed; probably, as Chevalley surmises, because he wanted to depict a golden age of the industry, such as had actually prevailed in the time of Henry VIII., and to bring out certain facts about the clothing trade and its dependence on royal protection, which it was dangerous to ventilate except under the cloak of a remote period. Henry, on the march against the Welsh, encounters great processions of wagons occupying the highways and blocking the way for his troops. Much incensed, he inquires what they are, and is more than appeased when he learns that he has subjects like Cole and Sutton, able to send these mighty trains of commodities up to London. "I always thought," quoth he, "that England's valour was more than her wealth, yet now I see her wealth sufficient to maintain her valour."

The six clothiers journey to London at their stated times, and forgather at an inn at Colnbrook, where they make good cheer. This hostelry is the scene of various diverting incidents, and of one tragic episode for which the book has had a fame perhaps even beyond its merits. Intertwined with their adventures Deloney has an underplot, concerned with the loves of Robert Duke of Normandy and a mythical daughter of the Earl of Shrewsbury. This, of course, is romance of the old-fashioned sort. Left destitute on the banishment of her father, who joins Duke Robert against the king, the Lady Margaret finds a place as a servant with the wife of Gray of Gloucester. Gray is inclined to be too attentive to the fair handmaiden; but Margaret's innocence mollifies even a jealous wife, and she remains under their protection. Meanwhile, the whole realm is disturbed by the strife between the royal brothers. Henry ingratiates himself with the powerful clothiers by granting them

Underplot: Robert of Normandy and Margaret

[1] Mann, 548.

certain privileges, and they in gratitude send aid in the campaign in Normandy. Duke Robert is captured and brought to England. It is while the king is being feasted by the clothiers that Robert first sees the beautiful Margaret. Later he escapes from his keepers and runs off with her. They are captured, and both sentenced to death. Robert is reprieved, but has his eyes put out; the lady receives pardon, but departs into a nunnery. All this is related with a superabundance of pathos.

Doings of the clothiers

More congenial to Deloney's pen are the hilarious chapters devoted to the doings of the cloth-merchants. They make merry at Colnbrook, on the way to London; they continue to make merry in the City, some playing at dice, some calling for music, others for wine or a venison pasty, another for merry tales. But Cuthbert of Kendal was of a different mind, "for no meat pleased him so well as mutton, such as was laced in a red petticoat." Bosom the innkeeper is a sour old fellow with a young wife, who is the object of Cuthbert's erotic proclivities. Old Bosom has his suspicions, which the erring pair endeavour to allay by pretending to have a grudge against each other. But the crafty husband lays a snare and catches them red-handed in the cheese-closet. To his wife, never at a loss for an excuse, he gives "as much credit as a crocodile"; but Cuthbert he has strung up in a basket in the smoky louver of the hall, and there leaves him hanging till the king's son begs for his pardon.[1] "And it is said," winds up Deloney, "the old man Bosom ordained that, in remembrance of this deed, every year once all such as came thither to ask for cheeses should be so served; which thing is to this day kept." Again we see him inventing an incident to explain a local story.

Traditional tales

The tale might have been told by Boccaccio. Another, describing the trick played on Sir William Ferrers, is imitated from the one in the *Decameron* about the way they cured the deluded Calandrino.[2] Sir William courts the fair maidservant Margaret, and to get rid of him she tells him she cannot away with his enormous nose. Terribly upset, the knight looks in the glass, and sure enough his nose, which he had always thought a handsome feature, appears hideously enlarged. His lady consults a physician, who devises a

[1] Louver = the cupola or lantern-shaped smoke-vent in a large hall

[2] *Decameron*, IX. iii.

remedy to cure the knight of his delusion. It is the earliest case on record of professional auto-suggestion. Having a bladder filled with blood concealed in his sleeve, the doctor pricks the offending nose. The bladder is squeezed and the blood runs into a basin in great abundance.

Immediately a glass was brought wherein he might behold himself.

"Yea, mary," quoth he, "I see my nose is come into some reasonable proportion, and I feel myself very well eased of the burthen thereof."

Whereupon the knight received great joy, and the doctor a high reward.

Tom Dove gets into trouble with his creditors, and is threatened with arrest. Now the office of catch-pole was so unpopular in London that no Englishman would undertake the duty. In this predicament a couple of Flemings are enlisted, and they try to seize Tom. One of the foreign catch-poles, fee'd by a creditor to arrest him, is so nervous that he comes up behind and fells him with his mace, then, thinking he has killed the man, takes to his heels. Tom seeks sanctuary at Westminster, and is smuggled out of town. But at last, ruined and bereft of his friends, he falls into utter destitution and is "made of as much account as Job when he sat upon his dunghill." Once more Deloney enlarges on the theme of the man in adverse circumstances deserted by servants and kindred, and this time the case is really pathetic. Happily, the rich clothiers hear of Tom Dove's distress, and subscribe to set him up again. "And riches being thus come upon him, his former friends came fawning unto him; and when he had no need of them, then every one was ready to proffer him kindness."

Petitions for the redress of grievances

In their negotiations with the king, the clothiers obtain three of their demands. He agrees to establish a single measure throughout the land, the length of his own arm constituting the yard; he orders all coins to be slit, because the merchants complain of cracked money; and he grants the town of Halifax the right to hang any man caught stealing cloth. A Scottish malefactor named Wallis is convicted and sentenced to be hanged; but nobody can be induced to carry out the sentence. Like Greene's Ned Browne, Wallis makes a defiant harangue at the foot of the gallows, and, refusing to be sent back to gaol to wait for a hangman, leaps from the ladder and throws the halter in Hodgkins' face. A friar presently devises a machine for cutting off heads "without man's help," a guillotine, in short; and Hodgkins, having told the king that "the privilege of Halifax was not worth a pudding," secures the right to employ it; "whereupon till this day it is observed in Halifax that such as are taken stealing of their cloth, have their heads chopped off with the same gin."

The murder of Thomas Cole

But the most memorable episode in *Thomas of Reading* is the murder of the eponymous hero. Here again Deloney worked up a traditional story. The inn at Colnbrook where Thomas Cole met his death is still in existence, and the room said to have had the collapsible floor is still pointed out.[1] The guest was put to bed in the fatal room, and whilst he slept his body was precipitated into a boiling cauldron in the basement.[2] It is a ghastly melodrama with tragic accompaniments that are really impressive. One thinks at once of the murder of Duncan, and can hardly credit that *Macbeth* was not yet written. Cole has mysterious premonitions before he retires to his pillow, though he has no reason to guess that the innkeeper and his wife harbour evil designs.

With that Cole beholding his host and hostess earnestly, began to start back, saying, "What ail you to look so like pale death? Good Lord! what have you done that your hands are thus bloody?"

"What my hands?" said his host. "Why you may see they are neither bloody nor foul. Either your eyes do greatly dazzle, or else fancies of a troubled mind do delude you."

"Alas, my host, you may see," said he, "how weak my wits are; I never had my head so idle before. Come, let me drink once more, and then I will to bed, and trouble you no longer."

With that he made himself unready, and his hostess was very diligent to warm a kerchief, and put it about his head.

"Good Lord!" said he, "I am not sick, I praise God, but such an alteration I find in myself as I never had before."

With that the screech owl cried piteously, and anon after the night raven sat croaking hard by his window.

"Jesus have mercy upon me!" quoth he, "what an ill-favoured

[1] Mann, 549.

[2] The same kind of incident has been in use from mediæval times to the present day; *cp.* Conrad's tale of terror, *The Inn of the Two Witches.*

cry do yonder carrion birds make!" and therewithal he laid him down in his bed, from whence he never rose again.

His host and hostess, that all this while noted his troubled mind, began to commune betwixt themselves thereof. And the man said, he knew not what were best to be done.

"By my consent," quoth he, "the matter should pass, for I think it is not best to meddle on him."

"What, man," quoth she, "faint you now? Have you done so many, and do you shrink at this? Then showing him a great deal of gold that Cole had left with her she said, "Would it not grieve a body's heart to lose this? Hang the old churl! what should he do living any longer? He hath too much, and we have too little. Tut, husband, let the thing be done, and then this is our own."

Deloney's merits and defects

Deloney's occasional success in the use of dramatic effect; his liking for a sub-plot, or at any rate for a subordinate story, to diversify interest and connect a rambling series of incidents and racy characterizations into something like a sustained narrative; and, above all, his pungent and lifelike dialogue, indicate that he had made an intelligent study of the methods employed on the contemporary stage. Not one of his novels taken as a whole would make a good play; but many single chapters would go admirably as comic scenes, the brief lengths of narrative serving as stage directions. Dekker, with a little manipulation, made first-rate low comedy out of the story of Simon Eyre. Such dramatic qualities as concentration and suspense were beyond him, but Deloney was a capital hand at a story—a story, that is, of moderate compass and no great complexity. Take the rivalry of Haunce the Dutchman and John the Frenchman for that jolly wench Florence, and the illusive tryst at Islington, from *The Gentle Craft*, as a good example. Deloney came to grief when he was called upon to show constructive skill. So admirable in the parts, he could not produce anything recognizable as a unified whole, not even in *Thomas of Reading*. The other two books are only strings of episodes or aggregates of detachable stories. In this respect they fall far below *Euphues*, the *Arcadia*, and *The Unfortunate Traveller*.

But when we turn to character-drawing, neither Lyly nor Sidney, not even Nashe, with his fierce portraits in the malevolent style of a lampoon, has a leg to stand on in comparison with Deloney. Master and Mistress Eyre, Richard the Cock of Westminster, Long

Meg and Gillian, Riming Robin, Tom Drum, Tom Dove, and Mistress Farmer, to name only some of them, make a long row of distinguishable portraits such as had not appeared in English literature since Chaucer, with whom, however, Deloney can sustain no serious comparison. They have individuality ; they behave like real people of their place and time ; they are humorous without being mere humours. Deloney's limitations are obvious. His character-drawing is entirely superficial ; he does not get down to the inner springs ; he gives idiosyncrasy but not motive. For the drama of character in action he had no capacity whatever. A few resemblances have been pointed out to Shakespeare, in the dialogue and in the mounting and atmosphere of a scene ; but this is of small significance. In truth, there is always something lacking in Deloney which is fundamental, something that cannot be dispensed with in a story, as distinguished from what is at best only an amusing display of manners and peculiarities. There is nothing much going on in his tales ; there is no real business, except business in the particular sense, and of that there is too much. Allowance must of course be made for one of his main incentives in writing. He put himself forward as the eulogist and defender of the trading corporations. Hence the economic element, which many writers tend to overlook, essential part though it be in the structure of life, all but monopolizes the story interest. If we now read his books simply as novels, we shall find our chief entertainment in the by-play. Fortunately, this is so good that we can ignore the economic side altogether and yet find Deloney well worth reading.

Chap-book literature

He owed little or nothing to Greene, Nashe, Lodge, or other writers of contemporary standing. He was not a puritan or a satirist, and did not concern himself with the ugly and reprehensible aspects of the world. Deloney fell into line rather with the anonymous makers of chap-book biographies, the last degenerate offspring of the mediæval romances and the ballads. His novels competed for popularity with the histories of Robin Hood, George à Green and Friar Bacon, and of such foreign celebrities as Robert the Devil, Fortunatus and Dr Faustus,[1] all of which were read with avidity, as the multiplication of editions proves. Stories of this class had an appeal denied to those of higher pretensions. Whatever the supposed

[1] *Cp.* Volume I., pp. 292-293.

date of the events recounted, they were a pretty faithful mirror of life and manners to the classes who read them. Usually they had a plebeian hero, or at least one frankly impersonating the democratic spirit; the ideas and sentiments were those of the masses, emphatically distinguished from those of the classes. Still more important, the hero was already a household figure, and the historical colour was of the inaccurate but familiar kind that is learned from tradition. Then, without in the least abstaining from the turgid and high-flown, any more than their congeners of the present day, the authors provided easy reading. No marvel if they were rewarded with the honour of endless reprintings—an empty honour, probably, since it is not to be supposed that they drew royalties every time.

Some account has already been given[1] of several such popular histories, which became current soon after printing came into England. The oldest prose versions of some of the other stories have vanished, and even the dates are not very certain. No edition is extant of a prose life of Robin Hood earlier than that of 1662, which is merely a redaction of certain ballads from the common garland, put together by "an Ingenious Antiquary." But a much older prose paraphrase exists in manuscript of the famous *Lytle Geste of Robyn Hode*,[2] and this is far less extravagant than the ballad material reproduced in the recension. In the Tudor versions of the story Robin Hood is boldly stated to have been outlawed by Henry VIII., and to have won the favour of Queen Katherine by his archery. So much for popular chronology. Time-honoured tradition fares no better. Little John's name was originally bestowed in irony—witness the gigantic proportions of his supposed grave in Hathersage churchyard; but we are here told that it was given him "by reason of his low stature." There is indeed more of the jest-book hero than the generous and chivalrous outlaw about the Tudor edition of Robin Hood, and he has humiliating misadventures which detract from his romantic prestige. Although as an archer he beats every competitor, he comes off second-best in several duels with sword or quarter-staff. The Tanner of Nottingham trounces him severely; he is not only thrashed but also robbed of

Robin Hood

[1] See pp. 52-53.
[2] In the Sloane Collection; printed in W. J. Thoms's *Early English Prose Romances*, pp. 521-555.

his clothes by a valiant beggar; and the Curtal Friar of Fountains Abbey, *alias* Friar Tuck, of uncanonical prowess, brings him single-handed into such straits that he has to wind his horn and summon fifty men in Lincoln green to his succour. The hero of Sherwood, though the son of a belted earl, has little sense of fair play. In the account of "a gallant combat fought between Robin Hood, Little John, and William Scarlocke, and three of the keepers of the king's deer," the wily outlaw, when palpably getting the worst of it, takes advantage of a pause in the fighting to propose a complete change of weapons. "Come and go with me to Nottingham, and there we will fight it out at the King's Head Tavern with good sack and claret." Tarlton or Peele should have taken his place in the episode of Robin Hood and the Butcher, in which Robin buys from a butcher his horse and the meat with which it is laden, and selling the meat at a loss in Nottingham, tempts the Sheriff out of bounds with the offer of a much more attractive bargain. When the unfortunate magistrate finds himself in Sherwood, and sees that the fields supposed to be for sale are rather too heavily timbered and that the horned beasts are fallow deer, he is glad to get away home with the loss of three hundred pounds that he had brought for purchase money. And in his battle with the Tanner, Robin gets nothing but dry blows, and the promise that if ever he comes to Nottingham he will have his hide tanned for naught.

"George à Greene"

Closely associated in common repute with Robin Hood was George à Green, the Pinder or Pound-keeper of Wakefield. The comedy, *George à Greene, the Pinder of Wakefield*, played by Lord Strange's company in 1593, was based on two ballad cycles, dealing respectively with the Pinder and with Robin Hood.[1] It is attributed to Robert Greene. The extant prose tale, *The Pinder of Wakefield: Being the Merry History of George à Greene the lusty Pinder of the North*, is dated as late as 1632; but the editor of another version, printed in 1706,[2] asserts that the manuscript was at least as old as the reign of Elizabeth. The play is based on the same authorities as the prose tale, which was probably written later, and may perhaps have been derived, at least in part, from the play. Three threads of interest are woven into the somewhat clumsy fabric of the tale—

[1] Greene's *Dramatic Works*, ed. J. Churton Collins; i. (Introduction), p. 215.
[2] Reprinted by Thoms.

the love-adventures of George and Beatrice, a wealthy justice's daughter; the Pinder's stout resistance to the Earl of Kendal's insurrection against Prince John and the Bishop of Ely, while Richard the Lion-hearted was in the Holy Land; and the coming of Robin Hood to Wakefield, because "Mariana could not be in quiet, till it could be tried whether Robin or George were the valientest, or she and [or] Beatrice the fairest." The taunts of the rival beauties and the vicissitudes of the combat are related in a style meant to vie with the romance of chivalry. One of George's feats was to compel a messenger sent by the rebels to swallow the three seals attached to his commission, and wash them down with a flagon of ale; another was the capture by stratagem of a spy, whom he inveigled into a sack and then hanged up before the castle he had tried to betray. But the best thing is a tag to the main story, and follows after the *dénouement* consequent on the king's return. This is the narrative of a great fight in the "Town of Merry Bradfield," where the shoemakers have a custom that any stranger shouldering his staff in the town must have a bout with some one or another of the gentle craft. Robin and George take up the challenge, and there is a battle royal, the fervid historian finding vent for his ardour in copious alliteration and a turbid stream of puns.

There was nothing now thought on but havoc and pall mall; the Pinder himself seemed to be pounded in amongst them, and many a shoemaker was brought to his last, and many a shaft was shivered and made skewers: cracked crowns went current, though many were found to take them against their wills: the shoemakers themselves thought fit to give ground, who had vowed to lose bodies and souls in the quarrel, and run to shelter themselves most shamefully.

It happens at this moment that the king, with the Earl of Leicester and Cuddie Musgrave, is passing through the town incognito. When the two champions are recognized, for they had fought in disguise, there is wild enthusiasm, and then a high-flown scene of reconciliation, in which the king restores Robin Hood to his earldom of Huntingdon and offers knighthood to George à Green.

Another play of Greene's, *Friar Bacon and Friar Bungay*, produced about 1589-1590 and published in 1594, was also derived from a prose story, of which the earliest edition known, *The*

"Fryer Bacon and Fryer Boungaye"

Historye of Fryer Bacon and Fryer Boungaye, was licensed in 1594. Greene was influenced by Marlowe's *Doctor Faustus*, which for its part had been influenced to a considerable extent by the English legends of Roger Bacon. Hence the solemn tone of the scene in which Bacon repents of his dealings with the infernal hosts, a serious motive that is absent from the prose story. In this, the philosopher is regarded as the great English thaumaturge, the national rival to Paracelsus and Cornelius Agrippa, performing feats evidently meant to surpass the prodigies recorded in Continental legend. Assisted by Friar Bungay he constructs a brazen head that, by the help of the Devil, is made to speak ; he would have walled all England round about with brass and done many further wonders, but for the carelessness of a servant. By his arts he takes a town without a blow, which the king had fruitlessly besieged for three months. Lastly, he triumphs over the foreign necromancer, Vandermast, who had previously beaten the less accomplished Bungay. Bacon had a marvellous glass, in which he could see everything that was going on within a radius of fifty miles. Through an untoward accident the mirror causes the death of two fathers, who, unperceived, had witnessed a quarrel of their own sons ; whereupon Bacon shatters the mirror and abjures magic. Probably this was the source of Nashe's scene of clairvoyance in *The Unfortunate Traveller*.

The story begins, methodically enough, with the parentage and birth of the great Franciscan, tells of his upbringing, his studies, and then his feats, and it ends with his death. But its continuity is merely that of a string of anecdotes in the order of date ; the narrative is as artless as the rest of its class. In a prosaic, matter-of-fact style the writer plods soberly along, from humdrum domestic incidents to conjurations of the Devil and like monstrous events, taking everything as it comes. The Devil enters with fearful noises, but on the whole behaves himself with great moderation. After all, the poor Deuce had not yet shaken off entirely the harlequin's garb in which the mystery-plays had attired him. Greene in his play could introduce tragedy and carry on a philosophical debate ; the compiler of the prose tale had to furnish an adequate allowance of buffoonery. Can it be that one comic scene, where Bacon's serving-man leads the thieves who have robbed his master over dike and swamp, dancing after the sound of his tabor, till they are mired from head to foot, gave Shakespeare the notion of his Ariel leading the spellbound seamen to the filthy-mantled pool?

In the regular manufacture of this literature for the groundlings Deloney had one competitor who was not anonymous, and who appears to have driven an equally lucrative trade with the booksellers. Richard Johnson (1573?-1659) was a writer for the illiterate. We can imagine his *Seauen Champions of Christendome* or his *Tom à Lincoln, the Red Rose Knight*, declaimed aloud to circles of those who could not read, and had no more sense of historical verisimilitude than children. Ritson roundly said of *The Most famous History of the Seauen Champions of Christendome* (1596-1597), that it contained "all the lyes of Christendom in one lye." This ingenuous, or fraudulent, work went, however, through edition after edition every few years, for a century and a half. Only a shade less beloved of the multitude was another rehash, *The most pleasant History of Tom à Lincolne,*[1] *That renowned Souldier, the Red-Rose Knight, who for his Valour and Chiualry was surnamed The Boast of England* (1599). The book is trash, and an egregious example of what delighted the mob in the early seventeenth century. It is a vulgarization, in high-flown language, of the romantic figures, the chivalric ideals, and the poetic fancies that had given beauty to the *Morte Darthur*, the *Amadís*, the *Faerie Queene*, and even *Euphues*. Johnson's "Fayerie-land" is a country of Amazons, the queen of which falls in love with the hero Tom, and is basely deserted by him. This ignoble episode is not meant for burlesque. Worse still is the behaviour of Arthur's jealous queen when the dying king confesses that Tom is his son by a nun of Lincoln. With misplaced puritanism the author reviles and maltreats the unfortunate nun in a manner that is a repulsive contrast to Malory's humanity. The history and the geography are unintentionally comic. After conquering Portingale and assailing the Turks, the Red-Rose Knight marches his army home without expense of shipping. Flanders "borders upon" Fayerie-land, which is described as an island in the western parts of the world. A later book of like nature was *The History of Tom Thumbe, for his small stature surnamed King Arthur's Dwarfe: Whose Life and Adventures containe many strange*

Richard Johnson's stories

[1] The name was stolen from, not given to, the famous bell in memory of the hero, as might have been believed by Johnson's readers.

and wonderfull accidents, published for the delight of Time-spenders (1621), the only interest of which is that it gravely propounded the story which was the basis of Fielding's admirable extravaganza.

From this sketch of Johnson's achievements as a romancer it would appear that he was hardly to be dreaded as a rival to Deloney. Happily, although he was first in the field, and in spite of the depravity of readers, his two London story-books did not set the Thames on fire. His first work of fiction, *The nine Worthies of London: Explaining the honourable exercise of Armes, the vertues of the valiant, and the memorable attempts of magnanimous minds* (1592), came half a decade before John Winchcomb. It is a feeble attempt to extract martial interest, akin to that of a story of chivalry, out of a fanciful history of the London companies. *The Pleasant Conceites of Old Hobson the merry Londoner* (1607)[1] appeared ten years after *The Gentle Craft*, and the witty and eccentric tradesman (*d.* 1581), with his shop in the Poultry, has been properly described by Chevalley as *un personnage vraiment delonesque.*[2] But the book is a mere scrapbook of well-worn anecdotes and jests attributed to this old original, who had recently been utilized for humorous purposes on the stage by Heywood, in *If you know not me, you know Nobody* (1606), and held a minor place in popular esteem beside Scoggin, Peele, and Long Meg of Westminster.

Henry Roberts

Deloney suffered from an impudent theft at the hands of another romancer, the prolific Henry Roberts (or Robarts) (*fl.* 1585-1616), in *Haigh for Devonshire. A pleasant Discourse of sixe gallant Marchants of Devonshire. Their Lives, Adventures and Travailes: with sundrie their rare showes and pastimes shewed before the King in Exeter* (1600). This is taken direct from *Thomas of Reading.*[3] The writer, who held some diplomatic office at the court of James I., was also the author of *A Defiance to Fortune: Proclaimed by Andrugio, noble Duke of Saxony. . . . Whereunto is adioyned the honourable Warres of Galastino, Duke of Millaine* (1590); *Phaeander, the Mayden Knight* (1595); and *Honours Conquest. Wherin is conteined the famous Hystorie of Edward of Lancaster* (1598). The popular appetite for history, especially localized

[1] Ed. J. O. Halliwell, Percy Society, ix., 1843.
[2] Chevalley, 138. [3] *Ibid.*, 137.

history, evinced by these and so many of the foregoing tales, is remarkable. The very badness of what passed for history is a testimony to the general desire to know about bygone times ; it proves the strength and vitality of tradition. So, too, the immense number of chronicle plays acted on the Elizabethan stage shows the direction of popular interest. But the interest was in persons rather than events ; the craving was to behold the man, whether king, hero, mighty magician, or mighty scoundrel. Deloney did a good deal to satisfy this demand, whilst pursuing his principal aim, the glorification of two important industries ; incidentally he left us the most faithful and intimate delineation of a whole stratum of society in his time.[1] The profitable vein of domestic fiction which he tapped has been worked pretty continuously ever since, and shows as yet no signs of exhaustion.

[1] M. Chevalley has discovered another biographical novel akin to *John Winchcomb* and *Thomas of Reading*. It is entitled : *The Honourable Prentice ; or Thys Taylor is a Man* (1615), and was written by a William Vallans, a Hertfordshire salt merchant, antiquary and poet. The extant copy is in the Bodleian. This is nothing more than a romanticized life of the famous condottiere, Sir John Hawkwood, first buried in the Duomo of Florence, about whom there was a false tradition that he had been a tailor's apprentice in London (see Chevalley, 138-139).

CHAPTER XII

FICTION AND DISCURSIVE LITERATURE

Affinity of the novel and the essay

THERE have been cases enough in the foregoing chapters of works that were not so much plain fiction as didactic or damnatory tractates on phases of contemporary life, using fictitious characters and incidents to enforce the argument. When one writer tells a set of stories for the sake of enlarging on them like a Puritan homilist, and another anatomizes the world as he sees it and illustrates his points with seasonable tales, it is exceedingly difficult to draw the line between what is primarily fiction and what something else. Fenton, not inaccurately, described his heavily moralized versions of Bandello as " discourses " ; Barnaby Rich and Whetstone used the same term ; and Pettie announced that his " pretty histories " were " most delightfully discoursed." The affinities of *Euphues*, more a philosophical commentary on life than a story, is rather with Sir Thomas Elyot's *Governour* and the *Scholemaster* of Roger Ascham than with the novel. And the framework into which Greene put his neat assortments of stories was of a similar nature. But Greene of the *Groats-Worth* and of the cony-catching series, together with Nashe, Rowlands and Breton, comes nearer, now to the sociological attempts of Awdeley and Harman and to the *Liber Vagatorum*, and now to the essay or commentary on life, or to the satire, in verse or prose. The analytical epitomes of character which became such a fashion at the beginning of the seventeenth century, with amateurs of literature who had less ability or zest for story-telling than a semi-scientific interest in the variations of human nature, are manifestly closer akin to the essay than to the novel ; although, in spite of the absence of narrative, their relation to the art of the novelist is obvious, and they contributed in no small degree to its development.

At a time when writers were hazy about the difference between prose and poetry, they were not likely to make clear distinctions between this method and that of expounding a view of life. Only when they had gained experience, and began to realize the capacities of a particular form, would there be specialization of technique. In that sense there is in truth an evolution of genres. Before it takes place there are these blundering mixtures of narration and reflection, characters coming to the footlights in the middle of the play to deliver harangues on behalf of the author, dialogue degenerating into a debate, and the action terminating in a lecture. Not until fiction has established itself as a well-defined art does the novelist see that his proper business is to submit his mature vision of life, not to talk about the people he has invented and what they do, or to proffer judgments and generalizations. If he holds strong opinions and is anxious to ventilate them, he can do it more effectively by making us see life as he himself sees it than by any amount of laying down the law. If he finds the portraiture of life an inadequate means, he has the alternative of putting his reflections into the form of an essay; and, like Fielding, he may venture to interpolate such essays between the successive chapters of his novel, like Thackeray, interject them in confidential asides, or, like George Eliot or George Meredith, have a witty aphorist among his characters to pronounce them. He may be wiser still, and, leaving conclusions to the reader, stick religiously to concrete statement. This requires the finer art; but when such art is at command even the unexpressed may be conveyed, and conveyed more persuasively than if it had been made explicit. As the sphere of the artist and the sphere of the expositor become more rigidly defined, the purist who insists on rules without understanding the principles for which they exist may go so far as to deny that it is within the province of the novelist to express himself in any way on the issues involved in the relations of his imaginary personages. This is to assert a human impossibility. Even those creative writers who are least conscious of a meaning to transmit, cannot help revealing a meaning; unformulated as a logical proposition, it is formulated in another way, the way that comes naturally to such minds. Fielding and Thackeray were equally skilled in the essay and in the novel. But there have been numberless writers who could express their philosophy of life, or, if that is too weighty a term, their sentiments and convictions, in no other way but through the medium of characters and incidents and spontaneous dialogue. So there are, of course, people who write verse with ease and prose with infinite labour. None have succeeded less in concealing their particular views of life and conduct than the most admired exponents of the doctrine that art should have no meaning.

The discursive function of prose

Right as it is, however, to keep the two modes of interpreting the phenomena of life clearly distinct, the essential affinity between the essay and the novel, between the interpretation of life through sentiments and reflections and its interpretation through concrete portraiture and imaginary action, remains. As fiction is obviously parallel to narrative poetry, so is the essay parallel to meditative and didactic poetry and to the lyric. And as the epic is related to the lyric, so is the novel to the essay, which fundamental affinity shows more conspicuously as prose literature and poetic literature move further and further apart. The distinction between verse and prose is a formal and external difference marking the distinction between profoundly different attitudes of mind. During the Elizabethan period, when imagination had the upper hand, when the scientific spirit was in abeyance, the distinction had no chance of making itself adequately felt. Prose is for the intellectual treatment of life, for the registration of facts rather than imaginative truth. Prose—that is, a really prosaic prose—is the appointed medium for an age of scientific investigation. It was ere long to be the medium of a more matter-of-fact realism than had hitherto emerged. But already, in the analytical and critical and the less emotional work of the essayists, character-writers and satirists, this proper function of prose was to find exercise, and the prose so used at once began to clear itself of foreign elements and to become better adapted for its proper function.[1]

The essay

Montaigne published his first two books of *Essays* in 1580, and to the second edition in 1588 he added a third.[2] He was the founder of an English school of essayists that is still flourishing. Montaigne's genius was as distinctively French as that of Voltaire or Anatole France; but the form which he initiated did not prove particularly congenial to the French mind. There has been no second Montaigne,

[1] See Volume I., introduction, especially pp. 15 and 18-21, on the different mental attitudes of the poet and the novelist.

[2] Florio's translation of Montaigne's *Essays* appeared in 1603, the second edition in 1613.

except perhaps in England. The list of his English disciples contains the names of most of the greatest writers of essays, and there is no reason why it should now be rolled up and put away. When Bacon, in 1597, published his first thin volume of *Essayes, Religious Meditations, Places of Perswasion and Disswasion,* he was no doubt encouraged to do so by the example of Montaigne. He adopted the name, and something of the method. Yet these ten brief jottings of detached thoughts were in manner and content not much like the fluid, digressive, self-revealing discourses of his French predecessor, nor did he come very much nearer in the longer and more carefully finished pieces that he added later.

Bacon's "Essays"

They were composed of the thoughts that occurred to him from day to day on such topics as Study, Ceremonies and Respects, Followers and Friends, Honour and Reputation, Faction, Negotiating—that is to say, they were reflections, counsels and maxims that appeared to him of value in the life of one engaged in affairs of state. He said in the dedication of the enlarged edition (1612) that he had divided his life "into the contemplative and active parts," and that these discourses were the fruit of both. But from first to last it was the active part that yielded him his themes, and the spirit of his meditations is uniformly practical and even utilitarian. Twenty-nine essays were added to the original ten in this second edition, and the final quarto brought the number up to fifty-eight (1625). *Essayes or Counsels, civill and morall,* was the title ultimately chosen, and it is aptly descriptive. As a statesman, a jurist, and a philosopher, Bacon centred attention on the graver problems of life, the public and private relations of humanity, especially of the man of affairs or the thinker towards his inferiors. The principal lesson to be gathered from the whole series is how such a one should so manage those under and about him as to husband his private energies, utilize the good and also the evil qualities of others to serve his own loftier aim in life, and provide himself with leisure for thought and rational enjoyment. He has many wise things to say on matters of public policy. But for the most part he is a self-centred moralist, concerned with his own development and the pursuit of his higher calling. For the finer distinctions of ethics, for nobility of character or any other ideal, for love of his fellow-men, Bacon shows no solicitude. Judged from a modern standpoint, he seems obtuse, cold-blooded, almost ignoble.

It is not a moral philosophy but the calculation of worldly wisdom that is apparent in such an essay as the one "Of Simulation and Dissimulation."

> The great advantages of simulation and dissimulation are three. First, to lay asleep opposition and to surprise. For where a man's intentions are published, it is an alarum to call up all that are against them. The second is, to reserve to a man's self a fair retreat. For if a man engage himself by a manifest declaration, he must go through or take a fall. The third is, the better to discover the mind of another. For to him that opens himself, men will hardly show themselves adverse, but will fair let him go on, and turn their freedom of speech to freedom of thought. And therefore it is a good shrewd proverb of the Spaniard: Tell a lie, and find a truth.

Love is the child of folly. "They do best who, if they cannot but admit love, yet make it keep quarter, and sever it wholly from their serious affairs and actions of life; for if it check once with business, it troubleth men's fortunes, and maketh men that they can no ways be true to their own ends." That is from the essay "Of Love"; this from the essay "Of Expense," in the passage concerning the management of servants: "He that cannot look into his own estate at all had need both choose well those whom he employeth, and change them often; for new are more timorous and less subtle. He that can look into his estate but seldom, it behoveth him to turn all to certainties." The same hardness characterizes the essay "Of Negotiating":

> It is better dealing with men in appetite than with those that are where they would be. . . . All practice is to discover or to work. Men discover themselves in trust, in passion, at unawares; and of necessity, when they would have somewhat done, and cannot find an apt pretext. If you would work any man, you must either know his nature and fashions, and so lead him; or his ends, and so persuade him; or his weakness and disadvantages, and so awe him; or those that have interest in him, and so govern him.

Had Bacon chosen the novel for the expression of such sentiments, the character giving them utterance would hardly have engaged the reader's sympathies. But the nature of the sentiments matters less than the clearness and concision with which they are enunciated. Bacon had found a vehicle for the definite and lucid exposition of what is a main element in fiction. He did not take typical characters and anatomize them; but his method points to the results of such analysis; and the character-writers, who went to work in a like methodical way, showed future novelists the need for the sifting and classifying of human qualities and motives in any reasonable interpretation of life.

His example to other writers in prose

This was one invaluable service for the benefit of other writers than essayists. A further and perhaps a greater service was to have introduced a new model of prose. The style of his first ten essays is terse and bare to the point of obscurity. But, having realized that he had begun a work which was worth doing, he took more pains with form and composition as he went on. He never abandoned the oracular manner. All his essays are full of compact aphorisms. He did not write to charm or persuade, but to set down in memorable phrases the truths that were the result of experience and reflection. And in their final shape his essays are as notable for their masterly style as the more stately passages in *The Advancement of Learning* are for their eloquence. Without detriment to the poetic qualities of prose, qualities to which an undue and delusive attention was paid by self-conscious young men of letters, he eschewed euphuism and romantic rhetoric, together with the wordy antics of the writers who scoffed at euphuism and would outgo it in their own way. Bacon gave prose the virtue of orderliness. His style was pointed, racy, flexible, good at both the epigram and the clinching illustration. He could be homely, he could write with majesty. His was the most satisfactory implement for the handling of both actualities and thought that had yet been forged. Those who followed him did not all, however, accept forthwith the new canon of prose. But at any rate they had it in front of them as a model of prose that made no pretence at being anything else, and the new standard of orderliness and suitability was effective in curbing the worst extravagances.

Other early essayists

Two writers whose collections of essays appeared between Bacon's first and second editions are worth a passing mention. Sir William Cornwallis published a volume of *Essayes* (1600) dealing with a wider range of topics than Bacon's, but without the same penetration.

He discusses such qualities as patience, vanity and ambition, introduces personal confidences in the fashion of Montaigne, and has much to say on that familiar subject, the miscellaneous interests of a gentleman of liberal culture. Robert Johnson's *Essaies or rather Imperfect Offers* (1601) were more narrowly educational in their interest. Cornwallis went on to publish *Essayes of Certaine Paradoxes* (1616) and *Essayes newlie corrected* (1638). But the only work of the period that can stand being placed side by side with Bacon's essays is the commonplace-book in which Ben Jonson wrote down thoughts encountered in his reading, sometimes as mere notes, sometimes connected into a discourse or the outline of an argument, and which was printed after his death. *Timber: or, Discoveries; made upon men and matter: as they have flow'd out of his daily reading; or had their refluxe to his peculiar notion of the times* (1641) might be compared, as the parenthetical work of a creative artist, with the essays or comments on things in general that have since come from the pen of several novelists. Possibly the dramatist had saved up these thoughts for a different use. Certainly, as rich a miscellany might be culled from his works for the stage. Jonson is as clear-headed as Bacon, and rivals him also in the severe beauty of his prose.

Ben Jonson's "Timber: or, Discoveries"

> No man is so foolish, but may give another good counsel sometimes; and no man is so wise, but may easily err, if he will take no other's counsel but his own. But very few men are wise by their own counsel, or learned by their own teaching. For he that was only taught by himself had a fool to his master (*Consilia*).
>
> A good man will avoid the spot of any sin. The very aspersion is grievous; which makes him choose his way in his life, as he would in his journey. The ill man rides through all confidently; he is coated and booted for it. The oftener he offends, the more openly; and the fouler, the fitter in fashion. His modesty, like a riding coat, the more it is worn, is the less cared for. It is good enough for the dirt still, and the ways he travels in. An innocent man needs no eloquence: his innocence is instead of it: else I had never come off so many times from these precipices, whither men's malice hath pursued me (*De bonis et malis*).

Jonson is tender and human, where Bacon was cold and aloof. He knew that "Science is not every man's mistress," and was tolerant of frailties. But his moral criterion was higher and more refined.

What a deal of cold business doth a man misspend the better part of life in! in scattering compliments, tendering visits, gathering and venting news, following feasts and plays, making a little winter love in a dark corner (*Jactura vitæ*).

He hath a delicate wife, a fair fortune, and family to go to be welcome; yet he had rather be drunk with mine host and the fiddlers of such a town than go home (*Maritus improbus*).

Half the entries in this well-stocked notebook are thoughts on the problems of life, half pertain to the literary art; and it is hard to say which are the more precious. As might be expected, the dramatist of the humours drops at times into the Theophrastian mode of charactery.

Jonson's charactery

A tedious person is one a man would leap a steeple from, gallop down any steep hill to avoid him, forsake his meat, sleep, nature itself with all her benefits to shun him. A mere impertinent; one that touched neither heaven nor earth in his discourse. He opened an entry into a fair room, but shut it again presently. I spake to him of garlic, he answered asparagus; consulted him of marriage, he tells me of hanging, as if they went by one and the same destiny (*Impertinens*).

It was wittily said upon one that was taken for a great and grave man so long as he held his peace: "This man might have been a counsellor of state till he spoke; but having spoken, not the beadle of the ward (*Argute dictum*).

These are flatterers for their bread, that praise all my oraculous lord does or says, be it true or false; invent tales that shall please; make baits for his lordship's ears; and if they be not received in what they offer at, they shift a point of the compass, and turn their tale presently tack about, deny what they confessed, and confess what they denied; fit their discourse to the persons and occasions. What they snatch up and devour at one table, utter at another; and grow suspected of the master, hated of the servants, while they inquire and reprehend and compound and delate business of the house they have nothing to do with. They praise my lord's wine, and the sauce he likes; observe the cook and bottle-man, while they stand in my lord's favour, speak for a pension for them; but pound them to dust upon my lord's least distaste or change of his palate (*Parasiti ad mensam*).

Selden, in his *Table Talk*, which might fitly be cited as a counterpart to Bacon and Jonson's essays or notebooks, James Howell of the *Epistolæ Ho-Elianæ*, Burton and Sir Thomas Browne, are all in direct succession from the first essayist. They in their several ways expound personal convictions on life and character, such as the sister art has expounded in other modes. Bacon's immediate successors, however, were the first systematic exponents of " charactery "—to adopt Joseph Hall's term for this minor art.[1]

[1] " A third sort in a mean course betwixt the two other (he is speaking of 'the divines of the old heathens' who discoursed of human felicity or made specific applications of moral precepts) and compounded of them both, bestowed their time in drawing out the true lineaments of every virtue and vice, so lively, that who saw the medals might know the face; which art they significantly termed Charactery " (Prefatory epistle to *Characters of Virtues and Vices*).

CHAPTER XIII

THOMAS DEKKER

Thomas Dekker

The typically Elizabethan pamphlets of Dekker seem an anachronism coming after Bacon and the birth of the sober and orderly essay. They show that Baconian methodology had not yet extinguished the exuberance, the gaiety, or the ribaldry of a world in which men grew old without losing the spirit of youth. Thomas Dekker (*c.* 1570-1641) in many respects, including his merry, irregular life—what little is known about it—but not his death—for he lived to a ripe age—is almost another Nashe. Several of his medleys of realism and fancy pair off singularly well with those of his senior, for whom he had a warm admiration, and to whom he would have been the last person to disavow his large indebtedness. He lacked the restless energy and the refractory spirit of Nashe, and perhaps he had less originality, for we must not forget that the "young Juvenal" never attained the maturity of his powers. Dekker's good sense and good nature were more inclined to acknowledge and profit by the excellences of other writers than to gibe at their absurdities. It is largely from this willingness to read, mark and learn that his work is generally more artistic and his satire more urbane. Dekker was also a poet, and not all his poetry was reserved for his plays. Touches of imagination in his cartoons of plague-stricken London, of pathos and lyrical emotion in his sketches of the poor and oppressed, and of moving eloquence in his prophecies of retribution for the age's sins, justify Lamb's remark that "he had poetry enough for anything."[1]

"The Wonderfull Yeare"

Three of his comedies, the boisterous *Shoemaker's Holiday, or The Gentle Craft*, the imaginative *Old Fortunatus*, and that effective burlesque, *Satiromastix*, had already appeared when Dekker wrote his first prose pamphlet, *The Wonderfull Yeare, 1603, Wherein is shewed the picture of London, lying sicke of the Plague* (1603).

[1] *Eng. Dram. Poets*, note on Massinger and Dekker.

Beginning with a funereal account of the passing of Elizabeth, followed by the rejoicings at the accession of James, he finds a more congenial subject in the story of the plague. It has often been alleged that Defoe borrowed ideas from Dekker's realistic descriptions of houses packed with the dying, streets full of coffins and death-carts, pits heaped with putrefying carcasses, and the horror and panic of the inhabitants; but the resemblances between this and the more famous account of a plague year are not so many as the contrasts. Dekker attempts no history of the terrible creeping progress of the visitation, but paints a few gruesome pictures and tells some seasonable and several grimly comic anecdotes. Defoe's is a tragic masterpiece; Dekker's is a lighter work. His was merely the journalistic aim to interest and amuse; and his heart is rather in the "merry epilogue" than the "dull play," as he puts it on his title-page—that is, in the tales "cut out in sundry fashions of purpose to shorten the lives of long winters nights, that lye watching in the darke for us." In these latter pages he tells the story of the wife who thinks herself at the point of death, confesses her frailties to her astonished husband, and then recovers; of the merry tinker who buries the corpse that the whole village shrank from in terror, and, making seven pounds by the transaction, comes back shouting: "Have ye any more Londoners to bury, hey down a down dery, have ye any more Londoners to bury?" *The Wonderfull Yeare* has many points in common with *Christes Teares over Jerusalem*; but there is a closer reminiscence of Nashe in Dekker's portrait of a rustic innkeeper, who might have been the army victualler in *Jack Wilton*, settled down in a village near London.

> A goodly fat burger he was, with a belly arching out like a beer-barrel, which made his legs (that were thick and short, like two piles driven under London Bridge) to straddle half as wide as the top of Paul's, which upon my knowledge hath been burnt twice or thrice. . . . He was an host to be led before an emperor, and though he were one of the greatest men in all the shire, his bigness made him not proud, but he humbled himself to speak the base language of a tapster, and upon the Londoner's first arrival, cried "Welcome! a cloth for this gentleman."

But the guest, next moment, is struck down by the plague, and all is panic and confusion.

My gorbelly host, that in many a year could not without grunting crawl over a threshold but two foot broad, leapt half a yard from the corse (it was measured by a carpenter's rule) as nimbly as if his guts had been taken out by the hangman. Out of the house he wallowed presently, being followed with two or three dozen of napkins to dry up the lard that ran so fast down his heels, that all the way he went was more greasy than a kitchen-stuff wife's basket.

This same year Dekker brought out the first booklet in which he broadly paraphrased a foreign masterpiece of popular drollery and adapted it to the peculiarities of his countrymen. That cynical eulogy of a young wife's humours, *Les Quinze Joies de Mariage* (*c.* 1464), attributed to Antoine de la Sale on the strength of an acrostic in one of the manuscripts, was a favourite satire in the days of the jest-books, the commonest butt of which was woman and marriage. A coarse English rendering, sold as a chap-book down to the eighteenth century, under the title, *The Fifteen Comforts of Rash and Inconsiderate Marriage; or, Select Animadversions upon the Miscarriages of a Wedded State.* The fourth edition, to which "Three Comforts" are added, is dated 1694. Dekker's free and masterly version of La Sale's fifteen chapters he entitled *The Batchelars Banquet*, "pleasantly," and it is the appropriate word, "discoursing the variable humours of women, their quickness of wits, and unsearchable deceits."

"The Batchelars Banquet"

His next tract, *The Seuen deadly Sinnes of London: Drawn in Seuen seuerall Coaches, through the seuen seuerall gates of the Citie, bringing the Plague with them* (1606), is largely the counterpart of Nashe's *Pierce Penilesse*, in which the Deadly Sins had been depicted in their latest modern guise.[1] Dekker likewise shows them at home in London, to which they are ceremoniously admitted in a seven days' triumph, and entertained by their devotees. Dekker gives them new names, answering to the newest fashions of vice and knavery —Apishnesse, or foppery; Candle-light, the sins of darkness; Shaving, or fraudulent dealing; Politick Bankruptisme, the process by which Bunyan's Mr Badman was to make himself rich; and Lying, Sloth, Crueltie. Under the old designations he paints the follies and vices of a more sophisticated and more turbulent age, in which, however, many iniquities were dissembled under the cloak

"The Seuen deadly Sinnes of London"

[1] See p. 156.

of respectability and puritanism. This account of "Politick Bankruptisme" is a fair example of Dekker's delineation of manners, in the now hackneyed form of the anatomy of social abuses and denunciation of the general depravity:

Whether he be a tradesman, or a merchant, when he first sets himself up, and seeks to get the world into his hands (yet not to go out of the City) or first talks of countries he never saw (upon the Change) he will be sure to keep his days of payments more truly than lawyers keep their terms, or than executors keep the last laws that the dead enjoined them to, which even infidels themselves will not violate: his hand goes to his head, to his meanest customer (to express his humility); he is up earlier than a sergeant and down later than a constable, to proclaim his thrift. By such artificial wheels as these, he winds himself up into the height of rich men's favours, till he grow rich himself, and when he sees that they dare build upon his credit, knowing the ground to be good, he takes upon him the condition of an ass, to any man that will load him with gold; and useth his credit like a ship freighted with all sorts of merchandise by venturous pilots: for after he hath gotten into his hands so much of other men's goods or money, as will fill him to the upper deck, away he sails with it, and politicly runs himself on ground, to make the world believe he had suffered shipwreck. Then flies he out like an Irish rebel, and keeps aloof, hiding his head, when he cannot hide his shame: and though he have feathers on his back pulled from sundry birds, yet to himself is he more wretched, than the cuckoo in winter, that dares not be seen. The troops of honest citizens (his creditors) with whom he hath broken league and hath thus defied, muster themselves together, and proclaim open war: their bands consist of tall yeomen, that serve on foot, commanded by certain sergeants of their bands, who for leading of men, are known to be of more experience than the best low-country captains. In ambuscado do these lie by day and night, to cut off this enemy to the City, if he dare but come down. But the politic bankrupt, barricadoing his sconce with double locks, treble doors, invincible bolts, and pieces of timber four or five stories high, victuals himself for a month or so; and then in the dead of night, marches up higher into the country with bag and baggage; parlies then are summoned; compositions offered; a truce is sometimes taken for three or four years; or (which is more common) a dishonourable peace (seeing no other remedy) is on both sides concluded, he (like the States), being the only gainer by such civil wars, whilst the citizen that is the lender, is the loser: *Nam crimine ab uno disce omnes*, look how much he snatches from one man's sheaf, he gleans from every one, if they be a hundred.

The victory being thus gotten by baseness and treachery, back comes he marching with spread colours again to the City; advances in the open street as he did before; sells the goods of his neighbours before his face without blushing: he jets up and down in silks woven out of other men's stocks, feeds deliciously upon other men's purses, rides on his ten pound geldings, in other men's saddles, and is now a new man made out of wax, that's to say, out of those bonds, whose seals he most dishonestly hath cancelled. O velvet-guarded thieves! O yea-and-by-nay cheaters! O civil, O grave and right worshipful cozeners![1]

"Newes from Hell"

Newes from Hell; brought by the Divells Carrier (1606), which he amplified next year and reissued as *A Knights Conjuring done in Earnest discovered in Jest* (1607), was also developed out of hints from *Pierce Penilesse*. Further grim descriptions of the corrupt life of London are balanced by the messenger's experience of Hell, where he finds London usurers and other evildoers being tried for their sins or still deliriously slaving at the tasks imposed by their own greed. Dekker's tale of Orpheus in this tract makes an excellent pendant to Nashe's sprightly story of Hero and Leander.[2]

That venturous but jealous musician of Thrace, Eurydice's husband, who being besotted on his wife . . . went alive with his fiddle at his back, to see if he could bail her out of that adamantine prison. The fees he was to pay for her were jigs and country-dances: he paid them; the forfeits if he put on yellow stockings and looked back upon her was her everlasting lying there, without bail or mainprize. The loving cockscomb could not choose but look back, and so lost her: perhaps he did it because he would be rid of her. The moral of which is, that if a man leave his own business and have an eye to his wife's doings, she'll give him the slip though she run to the devil for her labour.[3]

Leaving on one side some trifling compilations and other items we come to a pair of booklets in which Dekker took up the trite business, started by Awdeley and Harman and continued by Greene and Rowlands, of detecting and depicting professional roguery. There does not appear to have been anything left to discover; at

[1] "The Seven Deadly Sins of London" (*Non-Dramatic Works*, ed. E. Arber, 1885, pp. 21-24.)

[2] See p. 159.

[3] Dekker's *Non-Dramatic Works*, ed. A. S. Grosart, 1884, ii. 101.

any rate, Dekker simply appropriates all he wants from the earlier authorities. He obtained the whole of his enumeration of upright men, rufflers, anglers, wild rogues, Abraham men, and the like, from Harman's *Caveat*, the anecdotes and other touches of first-hand knowledge that make Harman's pages such lively reading being omitted.[1] Then Dekker takes the first and second parts of Greene's *Cony-catching* and Rowlands's pamphlet, *Greenes Ghost haunting Conie-catchers*, and finds there enough matter for the rest of his book.

"The Bel-man of London"

But the high-handedness is justified by the use to which Dekker put his borrowed material. He describes *The Bel-man of London* (1608) as "A Discoverie of all the idle Vagabonds in England: their conditions, their lawes among themselves, their degrees and orders, and their maners of living, both men and women." All this is stale enough; what is fresh is the unified picture that Dekker achieves of this outcast world, into which the narrator is suddenly pitched as he roams one day through a quiet rural solitude that makes him dream of fairies or hamadryads. All at once he happens upon a cottage in a wood, which looks like an inn. It is the headquarters of the "Damned Crew," the "Ragged Regiment," whose orgies he presently watches from a gallery where he bribes an old woman to conceal him. He sees the Grand Signior of the fraternity initiate a young squire into the order, emptying on his head a pot of ale, and listens to an allocution which is a catalogue of all their degrees and faculties. Further information is supplied by the old

[1] The closeness of Dekker's version may be judged from the following comparison of passages chosen at random:

Harman	Dekker
Then haue you iiij. more (refuges) in Middlesex, drawe the pudding out of the fyre in Harrow on the hyll parish, the Crose Keyes in Cranford parish, Saynt Iulyans in Thystell worth parish, the house of pyty in Northhall parysh. . . . The vpright men haue geuen all these nycke names to the places aboue sayde. Yet haue we two notable places in Kent, not fare from London: the one is betwene Detforde and Rothered, called the Kynges barne, standing alone, that they haunt commonly; the other is Ketbroke, standinge by blacke heath, halfe a myle from anye house.	In Middlesex likewise stand foure other Harbours for them, namely, Draw the pudding out of the fire, (which is in the parish of Harrow on the Hill.); The Crosse Keyes, (which is in Cranford parish,) Saint Julians, (which is in Thistleworth parish.) And the house of Pitty in Northall Parish. The Kinges Barne neere Darford (*sic*), and Ketbrooke neere Blackheath, are likewise houses of good receite for them.

crone, and after nightfall the traveller wends his way back to the city, where he encounters the Bel-man himself. This worthy demonstrates from what he knows by nightly experience that there is nothing to choose between town and country in the matter of wickedness, and enters on a detailed account of the various laws of cosenage.

A second and a third edition of the *Bel-man* were called for the same year, and Dekker pretended that he had a rival in the field, describing himself as the Bel-man's brother, who aspired to lead the attack on the army of disorder troubling the common weal.[1] So he came out at once with a sequel, *Lanthorne and Candle-Light, Or The Bell-mans second Nights walke* (1608), "bringing to light a Brood of more strange Villanies than ever were this yeare discovered." This time the setting is more trite and clumsy. Hell is alarmed by the Bel-man's revelations, and a council being summoned it is decided to send a devil to London to ensure that profligacy and crime go on as usual. But the result is only another enumeration of fraudulent practices. Knavery seems to be rooted in human nature and the interest for Dekker's readers lay evidently more in the amusing nature of the tricks exposed than in the need to be on the watch against them. Anyhow, they bought the book, which was reprinted twice the next year, and in a new edition in 1612, with the supplementary *O per se O, or a new Cryer of Lanthorne and Candle-light*, which recounted various rascalities perpetrated by daylight as an addition to the deeds of darkness.

"Lanthorne and Candle-Light"

A year after the *Bel-man*, Dekker produced the best of all his tracts, *The Guls Horn-Booke: or Fashions to please all sorts of Guls* (1609), which is another work based on a foreign masterpiece. It is an attempt to naturalize the peculiar vein of satire exploited by several German writers, of whom the best known was F. Dedekind, author of *Grobianus* (1549). Dekker made skilful plays with the sardonic method of Grobianism, but was bound to fail in trying to fit the caricature of German grossness, slovenliness and brutality to an English subject. He says in the preface:

"The Guls Horn-Booke"

This tree of gulls was planted long since, but not taking root could never bear till now. It hath a relish of Grobianism, and tastes very

[1] See p. 146.

strongly of it in the beginning; the reason thereof is that, having translated many books of that into English verse, and not greatly liking the subject, I altered the shape, and of a Dutchman fashioned a mere Englishmen."

Grobianism

Dedekind wrote his *Grobianus* in Latin, and it was turned into German by Kaspar Scheidt (1551), who was responsible for many additional features which Dedekind gladly accepted and made use of in the expanded *Grobianus et Grobiana* (1552), in which a new character, Grobiana, a sluttish and shameless quean, matches Grobian's uncouthness. The work was immensely popular; it went into numerous editions, and was repeatedly translated. An English translation, *The Schoole of Slovenrie: or Cato turned wrong side outward*, appeared in 1605. Grobianus was "the Cato of inverted etiquette."[1] All the dictates of good breeding are read backwards. He gets up lazily at midday, and if it is cold dresses himself without ceremony before the hall fire. He goes unwashed and with his hair uncut; he makes himself comfortable at whomsoever else's expense. Gluttony is his ruling passion, unmannerliness his pride. He is the grand exponent of what Scheidt called "the art of unseemly, riotous, and filthy behaviour."

The London gull

Grobianism was merely Dekker's starting-point. At first he keeps close to his original; but he rapidly finds that the scathing satire of boorish Germans falls flat when applied to his own countrymen. The London gallant was noted for excessive attention to his person and for ostentatious attire, not for dirt and slovenliness. The fault of his manners was rather affectation and mincing gentility than wilful and overbearing churlishness. Dekker therefore changes his plan, and, maintaining the style of ironical instruction, tells one of those raw youths who aspired to cut a figure among the town gallants how he should behave in a tavern, in an ordinary, at the playhouse, and in that resort of all that is elegant, Paul's Walk.

The gull had already appeared in *Lanthorne and Candle-Light*; he was, in fact, the indispensable dupe in all the tales of cony-catching. He was "the freshwater soldier" who had never before followed

[1] C. H. Herford, *Studies in the Literary Relations of England and Germany in the Sixteenth Century*, 1886, vii.: "Grobianus and Grobianism." Cp. *Camb. Hist. of Eng. Lit.*, iii., p. 82, and iv., pp. 355-356. *Cato* was a mediæval manual of etiquette.

these strange wars, who had just inherited some ten or twelve thousand in ready money and many hundreds a year, for whom scouts were to lie in ambush so that "the whole troop of weather-beaten gallants" might beleaguer him. "The eagle feathers his nest, the wood-pecker picks up his crumbs, the gull-groper grows fat with good feeding; and the gull himself, at whom everyone has a pull, hath in the end scarce feathers enough to keep his own back warm." Such callow young fellows, of whom there were numbers in London, attracted by its amusements and dissipations or by the desire of pushing their fortunes, offered the best substitute for the conceited bumpkins castigated by Dedekind and his coadjutor.

Lying abed was certainly one of the chief observances of Grobianism. Dekker recommends his pupils to stay between the sheets till noonday.

By the opinion of all philosophers and physicians, it is not good to trust the air with our bodies till the sun with his flame-coloured wings hath fanned away the misty smoke of the morning, and refined that thick tobacco breath which the rheumatic night throws abroad of purpose to put out the eye of the element; which work questionless cannot be perfectly finished till the sun's car-horses stand prancing on the very top of highest noon; so that then, and not till then, is the most healthful hour to be stirring. Do you require examples to persuade you? At what time do lords and ladies use to rise but then? Your simpering merchants' wives are the fairest lyers in the world; and is not eleven o'clock their common hour? They find, no doubt, unspeakable sweetness in such lying, else they would not day by day put it so in practice. In a word, midday slumbers are golden; they make the body fat, the skin fair, the flesh plump, delicate, and tender; they set a russet colour on the cheeks of young women, and make lusty courage to rise up in men; they make us thrifty, both in sparing victuals (for breakfasts thereby are saved from the hell-mouth of the belly) and in preserving apparel; for while we warm us in our beds, our clothes are not worn.

The casements of thine eyes being then at this commendable time of the day newly set open, choose rather to have thy wind-pipe cut in pieces than to salute any man. Bid not good-morrow so much as to thy father, though he be an emperor. An idle ceremony it is, and can do him little good; to thyself it may bring much harm; for if he be a wise man that knows how to hold his peace, of necessity must he be counted a fool that cannot keep his tongue.

Speedily dropping mere Grobianism, Dekker conducts his aspiring novice to the Englishman's promenade in St Paul's.

Now for your venturing into the Walk, be circumspect and wary what pillar you come in at, and take heed in any case, as you love the reputation of your honour, that you avoid the serving-man's log, and approach not within five fathom of that pillar ; but bend your course directly in the middle line, that the whole body of the church may appear to be yours ; where, in view of all, you may publish your suit in what manner you affect most, either with the slide of your cloak from the one shoulder, and then you must, as 'twere in anger, suddenly snatch at the middle of the inside (if it be taffeta at the least) and so by that means your costly lining is betrayed, or else by the pretty advantage of compliment. But one note by the way do I especially woo you to, the neglect of which makes many of our gallants cheap and ordinary, that by no means you be seen above four turns ; but in the fifth make yourself away, either in some of the sempsters' shops, the new tobacco-office, or amongst the booksellers, where, if you cannot read, exercise your smoke, and inquire who has writ against this divine weed, etc. For this withdrawing yourself a little will much benefit your suit, which else, by too long walking, would be stale to the whole spectators. But, howsoever, if Paul's Jacks be once up with their elbows, and quarrelling to strike eleven, as soon as ever the clock has parted them, and ended the fray with his hammer, let not the Duke's gallery contain you any longer, but pass away apace in open view. In which departure, if by chance you either encounter or aloof off throw your inquisitive eye upon any knight or squire, being your familiar, salute him not by his name of Sir such a one or so, but call him Ned or Jack, etc. This will set off your estimation with great men ; and if (though there be a dozen companies between you 'tis the better) he call aloud to you (for that's most gentle) to know where he shall find you at two o'clock, tell him at such an ordinary or such, and be sure to name those that are dearest, and whither none but your gallants resort. After dinner you may appear again, having translated yourself out of your English cloth coat into a light Turkey grogram, if you have that happiness of shifting, and then be seen, for a turn or two, to correct your teeth with some quill or silver instrument, and to cleanse your gums with a wrought handkerchief. It skills not whether you dined or no (that's best known to your stomach) or in what place you dined, though it were with cheese, of your own mother's making, in your chamber or study.

At the ordinary, he must walk up and down as scornfully and carelessly as a gentleman-usher, with a friend who is dressed if may be less expensively than himself, so as to be a foil ; "and this will be a means to publish your clothes better than Paul's, a tennis court, or a playhouse. . . . Discourse as loud as you can, no matter to what purpose if you but make a noise, and laugh in fashion, and have a good sour face to promise quarrelling, you shall be much observed." Than, after more directions as to ostentatious behaviour, comes another touch of grobianism :

When you are set down to dinner, you must eat as impudently as can be, for that's most gentlemanlike ; when your knight is upon his stewed mutten, be presently, though you be but a captain, in the bosom of your goose ; and when your justice of peace is knuckle-deep in goose, you may, without disparagement to your blood, though you have a lady to your mother, fall very manfully to your woodcocks.

In a tavern he will vary his fare with the season and be careful not to confine himself to one particular liquor, "but rather be a general scholar, that is, have a lick at all sorts of learning and away."

Your discourse at the table must be such as that which you utter at your ordinary ; your behaviour the same, but somewhat more careless ; for where your expense is great, let your modesty be less; and, though you should be mad in a tavern, the largeness of the items will bear with your incivility : you may, without prick to your conscience, set the want of your wit against the superfluity and sauciness of their reckonings. . . .

When the terrible reckoning, like an indictment, bids you hold up your hand, and that you must answer it at the bar, you must not abate one penny in any particular, no, though they reckon cheese to you, when you have neither eaten any nor could ever abide it, raw or toasted ; but cast your eye only upon the totalis and no further ; for to traverse the bill would betray you to be acquainted with the rates of the market, nay more, it would make the vintners believe you were paterfamilias and kept a house, which, I assure you, is not now in fashion.

Still intent on rallying the fop's desire to make himself conspicuous, Dekker takes him through the streets, giving similar advice for his conduct in all emergencies, and brings him to the theatre. There he must occupy a seat on the stage itself, where, full in the public eye, he can talk loudly while the play is going on, laugh outright at the crisis of a tragedy, and win further notoriety by freely abusing the author. The book is as complete a picture of one phase of London life as Deloney's is of another; but it suffered the usual fate of ironical writing; it failed to sell to anything like the same extent as the plainer-spoken *Newes from Hell* and the *Bel-man.*

Other miscellanies of fact and fiction

Dekker's pamphlets, and also his plays, belong to a mass of literature about London life which at a later date would inevitably have taken the form of fiction. The forms it actually took were miscellaneous in the extreme. There were medleys of anecdote and descriptive sketches, appealing to the sense of curiosity or love of the queer and picturesque; there were further collections of jests, assuming more and more the shape of picaresque adventures; ballads and other occasional verse; and books of travel in London and the suburbs, which began apparently in journeys for a wager, such as that recounted in *Kemps nine daies wonder. Performed in a daunce from London to Norwich* (1600). The author of this, William Kemp, went on a morrice dance between the two cities, and writes a lively report "to satisfy his friends the truth against all lying ballad-makers." One of Deloney's characters, the eccentric Green King, had gone all the way from London to Bristol in one of these escapades. An even earlier example was *The most dangerous and memorable adventure of Richard Ferris* (1590), the account of a voyage in a small wherry by a man who undertook to row from Tower Wharf to Bristol.

John Taylor, the Water-Poet.

John Taylor, the Water-Poet, whose voluminous writings in verse and prose are a veritable encyclopædia of popular lore about London and the Home Counties, wrote several such serio-comic narratives.[1] One of the best accounts of such a frolic is Richard Brathwaite's *Barnabee's Journall* (1638), a picaresque narrative that happens to be in rhymed Latin and English verse.[2] *Westward*

[1] E.g. *The Pennyless Pilgrimage, or the Money-lesse Perambulation* (1618), a record in both prose and verse of such a journey from London to Edinburgh; *A Very Merry Wherry-Ferry-Voyage: or Yorke for my Money* (1622), this was in verse; *John Taylor the Water-Poet's Travels through London to visit all the Taverns* (1636), a directory full of information for the modern antiquary; *Taylor's Travels and Circular Perambulation, through . . . the Famous Cities of London and Westminster* (1636) and *John Taylor's Wanderings to see the Wonders of the West. How he travelled neere 600 miles, from London to the Lands End, and Home again* (1649). See *Works of John Taylor the Water-Poet* (Spenser Society, from folio of 1630, 3 vols., 1869, other works, 5 vols., 1870-1877). The best account of Taylor is in Southey's *Lives and Works of the Uneducated Poets*, new ed., 1925.

[2] *Barnabæ Itinerarium or Barnabee's Journal*, ed. J. Haslewood, rev. W. C. Hazlitt, 1876.

for Smelts (1620) also is slightly connected with the genre; but its special feature is the tales from the *Decameron* and other old sources, all in an English setting, which are put in the mouths of seven merry fishwives on a trip up Thames.[1]

Taylor dealt in jests, as in his *Wit and Mirth. Chargeably collected Out of Taverns, Ordinaries, Innes. . . . Made up and fashioned into Clinches, Bulls, Quirkes, Yerkes, Quips, and Jerkes* (1629); in characterizations, midway between the Theophrastian character and such pieces as Greene's *Disputation*, like *A Bawd, a vertuous Bawd, a modest Bawd: as Shee Deserves, reproove, or else applaud* (1635); with which may be grouped two others in heroic verse, *A Whore* and *A Thief*; in broadsheet reports of murders, like *The Unnatural Father*, or of local celebrities, such as *The Great Eater of Kent*, an earlier prodigy than the Nottinghamshire Gideon Giles. A growing preference for fact to fiction is evinced by the abundance of ephemeral work like Taylor's.[2]

[1] *Westward for Smelts*, ed. J. O. Halliwell (Percy Society Reprints, xxii., 1843).
[2] *Works of John Taylor* (Spenser Society, 1869).

CHAPTER XIV

THE WRITERS OF CHARACTERY

Char-actery

THE outbreak of character-writing which took place at the beginning of the seventeenth century is commonly attributed to the interest excited by Isaac Casaubon's edition of Theophrastus, with a Latin translation (1592), and the English translation by John Healey that followed (1593). But the appearance of the Baconian essay probably had quite as much to do with it. Charactery is but a specialized kind of essay-writing, as Breton, Mynshul, Stephens, and other practitioners of the art were aware when they called their characters "essays." Apart from the new fashion of making whole books out of such inventories of human qualities, charactery itself was almost as old as English literature. Theophrastus was not entirely forgotten during the Middle Ages, nor his influence dead. Chaucer was a master of the art, both of hitting off tersely and wittily the points of a character, and of bringing out contrasts[1]; and anyone reading Langland with open eyes can but see that he too understands the uses of charactery. But in these two cases the character was subordinate to the purposes of a higher kind of art, not a sufficient object in itself. On the other hand, in satirical works, such as Barclay's *Shyp of Folys* or *Cocke Lorelles Bote*, or in *The Hye Way to the Spyttel Hous*, the on eaim was to present the characters in all their grotesque variety, and to show them off.

Char-actery in Awdeley and Harman, Greene, Nashe, etc.

A nearer approximation to the formal classification of character will have been noticed in Awdeley and Harman's catalogues of the vagrant tribe. Greene gave an example of charactery in his *Quippe for an Upstart Courtier*, where he reviews a large crowd of contemporary types. Nashe's Mistress Minx, in *Pierce Penilesse* (1592)[2]

[1] E. C. Baldwin points out an allusion to "Theofraste" in *The Wife of Bath's Prologue*, 671.

[2] See p. 157.

anticipates Hall and Overbury; and *Christes Teares* (1593), whereunto, he says, "is annexed a comparative admonition of London," slips naturally into the same procedure. See, for instance, his sketch of the making of a usurer:

Being a young trader, and having of old Mumpsimus, his avaricious master, learned to be his craftsmaster, for a year or two he is very thrifty and husbandly; he pays and takes as duly as the clock strikes; he seemeth very sober and precise, and bringeth all men in love with him. When he thinketh he hath throughly wrung himself into the world's good opinion, and that his credit is as much as he will demand, he goes and tries it, and on the tenter-hooks stretches it. No man he knoweth but he will scrape a little book courtesy of; two or three thousand pounds, perhaps, makes up his mouth. When he hath it all in his hands, for a month or two he revels it, and cuts it out in the whole cloth.

He falls acquainted with gentlemen, frequents ordinaries and dicing-houses daily, where, when some of them, in play, have lost all their money, he is very diligent at hand, on their chains, or bracelets, or jewels, to lend them half the value. Now, this is the nature of young gentlemen, that where they have broke the ice and borrowed once, they will come again the second time; and that these young foxes know, as well as the beggar knows his dish. But at the second time of their coming it is doubtful to say, whether they shall have money or no. The world grows hard, and we all are mortal; let them make him any assurance before a judge, and they shall have some hundred pounds, *per consequence*, in silks and velvets. The third time, if they come, they shall have baser commodities; the fourth time, lute-strings and grey paper; and then, I pray, pardon me, I am not for you; pay me that you owe me, and you shall have anything.[1]

Nicholas Breton's characters

Several of Nicholas Breton's stories, dialogues and nondescript pieces show a strong inclination towards formal charactery, and also the influence of the essay. Thus he has a weakness for contrasts. Take, for example, the two dialogues already noticed, *A Mad World my Masters* (1603) and *Grimello's Fortunes* (1604).[2] The cowards so extravagantly portrayed in the latter may well be

[1] *Works*, ii.: *Christes Teares*. Nashe may possibly have read Theophrastus in the original; at any rate, he alludes to "the golden book of Theophrastus" in his *Anatomie of Absurdities*; see "The Relation of the Seventeenth Century Character to the Periodical Essay," by E. C. Baldwin, who thinks Nashe had read him (*Mod. Lang. of America*, xix., 79 n.).

[2] See pp. 149-151.

compared with Breton's more Theophrastian method in *Characters upon Essaies* (1615):

A Coward

A coward is the child of fear: he was begotten in cold blood, when nature had much ado to make up a creature like a man: his life is a kind of sickness, which breeds a kind of palsy in the joints, and his death the terror of his conscience, with the extreme weakness of his faith: he loves peace as his life, for he fears a sword in his soul: if he cut his finger, he looketh presently for the sign, and if his head ache, he is ready to make his will: a report of a cannon strikes him flat on his face, and a clap of thunder makes him a strange *metamorphosis*: rather than he will fight he will be beaten, and if his legs will help him, he will put his arms to no trouble: he makes love commonly with his purse, and brags most of his maidenhead: he will not marry but into a quiet family, and not too fair a wife, to avoid quarrels: if his wife frown upon him he sighs, and if she give him an unkind word he weeps: he loves not the horns of a bull, nor the paws of a bear; and if a dog bark he will not come near the house: if he be rich he is afraid of thieves, and if he be poor he will be slave to a beggar. In sum, he is the shame of manhood, the disgrace of nature, the scorn of reason, and the hate of honour.[1]

[1] *Works*, ii.: *The Goode and the Badde*, 43 (p. 13). The earlier sketch, of the old lecher, in *The Miseries of Mavillia* (see p. 148), is also worth comparing. Theophrastus himself had dealt with the theme of cowardice, so let us put him and Breton side by side. The following, "Of Timidity or Fearfulness," is from Healey's translation from Casaubon's edition (reprinted with Earle's *Microcosmographie*, Temple Edition, 1899):

"Fearfulness may seem to be a timorous distrustful dejection of the mind. A fearful man is of this fashion: if he be at sea, he fears the promontories to be the enemies' navy; and at every cross gale or billow asketh if the sailors be expert, whether there be not some novices amongst them or no. When the pilot gives the ship but a little clout, he asketh if the ship hold a middle course. He knows not whether he should fear or hope. He telleth him that sits next him how he was terrified with a dream not long since. Then he puts off his shirt, and gives it the boy; entreats the sailors to set him on shore. Being in service at land, he calleth his fellow-soldiers unto him, and looking earnestly upon them saith, 'Tis hard to know whether you be enemies or no.' Hearing a bustling and seeing some fall, he tells them, that for pure haste he had forgotten his two-hand sword; and so soon as by running he hath recovered his tent, he sendeth the boy to scout warily where the enemy is, then hideth he his long sword under his pillow; then he spendeth much time in seeking of it. And if by chance he see any wounded brought over toward the tent, he runneth to him, encourageth him, bids him take a man's heart and be resolute. He's very tender over him, and wipes away the corruption of his wound with a sponge; he drives away the flies. He had rather do any work about the house than fight. He careth not how little blood he loseth himself; his two-heeled sword is his best weapon. When the trumpet sounds a charge, sitting in his tent, 'A mischief on him,' saith he, 'he disquieteth the poor wounded man, he can take no rest

In Breton's *Characters upon Essaies, Morall and Divine*, he follows Bacon the essayist rather than Bishop Hall, whose *Characters of Vertues and Vices* had appeared in 1608. It is a series of cogitations on such themes as wisdom, learning, knowledge, peace, war, truth, time, death. But in *The Goode and the Badde, or Descriptions of the Worthies and Unworthies of this Age* (1616), he prefers the analytical method of Hall. Instead, however, of placing the good and the bad in separate books, Breton ranges his virtuous and his vicious characters alternately: "A Worthy King" is followed by "An Unworthy King," "A Wise Man" by "A Foole," and so on. The pair given below are a fair illustration of his method of contrast:

A Worthy Merchant

A worthy merchant is the heir of adventure, whose hopes hang much upon wind. Upon a wooden horse he rides through the world, and in a merry gale makes a path through the seas. He is a discoverer of countries, and a finder out of commodities, resolute in his attempts, and royal in his expenses. He is the life of traffic, and the maintainer of trade, the sailor's master, and the soldier's friend. He is the exercise of the Exchange, the honour of credit, the observation of time, and the understanding of thrift. His study is number, his care his accounts, his comfort his conscience, and his wealth his good name. He fears not Scylla, and sails close by Charybdis, and having beaten out a storm rides at rest in a harbour. By his sea-gain he makes his land-purchase, and by the knowledge of trade finds the key of treasure. Out of his travails he makes his discourses, and from his eye-observations brings the models of architectures. He plants the earth with foreign fruits, and knows at home what is good abroad. He is neat in apparel, modest in demeanour, dainty in diet, and civil in his carriage. In sum, he is the pillar of a city, the enricher of a country, the furnisher of a court, and the worthy servant of a king.

An Unworthy Merchant

An unworthy merchant is a kind of peddler, who (with the help of a broker) gets more by his wit than by his honesty. He doth sometime use to give out money to gamesters, be paid in post, upon a hand

for him.' He loves the blood and glory of another man's wound. He will brag when he comes out of the field, how many friends he brought off with the hazard of his own life. He brings to the hurt man many of the same band to visit him; and tells them all that he with his own hand brought him into his tent."

at dice. Sometimes he gains more by baubles than better stuffs, and rather than fail will adventure a false oath for a fraudulent gain. He deals with no whole sale but all his honesty is at one word. As for wares and weights he knows how to hold the balance, and for his conscience he is not ignorant what to do with it. His travail is most by land, for he fears to be too busy with the water, and whatsoever his ware be he will be sure of his money. The most of his wealth is in a pack of trifles, and for his honesty I dare not pass my word for him. If he be rich 'tis ten to one of his pride, and if he be poor he breaks without his fast. In sum, he is the disgrace of a merchant, the dishonour of a city, the discredit of his parish, and the dislike of all.[1]

Breton's addiction to a mechanical symmetry of opposites is a weakness that had not seduced Theophrastus. The neater the antithesis, the less is it likely to carry conviction. Such apposition was, however, well suited to Breton's love of a witty sententiousness.

Ben Jonson's tendency to charactery

Ben Jonson was a skilled hand at charactery, and, as might be expected, many of the longer pieces in *Timber: or, Discoveries*, are specimens of the art.[2] He was, in truth, more likely than Nashe to have been acquainted with the work of Theophrastus, although he does not cite him by name. When he printed his comedy, *Every Man out of his Humour* (1600), he appended to the list of *dramatis personæ* a regular characterization of each individual. *Cynthia's Revels*, presented the same year, has more elaborate characters of a courtier, a traveller, a poet, and a bawd, set in the actual dialogue; and others are drawn at briefer length or taken by the handful together. He thus strays beyond the province of drama. Instead of attending to his work, which was to show men and women revealing their personalities in action, he takes it upon himself to analyse and describe their peculiarities. This is more than a fault in technique; it goes deeper. Charactery isolated idiosyncrasy, and made it more and more of an abstract quality. Even when it invented concrete acts and ways of behaving, in which the characters showed their particular foibles, it did not put life into them or make them real individuals. At the best it gave the animated presentment of a type; at the worst, a bundle of abstract qualities. In his earlier plays this is what Jonson was too often doing: it is the very principle of the comedy of humours, and its essential defect. Jonson

[1] *Works*, ii.: *The Good and the Badde*, pp. 24-25.
[2] See pp. 206-207.

at his weakest, along with his juniors, Beaumont and Fletcher, is merely a Theophrastian playwright.[1]

Bishop Hall

Joseph Hall (1574-1656), who, in his *Virgidemiarum* (1597), composed when he was still at Cambridge, announced himself, erroneously, as the first English satirist,[2] was the first to publish a volume of characters avowedly modelled on Theophrastus. His *Characters of Vertues and Vices* appeared in 1608. Since the date of the satires he had become a graver person, with the reputation of an accomplished preacher ; a wit, but also a theologian of some authority. His utopian *Mundus Alter et Idem*, though it was published as late as 1605, was written at the time of his satires, to which it is nearly related. An anonymous translation by John Healey came out in 1609, under the title, *The Discovery of a New World, or A Description of the South Indies. By an English Mercury.*[3] Other books of the interim were his religious *Meditations and Vowes* (1606), and divers poetical writings of an elegiac or ceremonial kind. In later life Hall took part in the Smectymnuus controversy, was bishop of Exeter and then of Norwich, and was treated contumeliously during the Civil War. But these later events do not concern us.

A Disciple of Theophrastus

Hall took Theophrastus as his model ; but it was impossible for a moralist and a divine in the age of puritanism to keep strictly to the line traced by the Athenian of two thousand years before. Theophrastus of Lesbos (371-287 B.C.), who succeeded Aristotle in the presidency of the Lyceum, called his book, of which twenty-eight chapters have survived, Ηθικοὶ χαρακτῆρες, ethical characters ; but it is a study of behaviour rather than conduct, of idiosyncrasies rather than morals. Without betraying either sympathy or malice, he noted down ingrained tendencies and peculiarities

[1] Jonson's comedy is "a grafting of the scientific theory of humours on the social portraiture of Plautus and Terence, the Roman descendants of Menander" (G. S. Gordon, *English Literature and the Classics*, p. 80).

[2] "I first adventure, follow me who list,
And be the second English satirist."—Prologue to *Satires*.

[3] Esdaile records another edition with the title, *The Travels of Don Francisco De Quevedo. Through Terra Australis Incognita, Discovering the Laws, Customs, Manners and Fashions of the South Indians* (1684), and an abridgment, *Psittacorum Regio. The Land of Parrots: Or, The She-Lands. With a description of other strange adjacent Countries, in the Dominions of Prince de l'Amour, not hitherto found in any Geographical Map. By one of the late most reputed Wits* (1669).

which he had observed in the Greek world of his day, the era of Menander and the New Comedy, and thus executed realistic portraits of certain representative types.

Compared with the loftier creations of the tragedians or the caricatures of Aristophanes, these doubtless are much more faithful representations of ordinary people, the men in the street and the market-place ; they belong, not to poetry, but to the world that a realistic novelist would have depicted. The method was to take a human quality—insincerity, meanness, stupidity, tactlessness, avarice, querulousness—define it, and then enumerate the tricks of behaviour by which it continually betrayed itself to a sharp-eyed observer. Theophrastus showed what a man is by telling us what he does. Consider this sketch of the diffident or distrustful man :

Diffidence or distrust is that which makes us jealous of fraud from all men. A diffident or distrustful man is he, who if he send one to buy victuals, sends another after him to know what he paid. If he bear money about him, he tells it at every furlong. Lying in his bed, he asks his wife if she have locked her casket, if his chests be fast locked, if the doors be fast bolted ; and, although she assure it, notwithstanding, naked without shoes he riseth out of his bed, lighteth a candle, surveys all, and hardly falls asleep again for distrust. When he comes to his debtors for his use-money, he goes strong with his witnesses. When he is to turn or trim some old gaberdine, he putteth it not to the best fuller, but to him that doth best secure the return of his commodity. If any man borrow any pots, any pails, or pans, if he lend them it is very rare ; but commonly he sends for them instantly again, before they are well at home with them. He biddeth his boy not to follow them at the heels, but to go before them, lest they make escape with them. And to those which bid him make a note of any thing they borrow, " nay," saith he, " lay down rather, for my men are not at leisure to come and ask for it."[1]

Healey's is a heavy and lifeless rendering, and does scant justice to the touches of humour that enliven these inventories of characteristics. Genuine humour there is, though it is subdued to the main purpose, accurate and lifelike exposition of a chosen trait.

The thankless man, when a friend has sent him something from his table, says to the servant who brings it, " He grudged me a dish

[1] J. Healey's translation (1609), reprinted in the Temple Edition of Earle's *Microcosmographie* (1899).

of soup and a cup of wine, I suppose, and so wouldn't invite me to dinner." When his sweetheart kisses him, he says, " I wonder if you really do love me so in your heart."

A bore is the sort of fellow who, the moment you open your mouth, tells you that your remarks are idle, that he knows all about it, and if you'll only listen, you'll soon find out. As you attempt to make answer, he suddenly breaks in with such interruptions as : " Don't forget what you were about to say "—" That reminds me "—" What an admirable thing talk is ! "—" But, as I omitted to mention "—" You grasp the idea at once "—" I was watching this long time to see whether you would come to the same conclusion as myself." In phrases like this he's so fertile that the person who happens to meet him cannot even open his mouth to speak. [1]

Hall regarded Theophrastus as primarily a moral philosopher, one of " the divines of the old heathens," who " received the acts of an inbred law, in the Sinai of nature, and delivered them with many expositions to the multitude." [2] That is, Hall thought him a moralizing Puritan like himself, and in his own characters assumed that he was following in the footsteps of his original without deviation. But Theophrastus was not a moralist in his disciple's sense of the word, nor was he a preacher. Charactery to him was simply a branch of natural history : he was, as Sainte-Beuve phrases it, " a botanist of minds." [3] What instantly strikes the modern who reads him is his neutrality, his complete detachment. If he thought that his delineations might lead to the recognition of faults and their amendment, he dropped no hint that this was his object or expectation. No doubt he was spurred in some measure by the impulse to satirize : his choice of vices and foibles instead of more sterling qualities is proof of it. But he carefully dissembled any malicious bias, and let his flatterers, cowards, braggarts, fools, cads, boors, and backbiters expose their own infirmities, without wasting an adjective in reproof or derision.[4]

[1] *The Characters of Theophrastus : a Translation.* With Introduction by C. C. Bennett and W. A. Hammond, New York, 1902.

[2] " A Premonition of the Title and Use of Characters " (*Characters of Vertues and Vices*).

[3] He was the founder of the science of Botany (see G. S. Gordon, *English Literature and the Classics,* Oxford, 1912, pp. 49-86 : " Theophrastus and his Imitators ").

[4] Professor G. S. Gordon takes a different view from that accepted here. He says : " The English Character," I conclude, " is in the main a by-product of the

Hall's puritanism and censoriousness

There is nothing of this scientific impartiality in Joseph Hall. He had been a satirist, hence he employed his wit to evolve epigrams stigmatizing the vicious. He was a Christian divine, to whom the indifference of a Theophrastus would have been a dereliction of his bounden duty. No one, in truth, in that age of moral conflict, could stand aloof from the fray and botanize on the battlefield of life. And, being more of a moral philosopher, and less of an artist, he could not manage the objective method of the Athenian. He was abstract, where the other was concrete ; he was analytical, where his predecessor was content to record a man's habitual doings without attempting to explain the state of mind which prompted them. Six of the eleven vices treated by Hall are from Theophrastus ; the eleven virtues are an innovation in charactery, standing for the Christian ideals of self-knowledge, self-control, and utter truthfulness. Thus his characters of virtues are eloquent appeals ; those of vices, denunciations and warnings. In both, the age's love of antithesis and conceit is very evident ; but in the panegyrics of the virtues, which were written last, these figures are subdued to the service of a fine and persuasive oratory.

Virtue is not loved enough, because she is not seen ; and vice loseth much detestation, because her ugliness is secret. Certainly, my lords, there are so many beauties, and so many graces in the face of goodness, that no eye can possibly see it without affection, without ravishment ; and the visage of evil is so monstrous through loathsome deformities, that if her lovers were not ignorant they would be mad with disdain and astonishment. What need we more than to discover these two to the world ? This work shall save the labour of exhorting and persuasion.[1]

There we have a clear statement of his didactic aim, and in the portrait of the wise man that heads the list of virtuous characters Hall indicates with equal clearness the cardinal points of his spiritual geography :

Comedy of Humours, accidentally determined, at an early moment in its history, by the opportune appearance of Theophrastus's model. Of these two strains in the Character, the Theophrastian and the Jonsonian, the first is most apparent in Hall, and the second, as we should expect from their life about town, in the work of Overbury and his friends" (*English Literature and the Classics*, p. 79: "Theophrastus and his Imitators").

[1] The Proem.

Of an Honest Man

He looks not to what he might do, but what he should. Justice is his first guide, the second law of his actions is expedience. He had rather complain than offend, and hates sin more for the indignity of it than the danger. His simple uprightness works in him that confidence which ofttimes wrongs him, and gives advantage to the subtle, when he rather pities their faithlessness than repents of his credulity. He hath but one heart, and that lies open to sight; and were it not for discretion, he never thinks aught whereof he would avoid a witness. His word is his parchment, and his yea his oath, which he will not violate for fear or for loss. The mishaps of following events may cause him to blame his providence, can never cause him to eat his promise: neither saith he, This I saw not; but, This I said. When he is made his friend's executor, he defrays debts, pays legacies, and scorneth to gain by orphans, or to ransack graves, and therefore will be true to a dead friend, because he sees him not. All his dealings are square and above the board; he bewrays the fault of what he sells, and restores the overseen gain of a false reckoning. He esteems a bribe venomous, though it come gilded over with the colour of gratuity. His cheeks are never stained with the blushes of recantation, neither doth his tongue falter to make good a lie with the secret glosses of double or reserved senses, and when his name is traduced his innocency bears him out with courage: then, lo, he goes on the plain way of truth, and will either triumph in his integrity or suffer with it. His conscience overrules his providence; so as in all things good or ill, he respects the nature of the actions, not the sequel. If he see what he must do, let God see what shall follow. He never loadeth himself with burdens above his strength, beyond his will; and once bound, what he can he will do, neither doth he will but what he can do. His ear is the sanctuary of his absent friend's name, of his present friend's secret; neither of them can miscarry in his trust. He remembers the wrongs of his youth, and repays them with that usury which he himself would not take. He would rather want than borrow, and beg than not to pay: his fair conditions are without dissembling, and he loves actions above words. Finally, he hates falsehood worse than death: he is a faithful client of truth, no man's enemy, and it is a question whether more another man's friend or his own; and if there were no heaven, yet he would be virtuous.[1]

The last pair of virtuous characters, the penitent and the happy man, are more suited for the pulpit than perhaps anything

[1] Joseph Hall, *Characters of Vices and Vertues*, Bk. I.

else in the many volumes of charactery. The latter has this fine peroration :

> He holds it no great matter to live, and his greatest business to die ; and is so well acquainted with his last guest that he fears no unkindness from him : neither makes he any other of dying than of walking home when he is abroad, or of going to bed when he is weary of the day. He is well provided for both worlds, and is sure of peace here, of glory hereafter ; and therefore hath a light heart and a cheerful face. All his fellow-creatures rejoice to serve him ; his betters, the angels, love to observe him ; God Himself takes pleasure to converse with him, and hath sainted him before his death, and in his death crowned him.

In the characterization of vices, Hall fears lest some should find his style " less grave, more satirical " ; and here the flowers of speech, the antitheses, the conceits, which his successors were to make the special ornament of the character, are most profusely strewn. " The estate " of the busybody " is too narrow for his mind, and therefore he is fain to make himself room in others' affairs, yet ever in pretence of love. No news can stir but by his door, neither can he know that which he must not tell. . . . His tongue, like the tail of Samson's foxes, carries firebrands, and is enough to set the whole field of the world on a flame." This is after Theophrastus,[1] and it is interesting to notice that Addison took up the old theme, in his sketch of the upholsterer who always has the latest intelligence of foreign affairs and the only solution for every imbroglio.[2] Hall at times keeps fairly close to the Theophrastian method, as in " The Hypocrite " :

> He rises, and looking about with admiration, complains on our frozen charity, commends the ancient. At church he will ever sit where he may be seen best, and in the midst of the sermon pulls out his tables in haste, as if he feared to lose that note ; when he writes either his forgotten errand or nothing. Then he turns his Bible with a noise to seek an omitted quotation, and folds the leaf as if he had found it, and asks aloud the name of the preacher, and repeats it, whom he publicly salutes, thanks, praises, invites, entertains with tedious good counsel, with good discourse, if it had come from an honester mouth.

[1] viii., " Of News-forging or Rumour-spreading."
[2] *Tatler*, 155.

But the last touch is foreign to the impartial manner of his original.

Theophrastus might have written of the superstitious man, "If he hear but a raven croak from the next roof he makes his will, or if a bittern fly over his head by night; but if his troubled fancy shall second his thoughts with the dream of a fair garden, or green rushes, or the salutation of a dead friend, he takes leave of the world and says he cannot live."[1] But the taste of the metaphysical poets is stamped on Hall's more ingenious definitions. "Superstition is godless religion, devout impiety"; "Flattery is nothing but false friendship, fawning hypocrisy, dishonest civility, base merchandise of words, a plausible discord of the heart and lips"; "Ambition is a proud covetousness, a dry thirst for honour, the longing disease of reason, an aspiring and gallant madness."

"The Man in the Moone"

Hall was speedily followed by other exponents of charactery. One of the queerest was an anonymous tract, entitled *The Man in the Moone telling strange fortunes; or The English Fortune Teller* (1609), the prefatory matter to which is signed by a certain W.M.[2] A traveller falls in with an aged hermit, Fido, who says that he has separated himself from the world, and is labouring to help those in need with consolation and counsel, though he is reputed among the vulgar to be a soothsayer or fortune-teller. He has two servitors—a pert juvenile, called Mockso, and one of riper years and more staid carriage, cognominated Opinion. Those who come to consult the sage are introduced by Mockso, with a ridiculous account of their personal appearance; Opinion then delivers his estimate of their characters, in a style more like that of Tom Nashe than of Theophrastus; finally, the old man, in a serious homily, tells each person what will be the probable consequences of his mode of life.[3] In this manner are passed in review a drunkard, a tobacconist, a prodigal, a serving-man, a lewd woman, a pander, an extortioner, a glutton, a parasite, and various others. Among the types of moral delinquency, it will be noticed that representatives

[1] E. C. Baldwin cites parallel passages from Hall and Theophrastus showing close study of the Greek original (*Modern Language Association of America*, xviii., 1903, pp. 418-421).

[2] Ed. J. O. Halliwell (Percy Society, 1849).

[3] Smollett's Cadwallader Crabtree and his myrmidons masquerade in a similar way in *Peregrine Pickle*, lxxxii.

of a calling are mingled. The example had been set by Hall, who included the portrait of a good magistrate among his characters of virtues. Probably the work was hastily put together on the appearance of Hall's *Characters*; the sermonizing style of the fortune-teller seems to be suggested by Hall, though the parts of the other speakers are in a different vein. The following is from Fido's oration to the Prodigal:

> Sir, you are generously descended, the greater is your shame to expose yourself to an ignoble course of living: much riches were you bequeathed, the more is the pity you have so little grace to mis-employ them; well are you featured, it is ill bestowed unless you would preserve your beauty better: for that which God and nature have ordained for your good, by your ill using you turn to your own overthrow. . . .You suppose it a great glory to lash your coin, you care not where, nor upon whom; though they will advance you, which receive benefits thereby, yet such as will not profit themselves by such means, resemble you to a candle, which wasteth itself to give others light. You esteem it an extraordinary happiness to be in favour with many and sundry beauties: you shall feel the contrary, pride will procure your fall, when you wot not of it; excess devour your riches ere you are aware; variety decay your body when you think it doth most delight it; and when your body is decayed, your wealth devoured, yourself fallen, go to your gossips, which now will hang like goodly jewels about your neck, and come with your purse empty: *stabis, Homere, foras*, you may stand like an impecunious whoremaster at their doors. Come to your tradesmen, which now cap and cringe you, and see if you shall receive any further comfort than moanful words, "Alas, it is pity, would we were able."

Sir Thomas Overbury and his co-adjutors

The posthumous volume, in which the twenty-one characters that first passed under the name of Sir Thomas Overbury (1581-1613) were published, appeared in 1614; but Fuller calls Overbury "the first writer of characters of our nation so far as I have observed," and it is very likely that these pieces were handed round among his friends some years before they went into print, and were therefore written not later than Hall's.[1] The sensational circumstances of

[1] The characters were incorporated with the second edition of his poem, *A Wife*, and the new title ran, *A Wife, now the Widdow of Sir Thomas Overburye. Being a most exquisite and singular Poem of the choice of a Wife. Whereunto are added many witty Characters and conceited Newes, written by himselfe and other learned Gentlemen his friends.*

Overbury's death, no doubt, had a good deal to do with the avidity with which the book was read. It was by far the most popular of the books of characters, reaching a twentieth edition in 1673, by which time the original score of essays had increased fourfold, many of them from other hands than Overbury's.

Their topical nature

Which are by Overbury and which by his learned friends it is impossible to say; in method and style all are like a series of prize essays on similar themes, each striving to outdo the others in cleverness, witty aphorism, and play upon words. They follow Theophrastus, but at a greater distance than Hall, and with altogether a different gait. Keeping clear of Hall's abstractions and his propensity for moralizing, they are more successful in recapturing something of the racy concreteness of the first character-writer. But, instead of the moral types chosen for review by Theophrastus and his clerical disciple, the Overbury group preferred to delineate the more striking figures that caught the eye in their own world, and to lay the emphasis not on morals but on manners, and even personal appearance. Subjects such as a country gentleman, a braggadocio Welshman, a serving-man, a host, an ostler, a sailor, a soldier, a Puritan, a mere common lawyer, an apparitor, an almanac-maker, an Inns of Court man, a waterman, a French cook, show the beginnings of a tendency to proceed from the type to the individual, which in due time goes on to the natural conclusion. Many of the so-called characters are really portraits, not, perhaps, from the life, but distinguished by individual traits rather than the general characteristics of a class.[1] This neglect of the type for the picturesque oddity, of the permanent and significant for the topical and ephemeral, went with an alert eye for visual peculiarities. Many of the personages are brought before us with extraordinary pictorial vividness. Compared with Hall's seriousness the Overbury

[1] Hall's *Characters of Vertues and Vices* was translated into French (1619) and stimulated charactery on the other side of the Channel. But, although La Bruyère translated Theophrastus and appended *Caractères* of his own, the tendency of French charactery has been in two directions markedly different from English, —*i.e.* towards the maxim or towards the portrait. The imaginary or pseudonymous portrait, of which there are celebrated examples in the romances of Mademoiselle de Scudéry, was probably not in the least indebted to Theophrastus. To what extent it was influenced later on by La Bruyère is a nice question, not to be settled here. The greatest master of the maxim is La Rochefoucauld, of the portrait, the Duc de Saint-Simon. Fuller's characters are portraits essentially, as much as those of Carlyle.

characters are light and trivial. They are often humorous, in spite of the unnatural effort at wit and sparkle ; and it has been rightly pointed out they are more nearly allied to the comedy of that time than to the puritanism which helped the early development of charactery.[1]

Epigrammatic in style

Still more artificial than Hall's definitions of vices are the opening phrases of almost any piece taken at random—"witty descriptions of the properties of sundry persons," as they are subtitled in the text. "A very woman is a dough-baked man, or a she meant well towards man, but fell two bows short, strength and understanding." "A timist[2] is a noun adjective of the present tense. He hath no more of a conscience than fear, and his religion is not his but the prince's." "A wise man is the truth of the true definition of a man, that is, a reasonable creature." "A fine gentleman is the cinnamon tree, whose bark is more worth than his body." "A braggadocio Welshman is the oyster that the pearl is in, for a man may be picked out of him. He hath the abilities of the mind *in potentia*, and *actu* nothing but boldness. His clothes are in fashion before his body, and he accounts boldness the chiefest virtue. Above all men he loves an herald, and speaks pedigrees naturally. He accounts none well descended that call him not cousin, and prefers Owen Glendower before any of the Nine Worthies." As to a pedant, "he treads in a rule, and one hand scans verses, and the other holds his sceptre. He dares not think a thought that the nominative case governs not the verb ; and he never had any meaning in his life, for he travelled only for words. His ambition is criticism, and his example Tully. He values phrases, and elects them by the sound, and the eight parts of speech are his servants. To be brief, he is a Heteroclite, for he wants the plural number, having only the single quality of words." This is all very brilliant, but by no means profound, although it has the look of profundity that hangs about the obscure. Style has become the object, to the sad detriment of meaning. It was a pity that Overbury and his coadjutors did not take to heart their own happy appraisement of false pedantry.

Nothing could be easier than to narrow down the focus of charactery to a definite object, such as a sect, a party, a social movement,

[1] E. C. Baldwin: "The relation of the seventeenth-century Character to the periodical Essay" (*Mod. Lang. Assoc. of America*, vol. xix., pp. 89-90).

[2] Time-server.

or the forces that tended to thwart it. In the course of time, the character was to be used as a weapon of controversy, a political pamphlet, a squib. In the Overbury collection this perversion of the art has already begun. The writers were men in close touch with the court, who had scholarship and literary taste, and held strong views on the need for a finer standard of manners and morals and for a more liberal culture, particularly in their own class. In such pieces as "A Good Woman," "A Wise Man," "A Noble Spirit," "A Reverend Judge," or "A Noble and Retired House-keeper,"[1] they put forward their ideals; in a far more numerous class of diatribe they expressed their contempt for the sordid motives of time-servers and pettifoggers, engrossing merchants and greedy tradesmen, and also of narrow-minded Puritans and precisians, the mere lawyer, the mere scholar, and the whole progeny of pharisaism and simulation. In brief, the character is taking over the mission of the Elizabethan anatomy of abuses. In this portrayal of a courtier the satire is moderate and gentle:

Satirical tendencies

A Courtier

A Courtier

to all men's thinking is a man, and to most men the finest: all things else are defined by the understanding, but this by the sense; but his surest mark is, that he is to be found only about princes. He smells; and putteth away much of his judgment about the situation of his clothes. He knows no man that is not generally known. His wit, like the marigold, openeth with the sun, and therefore he riseth not before ten of the clock. He puts more confidence in his words than meaning, and more in his pronunciation than his words. Occasion is his Cupid, and he hath but one receipt of making love. He follows nothing but inconstancy, admires nothing but beauty, honours nothing but fortune: loves nothing. The sustenance of his discourse is news, and his censure like a shot depends upon the charging. He is not, if he be out of court, but fish-like breathes destruction, if out of his own element. Neither his motion or aspect are regular, but he moves by the upper spheres, and is the reflection of higher substances.

If you find him not here, you shall in Paul's, with a pick-tooth in his hat, a cape-cloak, and a long stocking.[2]

[1] Galsworthy's "man of property."
[2] Sir Thomas Overbury, *Works*, ed. Edward F. Rimbault, 1890: *Characters*, pp. 52-53.

"An Ignorant Glory-Hunter," "An Intruder into Favour," and the like, are more roughly handled : the hatred for upstarts, snobs and tuft-hunters is as perennial as the species. The Puritan "is a diseased piece of apocalypse : bind him to the Bible, and he corrupts the whole text." The mere scholar is "an intelligible ass, or a silly fellow in black that speaks sentences more familiarly than sense." "Varnished rottenness" is the phrase applied to the precisian, who is defined as "a demure creature, full of oral sanctity and mental impiety ; a fair object to the eye, but stark naught for the understanding."

From this untempered invective it is refreshing to turn to that charming piece, sweet as a contemporary lyric, "A Fair and Happy Milkmaid," which Izaak Walton loved and many have quoted since, but which is too good not to quote again.

A Fair and Happy Milkmaid

The Milkmaid

is a country wench, that is so far from making herself beautiful by art, that one look of hers is able to put all face-physic out of countenance. She knows a fair look is but a dumb orator to commend virtue, therefore minds it not. All her excellencies stand in her so silently, as if they had stolen upon her without her knowledge. The lining of her apparel (which is herself) is far better than outsides of tissue, for though she be not arrayed in the spoil of the silk-worm, she is decked in innocence, a far better wearing. She doth not, with lying long abed, spoil both her complexion and conditions ; nature hath taught her, too immoderate sleep is rust to the soul : she rises therefore with chanticlere, her dame's cock, and at night makes the lamb her curfew. In milking a cow, and straining the teats through her fingers, it seems that so sweet a milk-press makes the milk the whiter or sweeter ; for never came almond glove or aromatic ointment on her palm to taint it. The golden ears of corn fall and kiss her feet when she reaps them, as if they wished to be bound and led prisoners by the same hand felled them. Her breath is her own, which scents all the year of June, like a new-made hay-cock. She makes her hand hard with labour, and her heart soft with pity : and when winter evenings fall early (sitting at her merry wheel) she sings a defiance to the giddy wheel of fortune. She doth all things with so sweet a grace, it seems ignorance will not suffer her to do ill, being her mind is to do well. She bestows her year's wages at next fair ; and in choosing her garments, counts no bravery in the world like decency. The garden and bee-hive are all her physic and chirurgery, and she lives the longer for it. She dare go alone, and unfold sheep in the night, and fears no manner of ill, because she means none: yet to say truth, she is never alone, for she is still accompanied with old songs, honest thoughts, and prayers, but short ones; yet they have their efficacy, in that they are not palled with ensuing idle cogitations. Lastly, her dreams are so chaste, that she dare tell them; only a Friday's dream is all her superstition; that she conceals for fear of anger. Thus lives she, and all her care is she may die in the spring-time, to have store of flowers stuck upon her winding-sheet.[1]

As a whole, the Overbury contribution to the portrayal of life is analogous to that of a novelist not of the first rank. It is a presentation of the salient figures in different spheres of society, bringing out the prevailing attitudes and motives, and criticizing by means both of satire and of contrast. Similar, but more specialized, are the contributions of two younger contemporaries, John Stephens, the lawyer, and Geffray Mynshul, another of the same profession who had been unlucky enough to see the inside of a debtors' prison. The major part of the former's *Satyricall Essayes, Characters, and others, or accurate and quick Descriptions fitted to the life of their Subjects* (1615), consists of lively miniatures of lawyers, or of such people as the shark, the informer, the gamester, and other disreputable characters with whom the lawyer would come into frequent contact. To his *New Essayes and Characters* (1631) Stephens appended "a new Satyre in defence of the Common Law, and Lawyers: mixt with Reproofe against their enemy Ignoramus." Like Lodge or Greene, he tries to show the temptations and the course of moral depravation by which such characters are produced, sometimes invoking the aid of incident to explain a man's life. So too, in *Essays and Characters of a Prison and Prisoners* (1616), Mynshul feelingly laments the corrupt influences of prison life, where more vice is learned than "in twenty dicing-houses, bowling-alleys, brothel-houses, or ordinaries." "A prisoner is an impatient patient, lingering under the rough hands of a cruel physician. . . . To his familiars he is like a plague, whom they scarce dare come nigh for fear of infection; he is a monument ruined by those which raised him; he spends the day with a *hei mihi! vae miserum!* and the night with a *nullis est medicabilis herbis*."

Stephens and Mynshul

[1] Sir Thomas Overbury, *Works*, ed. Edward F. Rimbault, 1890: *Characters*, pp. 118-119.

Parrot's "Cures for the Itch"; "Micrologia"

Little sympathy is wasted in the next two collections to be noted. The exaggerations and paradoxical epithets of the Overbury tradition are employed with what may be a personal animosity in Henry Parrot's *Cures for the Itch: Characters, Epigrams, Epitaphs* (1626),[1] and the *Micrologia: Characters or Essayes, of Persons, Trades, and Places*, (1629), by a writer calling himself R. M. Parrot, mingles a few general types with such personages as a ballad-maker, a tapster, a broker, and shows the tendency towards individuality in such pieces as "A Rectified Young Man," "A Young Novice's New Younger Wife," and "A Self-Conceited Parcel-Witted Old Dotard." His Scold is an early Mrs Gamp:

> There's nothing pacifies her but a cup of sack, which taking in full measure of digestion, she presently forgets all wrongs that's done her, and thereupon falls straight a-weeping. . . . Her manner is to talk much in her sleep, what wrongs she hath endured of that rogue her husband, whose hap may be in time to die a martyr.

Bishop Earle

The most coherent and balanced—almost the only one that tempers wit with urbanity—of all the Theophrastian books of characters was John Earle's *Microcosmographie or a Piece of the World Discovered, in Essays and Characters* (1628). Eight editions appeared in the author's lifetime, with which its popularity did not terminate. In the sixth (1633) the fifty-four characters of the original edition had grown to seventy-eight. John Earle (? 1601-1665) was a native of York, and he speaks of the work as "newly composed for the northern part of the Kingdom." He was a fellow of Merton College, Oxford, at the time of writing, and, of course, still a young man with a limited experience of the world. He was afterwards chaplain to Charles I., suffered and went into exile under the Parliament, and after the Restoration became bishop of Worcester, and later of Salisbury. Earle endeared himself to all who knew him by his gentleness and his delightful conversation. Even in those of his characters which castigate and ridicule, a profound charity is evident. He can be at once caustic and compassionate; he looks behind the surface tricks of behaviour for the motives that shape character; he penetrates

[1] The booklet is signed by H.P., who is identified as Henry Parrot, by Philip Bliss, who edited Earle's *Microcosmographie* (1811) and added a bibliography of character-writers. Parrot was the author of a series of epigrams, *Laquei Ridiculosi, or Springes for Woodcocks* (1613). His motto in *Cures for the Itch* is expressive, it runs, *Scalpat qui Tangitur.*

to the heart, and writes with the solicitude of one who feels himself to be a physician of souls.

Like that of the divine who had preceded him, Earle's interest is mainly ethical; and, again like Hall, he makes use of the method of contrast, though less obtrusively. He is of the Overbury school, however, in looking for his subjects in the world about him, and so evolving a picture of contemporary life; not so varied, indeed, as theirs, for the majority of his characters are obviously taken from the narrow range of a university town, but not less alive in the individual lineaments. Sympathetic insight more than made up for the limitation of his experience. Wit, with Earle, is not an object in itself, but the faithful servant of broad and humane wisdom. "A discontented man is one that is fallen out with the world, and will be revenged on himself. . . . He considered not the nature of the world till he felt it, and all blows fall on him heavier, because they light not first on his expectation. He has now forgone all but his pride, and is yet vainglorious in the ostentation of his melancholy." "A self-conceited man is one that knows himself so well that he does not know himself." "A sceptic in religion is one that hangs in the balance with all sorts of opinions, whereof not one but stirs him and none sways him." "Acquaintance is the first draft of a friend, whom we must lay down oft thus, as the foul copy, before we can write him perfect and true." "The best judgment of a man is taken from his acquaintance, for friends and enemies are both partial; whereas these see him truest because calmest, and are no way so engaged to lie for him. And men that grow strange after acquaintance, seldom piece together again, as those that have tasted meat and dislike it, out of a mutual experience disrelishing one another."

"A Young Man"

He is a practical moralist, teaching men the better way, as in the essay, "A Young Man," in which he shows how folly helps to make us wise:

He is now out of nature's protection, though not yet able to guide himself; but left loose to the world and fortune, from which the weakness of his childhood preserved him; and now his strength exposes him. He is, indeed, just of age to be miserable, yet in his own conceit first begins to be happy; and he is happier in this imagination, and his misery not felt is less. . . . Himself is his own temptation, and needs not Satan, and the world will come hereafter. . . . He leaves repentance for grey hairs, and performs it in being covetous. He is mingled with the vices of the age as the fashion and custom, with which he longs to be acquainted, and sins to better his understanding. He conceives his youth as the season of his lust, and the hour wherein he ought to be bad; and because he would not lose his time, spends it. . . . He does seldom anything which he wishes not to do again, and is only wise after a misfortune. He suffers much for his knowledge, and a great deal of folly it is makes him a wise man. . . . If he scape this age, he has scaped a tempest, and may live to be a man.

Earle's satire

When Earle is satirical, it is with the quiet satire of a true humorist, not the sarcasm and invective of the average delineator of character. He says of the mere formal man:

When you have seen his outside, you have looked through him, and need employ your discovery no further. His reason is merely example, and his action is not guided by his understanding, but he sees other men do thus, and he follows them. He is a negative, for we cannot call him a wise man, but not a fool; nor an honest man, but not a knave; nor a protestant, but not a papist. . . . He apprehends a jest by seeing men smile, and laughs orderly himself when it comes to his turn. . . . He hath stayed in the world to fill a number; and when he is gone, there wants one, and there's an end.

Here are some pithy opening phrases: "An idle gallant is one that was born and shaped for his clothes; and, if Adam had not fallen, had lived to no purpose"; "A constable is a viceroy in the street, and no man stands more upon't that he is the king's officer"; "Paul's Walk is the land's epitome, or you may call it the lesser isle of Great Britain. It is more than this, the whole world's map, which you may here discern in its perfectest motion, jostling and turning"; "A coward is the man that is commonly most fierce against the coward, and labouring to take off this suspicion from himself; for the opinion of valour is a good protection to those that dare not use it." A she precise hypocrite "is so taken up with faith she has no room for charity, and understands no good works but what are wrought on the sampler. She accounts nothing vices but superstition and an oath, and thinks adultery a less sin than to swear *by my truly*. . . . She overflows so with the Bible, that she spills it upon every occasion, and will not cudgel her maids without scripture. It is question whether she is more troubled with the Devil, or the Devil with her."

His idealism : "A Child" and "A Contemplative Man"

Earle strikes the chord of idealism at the outset, and reverts to it every now and again, evoking the beauty that resolves our human discords. The Overbury descant on the milkmaid is less pure and tender than the initial essay :

A CHILD

We laugh at his foolish sports, but his game is our earnest ; and his drums, rattles, and hobby-horses, but the emblems and mocking of man's business. His father hath writ him as his own little story, wherein he reads those days of his life that he cannot remember, and sighs to see what innocence he hath outlived. The older he grows, he is a stair lower from God ; and, like his first father, much worse in his breeches. He is the Christian's example, and the old man's relapse ; the one imitates his pureness, and the other falls into his simplicity. Could he put off his body with his little coat, he had got eternity without a burden, and exchanged but one heaven for another.

The complement whereto is the essay, "A Good Old Man," "the best antiquity, and which we may with least vanity admire." In between, the seven ages are chronicled, with a variety of feature that Shakespeare would not have disapproved. Here is one of them complete :

A CONTEMPLATIVE MAN

is a scholar in this great university the world ; and the same his book and study. He cloisters not his meditations in the narrow darkness of a room, but sends them abroad with his eyes, and his brain travels with his feet. He looks upon man from a high tower, and sees him trulier at this distance in his infirmities and poorness. He scorns to mix himself in men's actions, as he would to act upon a stage ; but sits aloft on the scaffold a censuring spectator. [He will not lose his time by being busy, or make so poor a use of the world as to hug and embrace it.] Nature admits him as a partaker of her sports, and asks his approbation, as it were, of her own works and variety. He comes not in company, because he would not be solitary ; but finds discourse enough with himself, and his own thoughts are his excellent play-fellows. He looks not upon a thing as a yawning stranger at novelties, but his search is more mysterious and inward, and he spells heaven out of earth. He knits his observations together, and makes a ladder of them all to climb to God. He is free from vice, because he has no occasion to employ it, and is above those ends that make man wicked. He has learnt all can here be taught him, and comes now to heaven to see more.[1]

Earle was less interested in rustic characters than were the Overbury group. But it is worth while comparing his country fellow with their franklin, drawn with such an air of warm approval :

"A Country Fellow"

He is taught by nature to be contented with little ; he is pleased with any nourishment God sends, whilst curious gluttony ransacks, as it were, Noah's ark for food only to feed the riot of one meal. He is never known to go to law ; understanding, to be law-bound among men is to be hide-bound among his beasts ; they thrive not under it, and that such men sleep unquietly as if their pillows were stuffed with lawyers' penknives. . . . He never sits up late but when he hunts the badger, the vowed foe of his lambs ; nor uses he any cruelty but when he hunts the hare, nor subtlety but when he setteth snares for the snipe or pitfalls for the blackbird ; nor oppression but when, in the month of July, he goes to the next river and shears his sheep. . . . He is lord paramount within himself, though he hold by never so mean a tenure, and dies the more contentedly, though he leaves his heir young, in regard he leaves him not liable to a covetous guardian. Lastly, to end him, he cares not when his end comes ; he needs not fear his audit, for his quietus is in heaven.

This is an idealized exemplar, not honest character-drawing ; and Earle, with his touches of Father Gammon and Dandie Dinmont, comes nearer the mark. His plain country fellow

is one that manures his ground well, but lets himself lie fallow and untilled. . . . He seems to have the punishment of Nebuchadnezzar, for his conversation is among beasts, and his talons none of the shortest, only he eats not grass, because he loves not sallets. His hand guides the plough, and the plough his thoughts, and his ditch and landmark is the very mound of his meditations. He expostulates with his oxen very understandingly, and speaks gee and ree better than English. His mind is not much distracted with objects, but if a good fat cow come in his way, he stands dumb and astonished, and though his haste be never so great, will fix here half-an-hour's contemplation. His habitation is some poor thatched roof, distinguished from his barn by the loop-holes that let out smoke, which the rain had long since washed through, but for the double ceiling of bacon on the inside, which has hung there from his grandsire's time, and is yet to make

[1] John Earle, *Microcosmographie*, xxxiii. The passage in square brackets was added after the first edition.

rashers for posterity. His dinner is his other work, for he sweats at it as much as at his labour ; he is a terrible fastener on a piece of beef, and you may hope to stave the guard off sooner. His religion is a part of his copy-hold, which he takes from his landlord, and refers it wholly to his discretion : yet if he give him leave he is a good Christian to his power, (that is,) comes to church in his best clothes, and sits there with his neighbours, where he is capable only of two prayers, for rain, and fair weather. He apprehends God's blessings only in a good year, or a fat pasture, and never praises him but on good ground. Sunday he esteems a day to make merry in, and thinks a bagpipe as essential to it as evening prayer, where he walks very solemnly after service with his hands coupled behind him, and censures the dancing of his parish. (His compliment with his neighbour is a good thump on the back, and his salutation commonly some blunt curse.) He thinks nothing to be vices, but pride and ill husbandry, from which he will gravely dissuade the youth, and has some thrifty hobnail proverbs to clout his discourse. He is a niggard all the week, except only market-day, where, if his corn sell well, he thinks he may be drunk with a good conscience. His feet never stink so unbecomingly as when he trots after a lawyer in Westminster Hall, and even cleaves the ground with hard scraping in beseeching his worship to take his money. He is sensible of no calamity but the burning a stack of corn, or overflowing of a meadow, and thinks Noah's flood the greatest plague that ever was, not because it drowned the world, but spoiled the grass. For death he is never troubled, and if he get in but his harvest before, let it come when it will, he cares not.[1]

By this time, charactery had become a favourite recreation among the intellectuals, and every clever person was publishing little collections of characters. In a bibliography by Mr E. C. Baldwin about a hundred and fifty books of the kind are entered for the seventeenth century.[2] Many of these are portraits or caricatures of actual persons ; others are odd essays in charactery prefixed or appended to a poetical or other work[3] ; many are sectarian or

[1] John Earle, *Microcosmographie*, xxii.

[2] Appended to his article on "The relation of the seventeenth-century Character to the periodical Essay" (*Mod. Lang. Assoc. of America*, xix., 1904).

[3] *E.g.* Habington's *Castara* (1635). George Herbert's very beautiful portrayal of a character in the various phases of his daily life, *A Priest to the Temple, or, the Country Parson, his Character, and rule of holy life* (1652), written in the sixteen-thirties, is not a Theophrastian essay but a complete picture, an ideal biography —perhaps we might say, an ideal autobiography. Goldsmith might have had it at the back of his mind in evolving his Vicar of Wakefield. See Herbert: *Works in Prose and Verse*, 1853, i. 142-252.

political diatribes. The strife of Cavalier and Roundhead was largely fought with such weapons, and at a later date they were used by Whigs and Tories with deadly effect. Few of Earle's contemporaries were as philosophic as he, or had insight enough to discern the general and permanent type beneath the surface traits of the characters they depicted. A pungent description of current actualities was the aim of Richard Brathwaite, in *Whimzies; Or, A new cast of Characters* (1631); of Wye Saltonstall, in *Picturæ Loquentes: or Pictures drawne forth in Characters* (1631); of Donald Lupton, in *London and Country Carnonadoed and Quartred into severall Characters* (1632); as of many others not worth mentioning here. Brathwaite's characters chiefly represent occupations—an Almanac-maker, a Ballad-monger, an Exchange-man, an Hospital-man, a Jailer, a Launderer, an Ostler, a Postmaster, and so on; a few, such as his Corranto-coiner, or state-newsmonger, exhibit those lasting foibles noticed by Theophrastus and by writers near our own day:

Brathwaite

Paul's is his walk in winter, Moorfields in summer, where the whole discipline, designs, projects, and exploits of the States, Netherlands, Poland, Switzer, Crimchan and all, are within the compass of one quadrangle talk most judiciously and punctually discovered. . . . Thanks to his good invention, he can collect much out of a very little; no matter though more experienced judgments disprove him, he is anonymous, and that will secure him. . . . Palisadoes, parapets, counterscarps, forts, fortresses, rampiers, bulwarks, are his usual dialect. He writes as if he would do some mischief, yet the charge of his shot is but paper. . . . He ever leaves some passages doubtful, as if they were some more intimate secrecies of state, closing his sentence abruptly with—"hereafter you shall hear more."

Saltonstall

Saltonstall followed in the Overbury track, and had a pretty wit of his own. He says of "The Term":

It is called the term because it does end and terminate business, or else because it is the *terminus ad quem*, that is, the end of the countryman's journey, who comes up to the term, and with his hobnail shoes grinds the faces of the poor stones, and so returns again. It is the soul of the year, and makes it quick, which before was dead. . . . The taverns are painted against the term, and many a cause is argued there and tried at the bar, where you are adjudged to pay the costs and charges, and so dismissed with "welcome, gentlemen."

In like manner he writes on a country fair, a country ale-house, and a horse race; thus preparing us for a new departure in Lupton's book, which gives the character of various localities, in town and country.

Thomas Fuller—his portraits

Thomas Fuller is sometimes numbered among the character-writers; but, as has been already said, his characters are almost destitute of the Theophrastian quality: he is a critic of human life whose mind dwells instinctively on the concrete, the personal, the historic. He is among the finest of literary portrait-painters, and his portraits are usually vivified by anecdotes that reveal the born story-teller; in retelling an old tale, his "fingers unwittingly itched (as Gibbon's did afterwards) to make the not yet born historical novel out of it."[1] His *Church History of Britain* (1648) and his *Worthies of England* (1662) are full of speaking likenesses of kings, statesmen, churchmen, and other historical personages. Few of his many books are devoid of some fragment of portraiture, some pithy anecdote, or much searching comment on man's inner and outer life, which would not have been in the wrong place had they occurred in the pages of a serious novel. All this, and the unlimited range of his curiosity, pertain to that attitude of mind which, allied with vivacity and humour—never wanting in Fuller—is the attitude that finds aptest and fullest expression there. Whether the novelists of the following century gained anything directly from Fuller or not, he did admirably many things that had to be done. Few of them may have read him; yet his familiar way of telling a story, the vitality of his portraits, which were no mere static characters, but walked and talked and looked and were sad or confident or hesitating, as people are in life, and, finally, the thought that often gave a fresh significance to the man he drew, all this could not but have taught a good deal to other chroniclers and critics of human activities, and so have reacted upon the novelists. After all, Fuller was read, when Deloney and others of that generation who had done some of these things before were dead and forgotten, except among those who had no connexion with the literary classes.

[1] Professor Saintsbury (*Camb. Hist. of Eng. Lit.*, vii., 248).

Here is a sketch of Tarlton the jester, from the *Worthies* :

Tarlton

Our Tarlton was master of his faculty. When queen Elizabeth was serious (I dare not say sullen) and out of good humour, he could *un-dumpish her* at his pleasure. Her highest favourites would, in some cases, go to Tarlton before they would go to the queen, and he was their usher to prepare their advantageous access unto her. In a word, he told the queen more of her faults than most of her chaplains, and cured her melancholy better than all of her physicians. Much of his merriment lay in his very looks and actions, according to the epitaph written upon him :

Hic situs est cujus poterat vox, actio, vultus,
Ex Heraclito reddere Democritum.

Indeed the self-same words, spoken by another, would hardly move a merry man to smile ; which, uttered by him, would force a sad soul to laughter.

In the *Church History* he says in his account of Hooker :

Hooker

Mr Hooker's voice was low, stature little, gesture none at all, standing stone-still in the pulpit, as if the posture of his body were the emblem of his mind, unmovable in his opinions. Where his eye was left fixed at the beginning, it was found fixed at the end of his sermon. In a word, the doctrine he delivered had nothing but itself to garnish it. His style was long and pithy, driving on a whole flock of several clauses before he came to the close of a sentence ; so that when the copiousness of his style met not with proportionable capacity in his auditors, it was unjustly censured for perplexed, tedious, and obscure.

The Rev. William Perkins

The next illustration of his pictorial faculty and his humorous insight is from his portrait of the Rev. William Perkins, a Calvinistic divine, celebrated for his *Discoverie of the damned Art of Witchcraft* (1608) ; it occurs in *The Holy State and the Profane State* (1642), a rich magazine of charactery[1] :

He had a capacious head, with angles widening and roomy enough to lodge all controversial intricacies ; and had not preaching diverted him from that way, he had no doubt attained to eminency therein An excellent surgeon he was at jointing of a broken soul, and at stating of a doubtful conscience. And, sure, in case-divinity

[1] The first part, "The Holy State," gives forty-eight characters—to be imitated—and the second part, "The Profane State," thirty-one—to be shunned.

Protestants are defective. For (save that a Smith or two of late have built them forges, and set up shop) we go down to our enemies to sharpen all our instruments, and are beholden to them for offensive and defensive weapons in cases of conscience.

He would pronounce the word *damn* with such an emphasis, as left a doleful echo in his auditors' ears a good while after; and when catechist of Christ-College, in expounding the Commandments, applied them so home, able almost to make his hearers' hearts fall down, and hairs to stand upright.

Portraits of types

In the same book will be found some characters more akin to those of Earle, as this idealistic example of a court lady, with its characteristic touches of meditative satire on modern fashions:

In discourse, her words are rather fit than fine, very choice, and yet not chosen. Though her language be not gaudy, yet the plainness thereof pleaseth, it is so proper, and handsomely put on. Some, having a set of fine phrases, will hazard an impertinency to use them all, as thinking they give full satisfaction for dragging in the matter by head and shoulders, if they dress it in quaint expressions. Others often repeat the same things; the Platonic year of their discourses being not above three days long, in which term all the same matter returns over again, threadbare talk ill suiting with the variety of their clothes.

She affects not the vanity of foolish fashions. But is decently apparelled according to her state and condition. He that should have guessed the bigness of Alexander's soldiers by their shields left in India, would much over-proportion their true greatness. But what a vast overgrown creature would some guess a woman to be, taking his aim by the multitude and variety of clothes and ornaments, which some of them use! insomuch as the ancient Latins called a woman's wardrobe *mundus*, "a world"; wherein, notwithstanding, was much *terra incognita* then undiscovered, but since found out by the curiosity of modern fashion-mongers.

"The Good Parent," "A Good Master of a College," an instance of the truth that "Sometimes ordinary scholars make extraordinary good masters," "The Good Wife," who "sets up a sail according to the keel of her husband's estate; and if of high parentage, she doth not so remember what she was by birth, that she forgets what she is by match," and "The Good Schoolmaster," who "studieth his scholars' natures as carefully as they their books," and "is, and will be known to be, an absolute monarch in his school," are other persuasive examples from this humane book.

Samuel Butler's sarcastic charactery

Passing over Cleveland, the Cavalier poet, who wrote three lengthy characters which he appropriately described as "anatomy lectures," and which were for the most part embittered criticisms of his foes, we come to one in the same camp whose analyses of character take high rank for their wit and general ability, though they digress widely from the Theophrastian highway. The *Characters* of Samuel Butler (? 1612-1680), author of *Hudibras*, were not published during his lifetime, but appeared for the first time in R. Thyer's edition of *The Genuine Remains in Verse and Prose of Mr Samuel Butler* (1759). In the second volume were included some hundred and twenty characters, which have recently been augmented by about sixty more, and a series of "Miscellaneous Observations and Reflections on various Subjects," previously unpublished.[1] Butler adopts the manner and the dimensions of the essay, not the Baconian, but the longer essay soon to be familiar in *Tatlers* and *Spectators*. And he strikes the attitude throughout of the cross-grained and disgruntled misanthrope. No ideal examples intrude to relieve the incessant bitterness. In the steady flaying of human follies, vices and pretences, Butler far outdoes the most savage Elizabethan censor of manners. Well might he have taken as his motto one of his own "Sundry Thoughts"—"There are more fools than knaves in the world, else the knaves would not have enough to live upon," or his fuller statement of the same doctrine :

> The reason why fools and knaves thrive better in the world than wiser and honester men, is because they are nearer to the general temper of mankind, which is nothing but a mixture of cheat and folly, which those that understand and mean better cannot comply with, but entertain themselves with another kind of fools' paradise of what should be, not what is ; while those that know no better take naturally to it, and get the start of them.[2]

"A Modern Politician"

In this spirit he writes of "A Modern Politician" :

> He believes there is no way of thriving so easy and certain as to grow rich by defrauding the public ; for public thieveries are more

[1] S. Butler, *Characters and Passages from Note-Books*, ed. A. R. Waller, Cambridge, 1908.

[2] *Characters*, p. 276 : "Miscellaneous Observations," etc.

safe and less prosecuted than private, like robberies committed between sun and sun, which the county pays, and no one is greatly concerned in. And as the monster of many heads has less wit in them all than any one reasonable person, so the monster of many purses is easier cheated than any one indifferent crafty fool. For all the difficulty lies in being trusted; and when he has obtained that, the business does itself; and if he should happen to be questioned and called to an account, a bawdy pardon is as cheap as a paymaster's fee, not above fourteen pence in the pound.

The Obstinate Man

"The Obstinate Man"

does not hold opinions, but they hold him; for when he is once possessed with an error, 'tis like the Devil, not to be cast out but with great difficulty. Whatsoever he lays hold on, like a drowning man, he never loses, though it do but help to sink him the sooner. His ignorance is abrupt and inaccessible, impregnable both by art and nature, and will hold out to the last, though it has nothing but rubbish to defend. It is as dark as pitch, and sticks as fast to anything it lays hold on. . . . The slighter and more inconsistent his opinions are, the faster he holds them, otherwise they would fall asunder of themselves; for opinions that are false ought to be held with more strictness and assurance than those that are true, otherwise they will be apt to betray their owners before they are aware. If he takes to religion, he has faith enough to save a hundred wiser men than himself, if it were right; but it is too much to be good; and though he deny supererogation, and utterly disclaim any overplus of merits, yet he allows superabundant belief, and if the violence of faith will carry the kingdom of heaven, he stands fair for it. He delights most of all to differ in things indifferent; no matter how frivolous they are, they are weighty enough in proportion to his weak judgment, and he will rather suffer self-martyrdom than part with the least scruple of his freehold. . . . He is resolved to understand no man's reason but his own, because he finds no man can understand his but himself.

He makes no bones of mentioning names. One of his most violent tirades is labelled "A Duke of Bucks"; and the biting critical dissertation, "A Small Poet," takes the unfortunate Benlowes as an apt illustration. Of the two samples of Butler given at full length below, the first is perhaps only a little harsher than previous characterizations by other writers of the genus pedant; the other is typical Butler—unerring in his insight, merciless in unveiling the base motives that lurk behind specious pretences.

A Pedant

"A Pedant"

is a dwarf scholar, that never outgrows the mode and fashion of the school, where he should have been taught. He wears his little learning, unmade-up, puts it on, before it was half finished, without pressing or smoothing. He studies and uses words with the greatest respect possible, merely for their own sakes, like an honest man, without any regard of interest, as they are useful and serviceable to things, and among those he is kindest to strangers (like a civil gentleman) that are far from their own country and most unknown. He collects old sayings and ends of verses, as antiquaries do old coins, and is as glad to produce them upon all occasions. He has sentences ready lying by him for all purposes, though to no one, and talks of authors as familiarly as his fellow-collegiates. He will challenge acquaintance with those, he never saw before, and pretend to intimate knowledge of those, he has only heard of. He is well stored with terms of art, but does not know how to use them, like a country-fellow, that carries his gloves in his hands, not his hands in his gloves. He handles arts and sciences like those, that can play a little upon an instrument, but do not know whether it be in tune or not. He converses by the book, and does not talk, but quote. If he can but screw in something, that an ancient writer said, he believes it to be much better than if he had something of himself to the purpose. His brain is not able to concoct what it takes in, and therefore brings things up as they were swallowed, that is, crude and undigested, in whole sentences, not assimilated sense, which he rather affects; for his want of judgment, like want of health, renders his appetite preposterous. He pumps for affected and far-fet expressions, and they always prove as far from the purpose. He admires canting above sense. He is worse than one, that is utterly ignorant, as a cock that sees a little, fights worse than one that is stark-blind. He speaks in a different dialect from other men, and much affects forced expressions, forgetting that hard words, as well as evil ones, corrupt good manners. He can do nothing, like a conjurer, out of the circle of his arts, nor in it without canting.[1]

The Affected or Formal

"The Affected or Formal"

is a piece of clockwork, that moves only as it is wound up and set, and not like a voluntary agent. He is a mathematical body, nothing but punctum, linea and superficies, and perfectly abstract from matter. He walks as stiffly and uprightly as a dog that is taught to go on his hinder legs, and carries his hands as the other does his fore-

[1] *Characters*, pp. 136-137.

feet. He is very ceremonious and full of respect to himself, for no man uses those formalities, that does not expect the same from others. All his actions and words are set down in so exact a method, that an indifferent accomptant may cast him up to a halfpenny farthing. He does everything by rule, as if it were in a course of Lessius's Diet, and did not eat, but take a dose of meat and drink, and not walk, but proceed, not go, but march. He draws up himself with admirable conduct in a very regular and well-ordered body. All his business and affairs are junctures and transactions; and when he speaks with a man, he gives him audience. He does not carry, but marshal himself; and no one member of his body politic takes place of another without due right of precedence. He does all things by rules of proportion, and never gives himself the freedom to manage his gloves or his watch in an irregular and arbitrary way; but is always ready to render an account of his demeanour to the most strict and severe disquisition. He sets his face as if it were cast in plaister, and never admits of any commotion in his countenance, nor so much as the innovation of a smile without serious and mature deliberation; but preserves his looks in a judicial way, according as they have always been established.[1]

It is obvious that Butler's scathing analyses of human failings, lying unprinted in his note-books, could have given no hints to the novelists who were shortly to scrutinize and interpret life in a different way. But the succession is complete from the general body of character-writers to the periodical essayists, who clothed the abstractions of charactery in flesh and blood and in them showed

> the very age and body of the time his form and pressure.

Halifax's *Character of a Trimmer* (1688) or the many polemical characters of Tories, Jacobites, churchmen, Whigs, latitudinarians, dissenters, etc., that kept appearing, do not concern us; the new application of the method to the sketching of real life, which we find in the *Tatler* and *Spectator*, emphatically do. These periodicals absorbed the essay, and with it the character.

"The Tatler"

In launching *The Tatler* (1709) Steele adopted the significant motto, "*Quicquid agunt homines, nostri est farrago libelli,*"[2] and in the dedication of the first volume described the general purpose of his paper as "to expose the false arts of life, to pull off the disguises

[1] *Characters*, pp. 184-185.
[2] Put at the head of each paper.

of cunning, vanity, and affectation, and to recommend a general simplicity in our dress, our discourse, and our behaviour."[1] But as the periodical went on, and especially when it was succeeded by *The Spectator*, a more liberal attitude was assumed by editor and collaborators, criticism and satire being, not discarded, but tempered with a more kindly appreciation of the many varieties of human idiosyncrasy and human foibles. The result was that in the character-sketches, the dialogues and soliloquies, the anecdotes and occasional short stories, the casual snatches of personal experience, and the reflective, critical, or satirical disquisitions, the two periodicals provided that portraiture of the realities of everyday life, combined with comment and interpretation, which was shortly afterwards to be more amply provided by the novel. The material for the novel of manners is all there, with the exception of continuity of action.[2]

"The Spectator"

Charactery becomes specific—the characters are named

Posing as spectators and commentators of everything that was going on around them, the writers were forced to eschew mere generalities and give everything a name. No matter whether the name were the real or a fictitious one; it served to individualize, which was the essential point. Sometimes, it is true, the formality is omitted, and the person is introduced as merely some one "of a vast estate, who is the immediate descendant of a fine gentleman," with other particulars; or "a very grave person, an upholsterer" who "lived some years since in my neighbourhood"; but it comes to the same thing, an individual is designated, not a mere generic being, like the "Humble Man," the "Busybody," the "Mere Pettifogger," the "Sergeant" or "His Yeoman," of established charactery. Steele's master-stroke was to borrow a recognizable character from Swift, the venerable moralist Mr Isaac Bickerstaff, and place him in the editorial chair, thus giving liveliness and dramatic appeal to what would otherwise have been the merely impersonal views of an anonymous journalist. The same device is apparent in the numerous letters which are received and discussed by Isaac Bickerstaff or the Spectator. The letter becomes a human

[1] *Tatler*, No. 1.

[2] The late Sir Walter Raleigh said: "It is no straining of language to speak of the *Tatler* (1709-1711) and *Spectator* (1711-1712) of Steele and Addison as brilliant examples of prose fiction. Here, for the first time, are the methods and subjects of the modern novel; all that is wanting is a greater unity and continuity of scheme to make of the 'Coverley Papers' in the *Spectator* a serial novel of a very high order" (*The English Novel*, second edition, 1895, p. 120).

document, because we have been made acquainted with the personality of the sender. An admirable instance is Steele's paper giving Sergeant Hall's letter written in the camp before Mons, with the editorial comments :

> If you will have my opinion, then, of the Sergeant's letter, I pronounce the style to be mixed, but truly epistolary ; the sentiment relating to his own wound in the sublime ; the postscript of Pegg Hartwell in the gay ; and the whole the picture of the bravest sort of men, that is to say, a man of great courage and small hopes.[1]

Charactery growing dramatic

With the accession of Addison, *The Tatler* extended the range of its good-humoured but telling criticism, and resorted more and more to the dramatic method of playing off character against character. Both writers collaborated in the spirited account of the visit paid to Isaac in his own apartment by Sir Harry Quickset, of Staffordshire, Bart., Sir Giles Wheelbarrow, Knight., Thomas Rentfree, Esq., Justice of the *quorum*, Andrew Windmill, Esq., and Mr Nicholas Doubt of the Inner Temple, Sir Harry's godson, in which the diverting struggle for precedence is suddenly pacified by the false alarm of fire. The very names are a reminder that the Country Gentleman, the Upstart Country Knight, the Inns of Court Man, and the other stock figures of charactery have not been left entirely behind.[2] The pair are found collaborating again in several numbers recording the proceedings of the mock court, where Isaac places himself in the chair of judicature, and deliberates on applications from all sorts of people for licences to carry canes, write high-flown love-letters, and indulge in other consecrated kinds of foppishness and affectation. Here, the review of a motley crowd of defendants has not a little in common with Robert Greene's *Quippe* and the string of challenged jurymen. Such humorous indictments of prevalent tricks and swindles as Addison's burlesque paper on the chymical operators engaged in fabricating choice wines out of the cheapest liquors[3] is only a modernized form of the attack on cony-catchers ; but how much finer is this satirical fooling than the old crude invective ! Again and again, the newsmonger and amateur

[1] *Tatler*, No. 87.

[2] Addison was "suspected of having revised and even written the translation of Theophrastus which his nephew, Eustace Budgell, published in 1714" (G. S. Gordon, *English Literature and the Classics*, p. 83).

[3] *Tatler*, No. 131.

politician, of ancient lineage in Theophrastian literature, is arraigned, nowhere more humorously than in the several passages with the upholsterer and his fellow-wiseacres who spend their leisure laying down the law on the state of Europe and the future of the Grand Turk.[1] That favourite of the character-writers, the pedantic critic, reappears in Tom Folio, the "learned idiot," who was convinced of the infallibility of Virgil, because he had read him several times in the edition of Heinsius, "and after the strictest and most malicious examination, could find but two faults in him: one of them is in the *Æneid*, where there are two commas instead of a parenthesis; and another in the third *Georgic*, where you may find a semicolon turned upside down."[2] Steele did yeoman's service for civilization in his censure of gambling, duelling, and the chartered licentiousness of the age, whilst Addison was not less efficacious in his appeals for a greater refinement of manners. Says the poet Gay, in *The Present State of Wit* (1711):

> Bickerstaff ventured to tell the town, that they were a parcel of fops, fools, and vain coquettes; but in such a manner, as even pleased them, and made them more than half inclined to believe that he spoke the truth. . . . Instead of complying with the false sentiments and vicious tastes of the age, either in morality, criticism, or good breeding, he has boldly assured them that they were altogether in the wrong, and commanded them, with an authority which perfectly well became him, to surrender themselves to his arguments for virtue and common sense. 'Tis incredible to conceive the effect his writings have had on the town; how many thousand follies they have either quite banished, or given a very great check to; how much countenance they have added to virtue and religion; how many people they have rendered happy, by showing them it was their own fault if they were not so; and, lastly, how entirely they have convinced our fops and young fellows of the value and advantages of learning.[3]

This was to continue the work of the manuals of polite culture so fondly compiled or translated from foreign idealists and propagandists in Tudor times, to make real progress on the road mapped out in *Euphues*; it was to be a hundredfold more effective than the efforts of the character-writers, rendered so barren by their deluded pursuit of verbal wit and intellectual hair-splitting. The programme of *The Spectator* was clearly announced by Addison in

[1] E.g. *Tatler*, No. 155. [2] *Ibid.*, No. 158. [3] Pp. 12-14.

the early numbers. Having acted "in all the parts of my life as a looker-on," that "is the character I intend to preserve in this paper." His magazine was to be an organ of social service, as Meredith was to conceive the novel to be.[1] "If I can any way contribute to the diversion or improvement of the country in which I live, I shall leave it, when I am summoned out of it, with the secret satisfaction of thinking that I have not lived in vain."[2] He resumes the subject a few days later, and having congratulated himself on the extent of his audience, he continues in the same strain:

Steele and Addison as social reformers

For which reasons I shall endeavour to enliven morality with wit, and to temper wit with morality, that my readers may, if possible, both ways find their account in the speculation of the day. And to the end that their virtue and discretion may not be short, transient, intermitting starts of thought, I have resolved to refresh their memories from day to day, till I have recovered them out of that desperate state of vice and folly into which the age is fallen. The mind that lies fallow but a single day, sprouts up in follies that are only to be killed by a constant and assiduous culture. It was said of Socrates that he brought Philosophy down from heaven, to inhabit among men ; and I shall be ambitious to have it said of me, that I have brought Philosophy out of closets and libraries, schools and colleges, to dwell in clubs and assemblies, at tea-tables and in coffee-houses.[3]

It is much more valuable "to be let into the knowledg of one's self, than to hear what passes in Muscovy or Poland." In a word, "Know thyself" is the adjuration with which essay and character, drama and novel alike, address themselves to mankind's attention. Literature has a social object, as Meredith was to contend, with particular reference to the novel.

And, like Lyly at the beginning and Meredith in the maturity of English fiction, Addison turns with special earnestness to women. "There are none to whom this paper will be more useful than to the female world. I have often thought that there has not been sufficient pains taken in finding out proper employments and diversions for the fair ones."[4] Fashions, dress, manners, sentiments and ideas are all paraded and reviewed with a quizzical eye. One of the *Spectator's* correspondents, in calling his attention to a modern example of the she cony-catcher who she hopes he will set up as a

Addison's criticism of women

[1] Preface to *Diana of the Crossways*. [2] *Spectator*, No. 1. [3] *Ibid.*, No. 10. [4] *Ibid.*

scarecrow for the benefit of the unwary, gives a catalogue of what he has done for the improvement of her sex :

> You have endeavoured to correct our unreasonable fears and superstitions, in your seventh and twelfth papers ; our fancy for equipage, in your fifteenth ; our love of puppet-shows, in your thirty-first ; our notions of beauty, in your thirty-third ; our inclination for romances, in your thirty-seventh ; our passion for French fopperies, in your forty-fifth ; our manhood and party zeal, in your fifth-seventh ; our abuse of dancing, in your sixty-sixth and sixty-seventh ; our levity, in your hundred and fifty-fourth and hundred and fifty-seventh ; our tyranny over the henpeckt, in your hundred and seventy-sixth. You have described the Pict in your forty-first ; the Idol, in your seventy-third ; the Demurrer, in your eighty-ninth ; the Salamander, in your hundred and ninety-eighth. You have likewise taken to pieces our dress, and represented to us the extravagances we are often guilty of in that particular. You have fallen upon our patches, in your fiftieth and eighty-first ; our commodes, in your ninety-eighth ; our fans, in your hundred and second ; our riding-habits, in your hundred and fourth ; our hoop-petticoats, in your hundred and twenty-seventh ; besides a great many little blemishes, which you have touched upon in your several other papers, and in those many letters that are scattered up and down your works. At the same time, we must own, that the compliments you pay our sex are innumerable, and that those very faults which you represent in us, are neither black in themselves, nor, as you own, universal among us.[1]

The reader who looks up these references may find it somewhat difficult to say whether Addison's criticism of manners is more akin to the obsolescent character or to the novel that was about to be. One thing he will be more sure about—namely, that Addison was of the same opinion as the great nineteenth-century novelist on woman's destined part in the effort towards a higher level of manners and intellectual life. He would have assented to the claim put forward in the *Essay on Comedy* that only " where women are on the road to an equal footing with men, in attainments and liberty," will there be a real civilization, or the atmosphere in which pure comedy flourishes.[2]

[1] *Spectator*, No. 205.

[2] G. Meredith, *An Essay on Comedy and the Uses of the Comic Spirit*, 1897, pp. 60-61.

The signal donation of the first periodical essayists to the substance of the novel was of a group of living and breathing characters who have become household figures in the imaginative life of the English. When *The Spectator* took over "the censorship of Great Britain" from among the duties of the deceased *Tatler*, it was decided that the counsels of the imaginary editor, residing at Mr Buckley's, in Little Britain, should be assisted by a club, meeting on Tuesdays and Thursdays, who had appointed a committee, meeting every night.[1] Addison having sketched the history and personality of the editor in the first paper, Steele followed in the next number with the first rough portrait of the other members. No doubt it had been settled between the friends what should be the particular features of these gentlemen, and what parts they should undertake in the ensuing episodes and discussions. But with some few lapses from perfect consistency, and even a contradiction or two, Steele and Addison, with the occasional help of Tickell and Budgell, proceeded in paper after paper to fill in the outlines and exhibit Sir Roger and his friends going about their affairs or exchanging views on the things of this world and the next.[2]

Sir Roger de Coverley

First in place and honour in this society was the immortal Sir Roger de Coverley, beyond challenge the most interesting and lifelike semblance of a man that had yet appeared in English fiction. Steele portrayed him at the outset as a man of brains, one who thought for himself, and put his ideas in striking phrases. Thus it is he who presently lets fall the remark that "none but men of fine parts deserve to be hanged," and from this paradoxical text discourses with learning and acuteness on the evils of abuse of the understanding.[3] Steele says: "He is a gentleman that is very singular in his behaviour, but his singularities proceed from his good sense, and are contradictions to the manners of the world only as he thinks the world is in the wrong."[4] Addison imparted

[1] Steele had already had his club in the pages of *The Tatler* (No. 132, 11th February 1709). It originally consisted of fifteen members, but these were now reduced to a third of that number, the three most remarkable being Major Matchlock, Dick Reptile, and the Bencher.

[2] Addison wrote sixteen of the Coverley papers, Steele seven, Budgell three, and one was by Tickell.

[3] *Spectator*, No. 6.

[4] *Ibid.*, No. 2.

the finer strokes of humanity to the portrait, explaining this singularity somewhat differently:

> I have observed in several of my papers that my friend Sir Roger, amidst all his good qualities, is something of an humourist; and that his virtues, as well as imperfections, are, as it were, tinged by a certain extravagance, which makes them particularly his, and distinguishes them from those of other men. This cast of mind, as it is generally very innocent in itself, so it renders his conversation highly agreeable, and more delightful than the same degree of sense and virtue would appear in their common and ordinary colours.[1]

Sir Roger is shown among his friends in town and in his manor-house in the country; he appears on the bench of justices, among his tenants, among the partridges, in church, in his Soho lodgings, at the playhouse, in Westminster Abbey among the tombs; and everywhere reveals those idiosyncrasies which give inimitable charm to his good sense and his fundamental humanity. He is, as critics have repeatedly noticed, Overbury's "Country Gentleman" drawn at full length, humanized, softened, and enriched, and brought upon the stage of actuality. Action of a limited nature has been added to character and sentiments; the art of charactery is developing into the art of fiction. It is noteworthy that this is the first creation in English fiction that has so fully come to life that his author has to put him to death, and the ties he had formed among those who read of him were so close and tender that they mourned him as a friend.

The Templar

Next in esteem and authority was "a man of great probity, wit, and understanding," who had been sent by his father to the Inner Temple to study law, but following his own bent was more learned in the art of the stage. "Aristotle and Longinus are much better understood by him than Littleton or Coke." "His familiarity with the custom, manners, actions, and writings of the ancients, makes him a very delicate observer of what occurs in the present world."

The Merchant

Next in consideration came Sir Andrew Freeport, "a merchant of great eminence in the City of London; a person of indefatigable industry, strong reason, and great experience." A man of noble and generous views on business and commerce, he says that "England may be richer than other kingdoms by as plain methods as he himself is richer than other men." Captain Sentry, "a gentleman

[1] *Spectator*, No. 106.

of great courage and understanding, but invincible modesty," has little to say, but his honest character and behaviour are much to the purpose.[1]

Captain Sentry

Then comes a person second only to Sir Roger in winning disposition and entertaining humour, "the gallant Will Honeycomb, a gentleman who, according to his years, should be in the decline of his life, but having ever been very careful of his person, and always had a very easy fortune, time has made but very little impression, either by wrinkles on his forehead or traces in his brain."

The man about town

He is very ready at that sort of discourse with which men usually entertain women. He has all his life dressed very well, and remembers habits as others do men. He can smile when one speaks to him, and laughs easily. He knows the history of every mode, and can inform you from which of the French king's wenches our wives and daughters had this manner of curling their hair, that way of placing their hoods; whose frailty was covered by such a sort of petticoat, and whose vanity to show her foot made that part of the dress so short in such a year: in a word, all his conversation and knowledge has been in the female world.[2]

Addison amplifies this account of Will by relating some of his misfortunes among the women and his rencounters among the men, and remarks: "The engaging in adventures of this nature Will calls the studying of mankind; and terms this knowledge of the town the knowledge of the world." In a debate with the Templar, "he told us, with a little passion, that he never liked pedantry in spelling, and that he spelt like a gentleman, and not like a scholar." He thought that a pedant was one "that does not know how to think out of his profession and particular way of life"[3]; and, after sorting out the varieties of this genus, sums up: "In short, a mere courtier, a mere soldier, a mere anything, is an insipid, pedantic character and equally ridiculous." Here, it will be observed, Addison is enlarging in a very lively manner upon a commonplace of Overbury, Butler, and the rest.[4]

Last but not least of the little group is the clergyman, "a very philosophic man, of general learning, great sanctity of life, and

The Clergyman

[1] *Spectator*, No. 2. [2] *Ibid.*, No. 2. [3] *Ibid.*, No. 105.
[4] See Overbury, pp. 235, 237; and Butler's "Pedant," p. 252.

the most exact breeding," who in a later paper of Addison's took part with the editor when the rest of the company remonstrated with him upon his free handling of those who happened to be in the same walk of life as themselves."

> He told us, that he wondered any order of persons should think themselves too considerable to be advised : that it was not quality, but innocence, which exempted men from reproof : that vice and folly ought to be attacked wherever they could be met with, and especially when they were placed in high and conspicuous stations in life. . . . He afterwards proceeded to take notice of the great use this paper might be of to the public, by reprehending those vices which are too trivial for the chastisement of the law, and too fantastical for the cognizance of the pulpit.[1]

Whereupon the writer promised his readers "never to draw a faulty character which does not fit at least a thousand people, or to publish a single paper that is not written in the spirit of benevolence and with a love to mankind." That doctrine was to be a saving and vitalizing principle to the future novel.

Approximation of attitude to that of the novel

Manifestly, the change of plan by which Isaac Bickerstaff was succeeded in his functions by the Club, not merely brought about an advance in the art of the periodic essay and in the efficacy of its censorship and gentle satire of mundane things, but was also a long stride towards the re-establishment of fiction on a new and more liberal basis. In the first place, the Club was intended to be representative of the contemporary world.

> The club of which I am a member is very luckily composed of such persons as are engaged in different ways of life, and deputed as it were out of the most conspicuous classes of mankind : by this means I am furnished with the greatest variety of hints and materials, and know everything that passes in the different quarters and divisions, not only of this great city, but of the whole kingdom. . . . There is no rank or degree among them who have not their representative in this club, and that there is always somebody present who will take care of their respective interests, that nothing may be written or published to the prejudice or infringement of their just rights and privileges.[2]

But, besides being representative of the larger world, the members of the Club were in themselves examples of a more

[1] *Spectator*, No. 34.

[2] *Ibid.*

genial human disposition than, for instance, the figures satirized in the sketches of convivial, political, or merely eccentric clubs which *The Spectator* attacked as a source of ill-manners and ill-feeling in the community. It was, as it were, the touchstone of a truly humane society: it preached the better way, and it illustrated the same in its own members. Addison, at least, had some inkling of that faith in the virtue of his craft soon to be announced by Fielding, who wrote: "An example is a kind of picture, in which virtue becomes as it were an object of sight, and strikes us with an idea of that loveliness, which Plato asserts there is in her naked charms."[1] The figures created by Steele and Addison are not dramatic, in that they are not doers or sufferers in any event of serious importance. Yet they do not merely perform to show off their peculiarities and entertain us with their humour. In the general outlook on the world they have a definite significance, standing for a philosophy of life and a certain level of good taste, good feeling, and polite behaviour; and this not merely through the sentiments they utter, but also by what they are in themselves and by what they do. The part taken by Defoe in the further treatment of the character in his periodicals, and the transition from the static character to the fictitious narrative, must be left to a later chapter. We have already been carried out of bounds in tracing the genre so far forward, and must now retrace our steps to earlier examples of fiction used for discursive or theoretic purposes.

[1] *Tom Jones*, dedication to Lyttelton.

CHAPTER XV

UTOPIAN FICTION

Utopian fiction

THE story of utopian fiction is of the nature of a digression, for it was not through works of this category that the art of fiction made any perceptible headway. Beginning with More's *Utopia*, first published in Latin, in 1518, and then in an English translation by Raphe Robinson, in 1551, a number of these works appeared before the end of the seventeenth century, and in later times there have been a great many more. Their historical importance is small, but they are a peculiarly good illustration of the close kinship between prose fiction and the essay or philosophical discourse on human life. The use of a story for conveying some intellectual, religious, or practical truth is as old as the art of story-telling, and the early philosophers were fond of it as an alternative or an auxiliary to abstract demonstration. Plato used myth and fable to elucidate theory, and dialogue, relieved by occasional incident and diversified with personal idiosyncrasy, for the lively conduct of discourse. In the *Republic* he availed himself of both devices, and provided More and other framers of imaginary polities with their original model. Thus, with an exception here and there, utopian fiction belongs to the category of applied art: the utopia, if a novel at all, is a novel of purpose. It is propagandist fiction. All great fiction must be philosophic. It is a mirror of life, but of life irradiated by mind, the luminous mind of the great novelist. On the other hand, utopian fiction, even when the author is a Plato, a More, or a Francis Bacon, is philosophic in a much narrower way, since it is not a survey of life but only a simulation of life-likeness for the sake of the doctrine to be enunciated.

Theoretically, the utopia should be a criticism of actualities by a hypothetical criterion, the utopian state. It should be an exposure of defects through the contrasts which the reader is enforced to draw; a plea for reform through the concrete presentment of a perfect, or at least an amended, condition. The utopia is the prose analogue to the idealistic visions of a Spenser or a Shelley. As the *Faerie Queene* or *Prometheus Unbound* is to the epic, so is the *Utopia* to *Tom Jones* or *Vanity Fair*. Poets, it might be said, are always evolving utopias, in that they are always imaging this world in the light of another. Spenser and Shelley, in their visionary poems, are in some sense more poetical even than the writers of great epic. Not so the author of the prose utopia. Despite its ideality, this is bound to be prosaic in the extreme. After all, it is a piece of dialectic, not an effort of the free imagination. Employing matter of fact for the sake of illustration, or weighing facts against hypotheses which themselves are made to look as much as possible like facts, utopias have to keep close to the ground in both matter and style. Bacon and Sidney could hardly have excluded them from their classification of Poesy, since they are assuredly a kind of writing that ranges "into the divine consideration of what may be and should be"; but as a user of inspired words and images, the other mark of Poesy, it is difficult to see who but Plato among the utopians could be awarded the bays.

The name utopia may be and has been applied to mere enunciations of an ideal scheme, without any story: works of that kind do not concern us, though we should note that in many of the others the story is a very perfunctory thing, a mere device for making description clearer. If the story is only an improvised vehicle on which the ideal scheme is loaded up, driven in, and shot down for inspection, we might as well have the scientific exposition which dispenses with the vehicle. At first blush, one would think that the spectacle of an ideal state of humanity might be made absolutely enthralling. But, apparently, with the elimination of evil there is an elimination of all that excites dramatic interest. Only a fierce satirical animus seems to be able to work the utopian machinery with perfect consistency. The mere theorist is too apt to forget what is the particular task he has undertaken, and to drop unwarily into argument or contentious criticism or mere categorical description, when he should have used the literary contrivance that he has hired for the purpose it was designed for. Even the supreme master of ironical narrative does not keep unswervingly to the method of implied comparison and contrast. The bitter caricature and savage denunciation to which Gulliver listens submissively from the mouth of the king of the Brobdingnagians is irony of the true dramatic order; but when Swift takes us to Laputa he often wanders from the path of either dramatic propriety or utopian indirectness. His disciple, Samuel Butler, is still oftener at fault in carrying out what was his accepted duty—to maintain the same ironical inversion throughout his account of the Erewhonians.

Sir Thomas More did not attempt anything so difficult as sustained irony: his ambition was to follow Plato, not to surpass Lucian. He accordingly put his direct criticism into one book, which is a Platonic dialogue in form, and his visionary republic into the second book, which is all narrative, told by one of the interlocutors. The *Utopia, a mendis vindicata* (1518), or, to adopt the English title of Robinson's translation, *A fruteful, and pleasaunt worke of the beste state of a publyque weale, and of the new yle called Vtopia* (1551), opens quietly with what purports to be an actual incident in More's own career. It was when he was sent into Flanders by that prince adorned with all the virtues that become a great monarch, our Henry VIII., that he and his old friend Peter Giles fell in at Antwerp with a picturesque stranger, who had been a companion of the navigator Amerigo Vespucci, and possessed a marvellous acquaintance with distant countries. Raphael Hythloday, this Portuguese, had, in the course of his voyages, been to Utopia, somewhere in the New World; and the book, in the orthodox manner, is resolved into the dialogue between the three. They first discuss the state of England; and the strictures on economic anomalies and the savagery of the penal system, the grasping avarice of the rich and powerful which was responsible for both, and the absurdity of war as the official expedient for composing international relations, are liberal and far-sighted, and remarkably outspoken from such a loyal subject of the King. More, however, puts his criticism into the other man's mouth, as he does the account of the Utopians which follows in the second book.

The happy republic is established on an almost inaccessible island, rendered more inaccessible by regulations framed to discourage intercourse with other peoples. Equality and uniformity are the salient characteristics of the Utopian economy. War is regarded as criminal folly, and the commonwealth enjoys perpetual peace. The people elect their sovereign and their magistrates. They have justice, and they have freedom, except that the system of universal regulations would be irksome to average humanity. All is calculated, at any rate, for the general welfare. Private gain does not exist; the Utopians live in common, without the use of money: they have no poor, "and though no man have anything, yet every man is rich." More's comment on this view of a socialist millennium is that, although he could not perfectly agree to everything that had been related of this nation, yet there were many things in their polity that he rather wished than hoped to see followed in our European governments.

Thus More's book consists of a political discussion of things as they are, followed by a sober description of things as they might be. He skilfully authenticates his account of the imaginary country by appealing to the memory of his friend Peter Giles to confirm or correct his report of Raphael's conversation, and also to another witness, his servant John Clement, who was present at the colloquy. One touch such as Defoe was to use later with unrivalled skill is the apparently frank admission that he cannot be quite sure whether the bridge over the Anider was five hundred paces wide or only three hundred paces, as John keeps affirming. And he adds, that Raphael did not think to mention, nor they to ask, exactly in what part of the western hemisphere Utopia was situated.

Bacon's *New Atlantis*, which appeared in *Sylva Sylvarum* (1627), is only a fragment, and that fragment depicts a utopia of advanced scientific activity. If, as his posthumous editor, Dr Rawley, Bacon's chaplain, explains in the preface, the author intended "to have composed a frame of laws, or of the best state or mould of a commonwealth," he left off when he had described his ideal of a great college, instituted by the state, "for the interpreting of nature and the producing of great and marvellous works for the benefit of man." Solomon's House, in the island of New Atlantis, is such an institution as might have carried out the vast schemes for the exploration and mastery of nature in the service of man which Bacon propounded in the *Novum Organum*. The discoveries and mechanical inventions are described with grave complacency. Some of them seem to be striking anticipations of modern achievements ; but the happy guesses are discounted by a number of unfounded and even absurd speculations.

Bacon makes much more play than More had done with the picturesque side of the imaginary voyage, and gives a loose to romance of a stately kind in such incidents as the miraculous epiphany of the Scriptures, the pillar of fire in the midst of the ocean breaking up and casting itself abroad, "as it were, into a firmament of many stars, which also vanished soon after, and there was nothing left to be seen but a small ark or chest of cedar," in which were contained all the canonical books of the Old and New Testaments. Strange to say, they included some portions "which were not at that time written," for the event took place three thousand years ago. Like More's Utopia, and other abodes of temporal felicity, New Atlantis was placed somewhere in the mystic region of the setting sun. The course by which the adventurers are driven there by tempests is long and perilous, and gives Bacon the opportunity for circumstantial narrative, in which he acquits himself ably.

These were the two most famous of early utopian romances in English. Many of the works sometimes placed in the same class have little right there : they are for the most part satires or coarse lampoons adopting the pretence of an unknown land, as they might any other form of allegory, for the sake of the equivoque. Such, for instance, is the work usually attributed to Bishop Joseph Hall, though it may have been by the Italian jurist Alberico Gentili, with the title *Mundus Alter et Idem, sive Terra Australis antehac semper incognita longis itineribus peregrini Academici nuperimme lustrata, auth. Mercurio Britannico.*[1] It is a satire, not unallied to the time-honoured encomium of folly, on the vices that distinguish

[1] Printed at Frankfurt (*c.* 1605), but undated. Utopian writers, from Plato downwards, had hitherto put their happy land somewhere in the Far West. But the West was now becoming well known ; hence, from this time onwards, we find a preference for the unexplored spaces of the South. That fabulous land, Terra Australis, reappears in a number of the imaginary voyages—*e.g.* those of Henry Nevile, Smeeks, Swift, etc. (see Geoffrey Atkinson : *The Extraordinary Voyage in French Literature before 1700* (Columbia University Studies), 1920). Atkinson mentions More, Bacon, etc., but not Bishop Hall, Henry Nevile, and other English writers who discovered the mythic Terra Australis earlier than the Frenchmen.

England, Germany, and other countries, with more pointed sarcasm towards the Roman Catholic Church. It describes Crapulia, the land of headaches, where there are laws against fasting; Yvronia, the land of drunkenness; Viraginia, the country of the viragoes, which is ruled by women; Moronia, the republic of fools; and Lavernia, that of thieves and rogues. John Healey did a close translation of this, with the title, *The Discovery of a New World, or a Description of the South Indies. Hetherto Vnknowne. By an English Mercury* (1609). Based on Healey's version, but much abridged, was a later book alleged to be from the Spanish, *The Travels of Don Francisco de Quevedo. Through Terra Australis Incognita, Discovering the Laws, Customs, Manners and Fashions of the South Indians* (1684). That mercenary and disreputable hack, Francis Kirkman, published a coarse and inaccurate version of the second book, that concerned with Viraginia, in what he called *Psittacorum Regio. The Land of Parrots: Or, The She-Lands. With a Description of other strange adjacent Countries, in the Dominions of Prince de l'Amour, not hitherto found in any Geographical Map. By one of the late most reputed Wits* (1669). Another prelate, Francis Godwin, Bishop of Hereford, took his cue from Lucian in *The Man in the Moone: or a discourse of a Voyage thither by Domingo Gonzales the speedy Messenger* (1638).[1] But in the more personal and scurrilous scandal-novels the pretence of a utopia, such as Mrs Manley's "Kingdom of Albigion" or "the New Atlantis, an island in the Mediterranean," or Mrs Haywood's "island adjacent to the kingdom of Utopia," is obviously but a device for avoiding the charge of libel.

Among the allegorical if not the utopian fiction may be placed James Howell's satirical Δενδρολογια, *Dodona's Grove, or, The Vocall Forest* (1640), with a second part (1650). The vivacious

[1] Godwin's picaresque story seems to have furnished ideas to several writers much more celebrated. The hero has Crusoe experiences on an uninhabited island, St Helena. Another bishop, John Wilkins of Chester, borrowed little more than his title, *The Discovery of a New World in the Moone* (1638). But Cyrano de Bergerac made use of a French translation of Godwin's romance, *L'Homme dans la Lune, on le Voyage Chimerique fait au Monde de la Lune*, and from Cyrano both Defoe in *The Consolidator* and Swift in *Gulliver* borrowed considerably. A more impudent creditor was that fraudulent quill-driver, Nathaniel Crouch, *alias* Burton, who supplemented his account of recent discoveries, *The English Acquisitions in Guinea and East India* (1728), by appending *The Man in the Moone* as a further piece of geographical erudition.

author of the *Epistolæ Ho-Elianæ* here gave an entertaining version of current European politics, introducing countries and their monarchs under Greek and Latin names for trees. Barclay's *Argenis* (1621) may have given him the idea ; this latter, in view of its affinities to heroic romance, must stand over for consideration in the next volume. A little later there fell from the press, anonymous and unnoticed, a Latin romance, *Nova Solyma libri sex* (1648), which remained in obscurity till, in 1902, a student of Milton, the Rev. Walter Begley, published an English translation, and attributed it to the author of *Paradise Lost.* This is not a political utopia, but, with some conventional and insipid romance, sets forth an ideal system of education, describing a model academy or university, an elaborate pattern of literary culture, with actual specimens of the yield of poetry, and a programme of religious and cosmological teaching.[1]

Amidst the controversies and agitations for reform of the revolutionary epoch, a number of doctrinaire utopias made their appearance. Samuel Hartlib's *Description of the Famous Kingdom of Macaria* (1641) was a tractate, pure and simple, on agricultural and educational projects. So too Gerard Winstanley, the digger or leveller, in his larger treatise, *The Law of Freedom in a Platform* (1652), dealt with agrarian and allied problems in a manner that was utopian in the theoretic rather than the literary sense. *Nova Solyma* belongs properly to the same group. James Harrington was another theorist of this polemical time who chose to put his views on reform into the shape of a story, but with as little artistic propriety as any of them. *The Common-Wealth of Oceana* (1656) is a dry but statesmanlike description of an England that has been thoroughly transformed by a new constitution. Harrington's object was to propound a scheme for national reconstruction that would approve itself to Cromwell, and be applied by him for the settlement of the realm. His lord archon Olphaus Megaletor stands obviously for the English Lord Protector, and is represented as spending sleepless nights in mental debate on the affairs of Oceana. Having called together a committee of experts, he

[1] See W. A. Neilson, "*Nova Solyma*, a Romance attributed to John Milton" (*Mod. Philology*, i., 1903-1904, pp. 525-546), for the case against Milton's authorship.

establishes the constitution worked out by them, and then retires. Thus Harrington's is the most directly practical of all these projects for a millennium, either then or at any other time, being a plan for rebuilding on a better design put forward in an actual emergency, when the walls were down and the scaffolding was still up. Nevertheless, it bore no more fruit than the others, and remains a curiosity of political theory, with minor claims to literary interest.

A continuation by a certain R.H. was added to Bacon's *New Atlantis* in the edition of 1660, in which year the cabalist, John Sadler, published his *Olbia, a new Island.* These and the Duchess of Newcastle's ingenuous anticipations of scientific discovery in *The Description of a New World, called the Blazing World* (1668) are worth a bare mention. This catalogue of utopian fiction—and it is not much more—suffices to show, at any rate, how obvious an instrument fiction had now become for purposes widely removed from those of pure art.

SELECT READING AND REFERENCE LIST

I. GENERAL

CHANDLER, F. W. *The Literature of Roguery.* 2 vols. 1907.
Romances of Roguery. Pt. I.: "The Picaresque Novel in Spain." 1899.

CROSS, WILBUR L. *The Development of the English Novel.* 1899.

DAVID-SAUVAGEOT, A. *Le Réalisme et le Naturalisme.* Paris, 1890.

DUNLOP, JOHN. *The History of Fiction.* Revised edition, 1896.

ERNLE, LORD. *The Light Reading of Our Ancestors: Chapters in the Growth of the English Novel.* [1927.]

ESDAILE, ARUNDELL. *A List of English Tales and Prose Romances printed before 1740.* 1912.

RALEIGH, WALTER. *The English Novel.* 1904.

REYNIER, GUSTAVE. *Les Origines du Roman Réaliste.* 1912.

TIEJE, A. J. *The Theory of Characterization in Prose Fiction prior to 1740.* (University of Minnesota Studies in Language and Literature. 1916.)

TUCKER, T. G. *The Foreign Debt of English Literature.* 1907.

WARD, A. W., and WALLER, A. R. *The Cambridge History of English Literature.* 15 vols. 1907-1917.

(See also the General List in Volume I.)

II. ELIZABETHAN FICTION

(*a*) TEXTS

ALEMÁN, MATEO. *The Rogue; or, The Life of Guzman d'Alfarache.* Translated by James Mabbe, with introduction by J. Fitzmaurice-Kelly. 4 vols. 1924.
Don Guzman de Alfarache. Translated by J. H. Brady. 1881.

An Alphabet of Tales. Edited by Mary Macleod Banks. Pts. I.-II. E.E.T.S., 1904-1905.

AWDELEY, JOHN. *The Fraternitye of Vacabones.* (*The Rogues and Vagabonds of Shakespeare's Youth.* Edited by E. Viles and F. J. Furnivall. 1907.)

BANDELLO, MATTEO, BISHOP OF AGEN. *Certaine Tragicall Discourses* [trans.] *by Geoffraie Fenton.* (Tudor Translations.) 2 vols. 1898.
Tragical Tales. Translated by Geoffrey Fenton. Modernized by Hugh Harris. 1924.
Histoires Tragiques. 2 vols. 1559.

BELLEFOREST, FRANÇOIS DE. *Histoires Tragiques.* 2 vols. 1565-1567 (vol. i., 1565; vol. ii., 1567).
18 *Histoires Tragiques.* 1564.
Histoires Tragiques. 7 vols. 1571-1604.

BRETON, NICHOLAS. *Works.* Edited by A. B. Grosart. 2 vols. 1879.

CELESTINA, *or the Tragi-Comedy of Calisto and Melibea.* Translated by James Mabbe. Edited by W. Warner Allen. 1923.

CHETTLE, HENRY. *Pierce Plainnes Seaven Yeres Prenticeship.* 1595.
Kind-Harts Dreame. 1592. (Bodley Head Quartos. 1923.)

COLONNA, FRANCESCO. *Hypnerotomachia : The Strife of Loue in a Dreame.* Edited by A. Lang. 1890.

DEKKER, THOMAS. *The Guls Horn-Booke ; The Bel-man of London ; Lanthorne and Candle-Light* (Temple Classics). 2 vols. 1904.
The Batchelars Banquet. 1603.
The Seuen deadly Sinnes of London. Edited by E. Arber, 1880. Edited by H. F. Brett-Smith. (Percy Reprints. 1922.)

DELONEY, THOMAS. *Works.* Edited by F. O. Mann. 1912.

DICKENSON, JOHN. *Prose and Verse.* Edited by A. B. Grosart. 1878.

ELYOT, SIR THOMAS. *The Governour.* Edited by H. H. S. Croft. 2 vols. 1883.

FORDE, EMMANUEL. *Parismus, The Renoumed Prince of Bohemia.* 2 vols. 1598-1599.
Vol. ii. contains "Parismenos."
Ornatus and Artesia. 1607.
Montelyon, Knight of the Oracle. 1633.

GASCOIGNE, GEORGE. *Complete Works*. 2 vols. 1904-1910.
Complete Poems. Edited by W. C. Hazlitt. 2 vols. 1869.
The Pleasant Fable of Ferdinando Jeronino and Leonora de Valasco. Edited by J. W. Cunliffe. 1907.

GREENE, ROBERT. *Life and Complete Works*. Edited by A. B. Grosart. (Huth Library.) 15 vols. 1881-1886.
Dramatic Works. Edited by J. Churton Collins. 2 vols. 1905.
Arcadia, or Menaphon (Archaica, ii., 1814).
Greene's Groats-Worth of Witte ; The Repentance of Robert Greene. 1592. (Bodley Head Quartos. 1923.)
A Notable Discovery of Coosnage. 1591. *The Second Part of Conny-catching*. 1592. (*Ibid.* 1923.)
The Thirde and Last Part of Conny-Catching ; with a Disputation betweene a Hee Conny-catcher and a Shee Conny-catcher. (*Ibid.* 1923.)
Pandosto : The Triumph of Time. Edited by P. G. Thomas. 1907.
Philomela (Archaica, i., 1814).

GUEVARA, ANTONIO DE. *The Diall of Princes, being select passages, with introduction and Bibliography*. Edited by K. N. Colvile. (English Scholars' Library. 1919.)

HALLIWELL, J. O. (*ed.*). *A Manifest Detection of the most vyle and detestable Use of Dyce Play*. 1532. (Percy Society, lxxxvii. 1850.)

HARMAN, THOMAS. *A Caveat or Warening for Commen Cursetors*. (*The Rogues and Vagabonds of Shakespeare's Youth*. Edited by E. Viles and F. J. Furnivall. 1907.)

HAZLITT, W. CAREW. (*ed.*). *Old-English Jest-Books*. 3 vols. 1864.
Vol. ii. : Merie Tales of Skelton ; Jests of Scogin ; Sackfull of Nerves ; Tarlton's Jests ; Merrie Conceited Jests of George Peele ; Jacke of Dover. Vol. iii. : XII. Mery Jests of the Wydow Edyth ; Pasquile's Jests with Mother Bunches Merriment ; The Pleasant Conceits of Old Hobson ; Taylor's Wit and Mirth, etc.

HURTADO, LUIS. *Palmerin of England*. Translated by Anthony Munday. 1581.

LAZARILLO DE TORMES. Translated by David Rowland. Edited J. E. V. Crofts. 1924.

LIBER VAGATORUM. Translated by J. C. Hotten (*The Book of Vagabonds and Beggars*, 1860).

LODGE, THOMAS. *Works*. Edited by E. Gosse. (Hunterian Club.) 4 vols. 1878-1882.

LODGE, T. *Rosalynde*. Edited by H. Morley. 1887.

LYLY, JOHN. *Works.* Edited by J. W. Bond. 3 vols. 1902.
Euphues. Edited by E. Arber, 1868. Edited by Morris William Croll and Harry Clemons, 1916.

MEXÍA, PEDRO. *The Foreste or Collection of Histories.* Translated by Thomas Fortescue. 1571.

MONTEMAYOR, JORGE DE. *Diana.* Translated by Bartholomew Yong. 1598.

NASHE, THOMAS. *Works.* Edited by R. B. McKerrow. 5 vols. 1904-1910.
The Unfortunate Traveller ; or, The Life of Jack Wilton. Edited by Edmund Gosse. 1892.
Pierce Penilesse his Supplication to the Divell. 1592. (Bodley Head Quartos. 1924.)

PAINTER, WILLIAM. *The Palace of Pleasure.* Edited by J. Jacobs. 3 vols. 1890.

PALMERIN D'OLIVA. Translated by Anthony Munday. 1588.

PETTIE, GEORGE. *A Petite Pallace of Pettie his Pleasure.* Edited by I. Gollancz. 2 vols. 1908.

PIUS II. (ÆNEAS SYLVANUS PICCOLOMINI), POPE. *De Duobus Amantibus.* 1430.
Historie of Eurialus and Lucretia. 1639.

REURE, O.-C. *La Vie et les Œuvres de Honoré d'Urfé.* 1910.

RICH, BARNABY. *Riche his Farewell to Militarie Profession.* Edited by J. P. Collier. 1846.

ROJAS, FERNANDO DE. See *Celestina.*

ROWLANDS, SAMUEL. *Complete Works.* Edited by E. Gosse. (Hunterian Club.) 3 vols. 1880.

SIDNEY, SIR PHILIP. *Complete Works.* Edited by A. Feuillerat. 1912, in progress.
The Countess of Pembroke's Arcadia. Edited by E. A. Baker. 1907.

SMYTHE, R. *Strange, Lamentable, and Tragical Histories.* 1577.

THOMS, J. W. (*ed.*). Early English Prose Romances. (Library of Early Novelists. 1906.)
Reynard the Fox, Robert the Devil, Virgilius, Hamlet, Fryer Bacon, Friar Rush, Thomas of Reading, Robin Hood, George à Green, Tom à Lincoln, Dr Faustus.

WARNER, WILLIAM. *Pan his Syrinx.* 1597.

WHETSTONE, GEORGE. *The Heptameron of Civil Discourses.* (Percy Society.) 1844.

WILSON, JOHN DOVER. *John Lyly.* 1905.

WROATH, LADY MARY. *The Countess of Mountgomerie's Urania.* 1621.

(*b*) STUDIES

AYDELOTTE, F. *Elizabethan Rogues and Vagabonds.* Oxford. 1913.

CHEVALLEY, ABEL. *Thomas Deloney: le Roman des Métiers au temps de Shakespeare.* Paris, 1926.

CONLEY, C. H. *The First English Translations of the Classics.* Yale University, 1927.

FEUILLERAT, ALBERT. *John Lyly: contribution à l'histoire de la Renaissance en Angleterre.* 1910.

FOSTER, F. M. K. *English Translations from the Greek: a bibliographical Survey.* (Columbia University Studies in English and Comparative Literature.) 1918.

GREG, W. W. *Pastoral Poetry and Pastoral Drama.* 1906.

HERFORD, C. H. *Studies in the Literary Relations of England and Germany in the Sixteenth Century.* 1886.

HUME, MARTIN A. S. *Spanish Influence in English Literature.* 1905.

JORDAN, JOHN CLARK. *Robert Greene.* 1915.

JUSSERAND, J. J. *The English Novel in the time of Shakespeare.* Translated by Elizabeth Lee. 1899.

SAINTSBURY, G. *Elizabethan Literature.* 1897.

SCOTT, MARY AUGUSTA. *Elizabethan Translations from the Italian.* (Vassar Semi-Centennial Series.) Boston. 1916.

SYMONDS, J. A. *Sir Philip Sidney.* (English Men of Letters.) 1885.

WARREN, F. M. *A History of the Novel previous to the Seventeenth Century.* 1908.

WOLFF, SAMUEL LEE. *The Greek Romances in Elizabethan Prose Fiction.* 1912.

III. SEVENTEENTH-CENTURY FICTION

(*a*) Texts

Addison, Joseph. *Works.* With notes by R. Hind. 6 vols. Bohn. 1854-1856.

Aldington, Richard (*ed.*). *A Book of Characters.* 1924.

Bacon, Francis, Lord Verulam. *Essayes, religious meditations, places of perswasion and disswasion ; from the 1st edition of 1597.* 1924.

Butler, Samuel. *Characters and Passages from Note-Books.* Edited by A. R. Waller. 1908.

Earle, John. *Microcosmographie.* Edited by W. H. D. Rouse. (Temple Classics. 1899.)

Godwin, Francis. *The Man in the Moone.* 1638.

Hall, Joseph. *Works.* Edited by J. Pratt and P. Wynter. 10 vols. 1863.

Mundus Alter et Idem. Edited by H. S. Anderson. With original maps. 1908.

Jonson, Ben. *Discoveries.* 1641. Edited by G. B. Harrison. (Bodley Head Quartos. 1923.)

Man in the Moone telling Strange Fortunes, The. Edited by J. O. Halliwell. (Percy Society.) 1849.

More, Sir Thomas. *Utopia : or, The Happy Republic.* Edited by J. A. St John. 1845.

Also Bacon's *New Atlantis*, an analysis of Plato's *Republic*, etc.

Overbury, Sir Thomas. *Works.* Edited by E. F. Rimbault. 1890.

Spectator, The. Edited by G. A. Aitken. 8 vols. 1898.

Tatler, The. Edited by G. A. Aitken. 4 vols. 1898-1899.

Theophrastus. *The Characters of Theophrastus : a Translation.* With introduction by C. C. Bennett and W. A. Hammond. New York, 1902.

This American rendering is probably the raciest and liveliest yet done.

Wilkins, John. *The Discovery of a New World in the Moon.* 1684.

(*b*) Studies

Gordon, G. S. *English Literature and the Classics.* Oxford. 1912.

Especially pp. 49-86 : "Theophrastus and his Imitators."

Gosse, Sir E. *Seventeenth Century Studies.* 1913.

Thomas Lodge, Samuel Rowlands, the Matchless Orinda, etc.

HERTZLER, J. O. *The History of Utopian Thought.* 1923.

MEREDITH, GEORGE. *An Essay on Comedy and the Comic Spirit.* 1897.

MORGAN, CHARLOTTE. *The Rise of the Novel of Manners.* 1911.
Full of errors and misprints: to be used with continual correction.

MORLEY, HENRY. *Character-Writings of the Seventeenth Century.* 1891.

MUMFORD, LEWIS. *The Story of Utopias.* 1922.

THOMAS, HENRY. *Spanish and Portuguese Romances.* 1920.

UNDERHILL, J. G. *Spanish Literature in the England of the Tudors.* 1899.

UPHAM, A. H. *The French Influence in English Literature from Elizabeth to the Restoration.* 1909.

INDEX

INDEX

A

B

C

D

E

F

G

H

I

J

K

L

M

N

Q

R

S

T

U

V

W

X

Y